THE ALEXANDER LETTERS

OLD FAMILY HOMESTEAD AT WASHINGTON, GEORGIA

Built by Felix and William Gilbert in 1808. Inherited by Sarah, only child of Felix, and in which her children, the ten Alexander brothers and sisters, were born and reared. Now owned by the family of Charles A. Alexander. The original photograph from which this reproduction is made was taken about the time of the Civil War.

THE ALEXANDER LETTERS

1787–1900

Edited by Marion Alexander Boggs

Foreword by
Richard Barksdale Harwell

BROWN THRASHER BOOKS

THE UNIVERSITY OF GEORGIA PRESS

ATHENS

Foreword by Richard Barksdale Harwell copyright © 1980 by the
University of Georgia Press, Athens, Georgia 30602

Printed in the United States of America

Library of Congress Cataloging in Publication Data

Boggs, Marion Alexander, 1877–1970, ed.
   The Alexander letters, 1787–1900.
   "Brown Thrasher books."
   Reprint of the 1910 ed. printed for G. J. Baldwin, Sa-
vannah, Ga.
      1. Alexander family.   I. Title.
CS71.A38 1980   929'.2'0973   79-5187
               ISBN 0-8203-0492-1
            ISBN 0-8203-0493-X pbk.

The original edition of *The Alexander Letters, 1787–
1900* was privately printed for George J. Baldwin in
Savannah, Georgia, in 1910. That edition was limited
to 131 copies, which were for distribution among the
descendants of those who wrote the letters.

To
Harriet Virginia Cumming, Mary Clifford Hull,
Edward Porter Alexander
and to
The Loved Memory of All Their Goodly Company
We Dedicate this Book
George J. Baldwin
Marion A. Boggs.

Foreword

Of the pioneers in the establishment of Georgia, Gov. George Gilmer wrote in his uninhibited and informative *Sketches of Some of the First Settlers of Upper Georgia* (1855):

> In tracing the causes of the present happy condition of Georgia to the character of the settlers, the Author infers that low, impotent, beggarly men had not the strength, activity, enterprise, nor spirit, to separate themselves from their accustomed haunts, their kindred and country, to encounter untried and unknown difficulties in a new land beyond a vast ocean. And that the strong, the brave, the determined to be free, must have made up the emigrating classes from Europe to the Colonies. He shows how the descendants of these emigrants . . . left the old states to form settlements in the new. . . . That they were descendants from the most vigorous and industrious classes of the Irish, Scotch, English, and Welsh, and how the Dutch, French, and Italian blood added to the crossings which gave value to the stock. He describes how these settlers formed the most intimate friendly social union ever known among the same number of persons; how exceedingly active they were in business; economical in their expenditures; honest in their dealings, and their prospering beyond example.

The family represented in *The Alexander Letters, 1787–1900* was among those outstanding families who, in Gilmer's words, "made Georgia the most prosperous of states" during the late antebellum period. The Alexander family combined the best of seaboard and up-country backgrounds.

The Georgia coastal region was settled, for the most part, directly from Europe. There the Alexander side of the family came in 1776 in the person of Dr. Adam Alexander, a surgeon at eighteen who had been born at Inverness, Scotland, and now joined the colonists' revolutionary army. His wife was Louisa Frederika Schmidt, born in Stuttgart in 1777. She came to Charleston with her parents about 1785. Adam Leopold Alexander was the son of Adam and Louisa Alexander.

The progenitors of the Gilbert family had been longer in America but not in Georgia. The first Felix Gilbert of this record moved from Virginia to Georgia shortly after the Revolution, settling a few miles northeast of Washington in Wilkes County. The Felix Gilbert who was the father of Sarah Hillhouse Gilbert, wife of A. L. Alexander, was described by Governor Gilmer as "one of the cleverest men of Georgia." He was a good businessman, prospering with his brother as a planter and in the business of ginning cotton, and an influential member of the Georgia Legislature.

Felix Gilbert married Sarah Hillhouse. Her parents, David and Sarah Porter Hillhouse, had removed from Connecticut to Washington in 1787. It is a letter from Sarah Hillhouse to her father, Col. Elisha Porter, that is the first of these *Alexander Letters*. Mrs. Hillhouse later became Georgia's first woman newspaper editor and was for a time the state printer. At his early death Felix Gilbert assigned the upbringing of his daughter, to whom he left a large fortune, to this capable woman, "a very sensible, well-informed, precise old lady."

"Miss Gilbert's education," according to Gilmer, "was perfected by passing some time with her intellectual and highly cultivated (Hillhouse) cousins in New Haven, and the neighborhood. Mr. Adam Alexander was then going through college. He was the handsomest youth of his class, intelligent and courteous, and like Miss Gilbert, a native Georgian. The young gentleman had not in the three years he had been in Yale, seen any one so beautiful and accomplished as his countrywoman. He made their admiration mutual, by the pleasing manner in which he pressed his admiration upon her. They became more and more attached to each other, until they felt that life would be lifeless unless spent together." Felix Gilbert had journeyed to Connecticut to secure permission from Senator James Hillhouse to marry his niece. Now his niece's daughter had unwittingly made a similar journey to find her husband. The two, she fourteen and he seventeen, were soon engaged. Three years later, on April 28, 1823, they were married in the old Gilbert home at Washington.

Thus were fortunately joined two prominent Georgia families, one from the seaboard and one from the upcountry—Middle Georgia, as the area stretching from Waynesboro to Athens and westward to Columbus came to be known in the nineteenth century. It was propitious circumstance that brought these young people together at New Haven. Otherwise they might never have met, for the two principal areas of Georgia were then still two very separate regions, with marked differences in manners and speech. (How Mrs. Hillhouse confirmed this in the letter to her son David of April 25, 1818!) Politics, intermarriages, the telegraph, and the railroads (especially the railroads) eventually broke down the regional barriers within Georgia—almost—

but there were few mergings of seaboard and Middle Georgia interests in the early days of the state, and the Alexander family is the most notable exception to the rule.

The lives of the children of Sarah and A. L. Alexander spanned nearly a century, from 1824 to 1914. They passed their distinguished heritage to a progeny that now numbers to three and four additional generations. The old Gilbert-Alexander home, built at Washington in 1808, still stands as a focal point for a widening clan. In like manner *The Alexander Letters* gives substance to the family's background.

These are the letters of the ten Alexander children, along with just enough of correspondence from the parents and grandparents to set their place within the family. The letters of this golden generation of Alexanders tell a story that could have happened in no other time or place. The central figure was Adam Leopold Alexander. The description of Alexander as a young man was supplemented in Gilmer's *Georgians* with a description of him at age fifty-one or fifty-two as a gentleman "as distinguished for his good understanding, cultivated taste, and excellent character, as when he was a collegiate for his fine person and regular features. He has done what few Southern men possessed of great riches in early life ever did before, devote his time constantly and industriously to laborious and useful employment. . . . He has constantly either instructed or superintended the education of his numerous family of children."

Adam Alexander was the pride of his children; so were they their parents' pride. The roll of the ten who make this book the wonderful story it is reads:

Louisa Frederika Alexander, 1824–1895; married Jeremy Francis Gilmer.

Sarah Gilbert Alexander, 1826–1897; married Alexander Robert Lawton.

Harriet Virginia Alexander, 1828–1910; married Wallace Cumming.

Mary Clifford Alexander ("Dearest May"), 1830–1914; married George Gilmer Hull.

William Felix Alexander, 1832–1907; married Louisa Toombs and after her death Lucy Grattan.

Edward Porter Alexander, 1835–1910; married Betty Jacqueline Mason and after her death Mary Landon Mason.

Charles Atwood Alexander, 1838–1907; married Ida Calhoun and after her death Rosa Calhoun.

3

James Hillhouse Alexander, 1840–1902; married Sarah Irvin.

Marion Brackett Alexander, 1842–1901; married William Ellison Boggs.

Alice Van Yeveren Alexander ("Dot"), 1848–1902; married Alexander Cheves Haskell.

There were two other children who did not live to become part of the family circle: Adam Leopold Alexander was born in 1837 and died after only seventeen days; Henry Leopold Alexander lived just six weeks in 1845.

The Civil War was the central event of nineteenth-century America. It is also the central event of *The Alexander Letters.* Despite his other very considerable accomplishments, Gen. Porter Alexander is best remembered for the part he played in the Battle of Gettysburg. His brothers, Felix, Charles, and Hillhouse, were all officers in Confederate service. Among his in-laws Louisa's husband, Jeremy Francis Gilmer, was a U.S. Army officer who resigned in 1861 to accept a Confederate commission as lieutenant colonel. He was made major general in 1863 and served as chief engineer of the Confederate States from 1862 to the end of the war. Sarah's husband, Alexander R. Lawton, also was graduated from West Point (1839) but resigned from the army in 1841 to practice law. He was made a Confederate brigadier general in 1861 and served as the Confederacy's quartermaster general from 1863 to 1865. Alice's husband, Alexander Cheves Haskell, served under Gen. Maxcy Gregg throughout the war, rising from private to assistant adjutant general and chief of staff to General Gregg. Douglas Southall Freeman called Porter Alexander "one of the ablest of the younger officers of the Confederate Army" and his book *Military Memoirs of a Confederate* (New York, 1907) "altogether the best critique of the operations of the Army of Northern Virginia." Freeman also praised Haskell as a particularly valorous officer.

The reader of Georgia, southern, and Civil War history will meet many friends in these pages: Polly Barclay, the first woman hanged in Georgia; Oliver Hillhouse Prince, the author of the "militia drill" sketch in Judge A. B. Longstreet's *Georgia Scenes;* Dr. William R. Waring of Savannah; the Sorrel family of Savannah; Eliza Bowen, the nineteenth-century historian of Washington, Georgia; Charles Colcock Jones, patriarch of *The Children of Pride;* Custis Lee, Richard Meade, Henry Halleck, Jefferson Davis, Alexander Stephens, James Longstreet, the LeContes, Richard Malcolm Johnston, and many more.

Ulrich B. Phillips wrote in reviewing *The Alexander Letters* in 1911: "The book is full of the intimate, sincere family-talk of unpretentious gentle folk. Numerous pen pictures occur, as of the giddy city life of Savannah in the flush times of 1818, of Saratoga Springs in 1841, of a rustic watering-place in western Georgia in 1846, of the dead town of Sunbury on the Georgia coast in 1853 . . . , of the wedding of Robert Toombs's daughter to one of the Alexander brothers in 1853, of military life at West Point on the eve of war, and of the battles of Fredericksburg and Gettysburg."

The reader doubtless wishes to hurry on to the letters and to the Alexanders themselves; he need be detained only a moment longer. *The Alexander Letters* was issued in a private edition of only 131 copies—just enough for the Alexander descendants and a few friends. A note prepared on June 20, 1909, by the three surviving Alexander children, Harriet Virginia Cumming, Mary Clifford Hull, and Edward Porter Alexander, tells how the book came to be. (When the book was finished the following year, Mrs. Hull was the only survivor.) That note, headed "How It Came About," was printed May 1, 1910, on a separate sheet to be sent to recipients of the book:

> At the Baldwins' tea table, one evening in the Fall of 1907 sat George and Lucy Baldwin [son-in-law and daughter of Mary Clifford Alexander Hull], Marion Boggs [daughter of Marion Brackett Alexander Boggs] and Mary Clifford Hull. The conversation turned on family letters, and some collections of them that had been published. Mrs. Hull remarked that she had kept a number of very delightful ones, with always a vague idea that some day they might be published and make pleasant reading for the descendants of the Alexander family. Marion Boggs immediately offered to edit the collection, and George Baldwin said that he would have the volume published.
>
> The idea was seized upon, and Marion at once began to collect letters from different members of the family. The idea grew and has expanded into this beautiful volume, which will be a treasure to all those who receive it, and an enduring monument to the cultivated literary taste of Marion Boggs, who has given so freely of her time and strength, as well as to the judgment and generosity of George Baldwin, who has planned the book and borne the expense of its production.
>
> We three last survivors of the family, to whom it is dedicated, wish to unite in this expression of our pleasure, gratitude, and

5

appreciation of the book, an invaluable possession to the whole connection, those present, those to come—and we venture to include those "gone before," whose children and grandchildren share with us in this noble gift from George to his wife's family— a proof of the affection which he holds for, and in which he is held by them.

RICHARD BARKSDALE HARWELL
Washington, Georgia

Foreword to the Original Edition

To those of the family connection who have been too far away to have taken part in the interesting work of collecting "The Alexander Letters" we wish to say a word of explanation concerning the purpose and design of this collection.

In the old days of the South, many of the small towns of Georgia contained highly educated, well trained families of gentlefolks, living on or near the cotton plantations which supported them and their dependent slaves. These families were connected by intermarriage with those of Virginia and New England, and from them has come much that is best in the South. Their members were well educated at the best institutions in this country or abroad, often possessed of large means, and charged with the grave responsibility, not only of caring for their many plantation slaves, but with the administration of large estates, at a time when nearly everything consumed on the plantation was made there, even the cloth with which the slaves were clothed. It is not strange that such responsibility and environment produced strong and interesting personalities.

The six sisters and four brothers, children of Adam Leopold Alexander and his wife, Sarah Hillhouse Gilbert, constituted such a typical family group, strongly bound together by ties of affection, and accustomed from early childhood to a very free and constant interchange of letters, in which have been recorded their history, their accomplishments, and their emotions; this correspondence includes charming word pictures of Southern plantation life and of the environment of the writers in the quarter century before the Civil War.

It had become a family custom to pass these interesting letters around from one member to another, and many of them were preserved, some because of their literary charm, others because of the recollections contained therein, or on account of some special historical value.

7

From these rich stores the following selections have been made, that they may be permanently recorded and preserved for the pleasure and benefit of the many descendants of Adam L. Alexander.

In order to clearly show the heredity and environment which produced this group of letter-writing brothers and sisters, certain additional matter has been included in this collection.

The genealogical table of ancestry and the record of descendants has been prepared by Lucy Harvie Baldwin.

A search has been made for the most interesting portraits of each member of the family, reproductions of which have been efficiently prepared by H. Davidson, engraver, of New York, so that this collection is thought to be the best one possible.

The "Settlement of the Family in Georgia" by Harriet V. Cumming leads up to the first letter, which gives a graphic picture of the early times of 1787. It is interesting to note that the Puritan ancestry of Sarah Porter and David Hillhouse were apparently satisfied by the manner in which he was making money!

This is followed by a series of letters showing the evolution from colonial life onward to the more modern period preceding the Civil War, and then the Alexander family are allowed to speak for themselves.

It will be evident that the later days and the younger members of the family are not fully represented, and the reason is not far to seek. After the Civil War the brothers and sisters, being all full grown and widely scattered, their more important letters passed about until many of them were lost. The modern sense of hurry makes itself felt in the decreasing spirit of the correspondence, which, to the lover of literature and human nature, is a sad result of modern progress.

It is to be regretted that no information is obtainable concerning the ancestry of Dr. Adam Alexander, but the character of the male branch of the family can be inferred, and, in fact, known, from information herein contained.

8

Adam Leopold Alexander, his son, was a ripe scholar, and active in all educational matters; he was a Trustee of the State University, and Founder of the Washington Female Seminary, so well known throughout the State, which gave a great impulse to female education and materially elevated its standard in Georgia.

In dedicating "The Reviewers Reviewed" to him, Alexander H. Stephens says of his friend:

"To the only survivor of my early benefactors, a gentleman distinguished for his integrity, piety, urbanity, and high culture, in all that pertains to Art, Science, and Literature, this volume is most respectfully and gratefully inscribed, with a fervent wish that his days may yet be continued for many years to come, in the enjoyment of that 'otium cum dignitate' which always imparts a hallowing charm to the crowning glory of a long, happy, prosperous, and well-spent life."

From "In Memoriam," a tribute written soon after Mr. Alexander's death by his fellow-townsman, Samuel Barnett, the following is quoted:

"His only sister, to whom he was attached with a peculiar love, was bathing his hands, and as she lifted them from the water, she said to him, 'How clean and white your hands always look.' He raised his hand, looked at it, and still holding it up, said, 'Yes, sister; these *are* clean hands. I, a dying man, am not afraid to say that they have never been soiled by a disreputable or dishonest action.' Then he added, 'I wish my children and my children's children to know that no dishonor lurks in these gray hairs.'"

How can we better carry out his wishes than by preserving these letters for his "children's children, even unto the third and fourth generation?"

Marion A. Boggs.
Geo. J. Baldwin.

Savannah, Ga.,
        September 6th, 1909.

The Alexander Letters.

Settlement of the Family in Georgia.*

My father's family (on his mother's side) came from Stuttgardt, in Germany. His maternal grandfather was Egydius Heinrich Schmidt, whose diploma, given when he graduated at the University of Leipsic, is still in the family. We know nothing of his life after graduation till he was a married man, with several children. He was then owner of ships trading between Amsterdam and the West Indies, carrying hardware to the latter place, where he spent a good deal of time. Having lost one or two valuable ships on the long voyage, he decided to leave the West Indies and settle in the United States. He went first to Charleston, S. C. There lived in Charleston at that time a man named Moloch, who was a younger son of a noble family, and had been sent to this country by his parents, because he had fallen into bad company and dissipated habits at home. The two families had been intimate in the Old Country, and when Egydius Schmidt arrived in Charleston, Moloch took him at once to his own house. He was unmarried, wealthy, and had a beautiful home in Charleston. He insisted that his friend should remain with him until he decided fully on his future plans, and till his family could join him.

The mother and children left Stuttgardt and went to Amsterdam to take vessel for this country. This was about 1789, according to the best information that I have. The family consisted (as far as I know) of five children,†

*Written by Harriet V. Cumming.
†Two sons and three daughters.

II

Heinrich, the eldest, remained in Germany, being already in the Army. A very handsome album of his is still in the family,* with etchings, silhouettes, pictures, verses, etc., written and drawn by his brother officers. He died in that country unmarried. Leopold,† after his arrival in this country, studied medicine in Philadelphia under the (then) celebrated Dr. Rush.

When the dreadful epidemic of yellow fever broke out in Philadelphia (about 1798) all the medical students fled but this one. He tarried by his master and died. Leopold Alexander, his namesake, has been given a most appreciative letter which Dr. Rush wrote after his pupil's death to the parents, speaking in the highest terms of him, both as to character and intellect, and his own affection for him.

The names of the daughters were Dorothea Christina, Carlotta Sybilla, and Louisa Frederika (who was our grandmother).

But something remains to be told of the voyage to this country. On the day when the family were to sail from Amsterdam, two vessels were loading for Charleston. One caught the tide at noon. The one on which this family was to go was not quite ready and waited for the next tide. That night came a great freeze, memorable for many years after. The harbor was frozen a long way out, and the belated vessel was held fast in the ice. The severe cold continued and the ice did not melt for months. It was late Spring before the vessel was thawed out and set sail. Her consort had reached Charleston months before, reporting that her mate was only one tide behind her; and when nothing was heard of her for months (for mails were only carried in the vessels) she was given up for lost, and the father was left to believe that his family had perished. When they at last reached Charleston, Moloch's house received them all, till the father finally

*The property of Mrs. J. F. Minis.

†The second son.

decided on Sunbury, Ga., as their future home. This now unknown place was then a thriving town, with a beautiful and very safe harbor, and was considered a dangerous rival to Savannah.

Louisa Frederika was then a girl of twelve or thirteen and Moloch fell desperately in love with her and wanted to marry her. She refused him, but when they moved to Sunbury he broke up his establishment in Charleston and followed them there. Being a rich man, he determined to build for himself a fine house there, and he sent to Amsterdam for a load of German bricks. Many years afterward some of those bricks that were left over were given to grandmother to build the sides of her husband's tomb, the top of the tomb being a heavy marble slab bearing the inscription. That tomb was moved to Laurel Grove, in Savannah, in 1880, and the man who moved it spoke to me of those bricks, asked where they came from, as he had never seen any like them, and said they were very small, not over four or five inches in length, but as hard as iron.

Grandmother's father urged her to marry Moloch, but she refused, though she promised her father to wed no one else during his (her father's) lifetime. He died when she was about twenty-three years of age, and not very long afterwards she married Dr. Adam Alexander, of Edinburgh, Scotland. That marriage was on March 10, 1802, at Sunbury, Ga. Her two children were Adam Leopold Alexander and Louisa Alexander (Mrs. Porter).

Of the other two sisters, Carlotta never married, and died young; and Dorothea Christina was Aunt Van Yeveren, who died at Mrs. Porter's house, in Savannah, in 1851, over eighty years of age.

About Dr. Alexander's family we only know that he was brought up by two maiden aunts named Jamieson and was educated at the University of Edinburgh. His diploma is still in the family.* He came alone to this country as a

*The property of Mr. Irvin Alexander.

young man, and was a surgeon in the United States Army. He was taken prisoner at the siege of Savannah, and was released on parole, because he was wanted to attend a wounded British officer of rank, who was not doing well under his own physician. He died in Sunbury on March 3, 1811, aged 53. His widow took her two children to New Haven, Conn., to educate them, there being few good schools at the South, though old Dr. McWhirr, of Sunbury, had taught the son (A. L. A.) evidently to good purpose, seeing that at the age of fourteen he entered the Junior Class at Yale College. He graduated at the age of seventeen, in the Class of 1821.

My mother (Sarah Hillhouse Gilbert) was an orphan, both parents having died before she was eight years old. Her parents were Sarah Hillhouse and Felix Gilbert. David, the father of Sarah Hillhouse, came to Georgia from Connecticut, and the Gilberts from Rockingham County, in Virginia. My mother was brought up by her grandmother, Mrs. Sarah Porter Hillhouse. Her mother (Mrs. Gilbert) died when this child was three years old, and is buried at the family home, in Washington, Ga. After that her father (Felix Gilbert) never stayed at home, but spent all his time in travel, till he died, in 1813. He left a large fortune, but divided much of it among his relatives, saying that he did not wish to make his only child an object for fortune-hunters. When mother was about ten or twelve years old, her grandmother carried her to New Haven (the grandmother's family home) to educate her, and there she met the young Yale student, Adam Alexander, who was likewise from Georgia. When she was fourteen and he seventeen they became engaged. They were married in Washington, Ga., on April 28, 1823, he aged twenty and she seventeen.

Their home was first in Sunbury, with his mother; but after they had been married about six months, they were recalled to Washington by her uncle, William Gilbert. The two brothers, William and Felix Gilbert, were wealthy men, and had never divided their property. They kept a bank account in the name of the firm, and each one drew on it as he pleased, without giving any account to the other. It so remained (in the name of the firm) even after the death of one partner, and Uncle Gilbert wrote that he had lost money heavily from having endorsed notes for some of his nephews, who had proved very unworthy, and that the property was so involved that mother could not get the $40,000 which her father had left her without taking the house and plantation in Washington as part of it. So Washington became their home and the birthplace of their twelve children. The place still remains in the family. Two little boys died in early infancy. The other ten, six girls and four boys, lived until the youngest child was fifty-four years of age. My mother died on February 28, 1855, aged forty-nine; father on April 9, 1882, aged eighty.

H. V. C.

Mrs. David Gillhouse to Col. Elisha Porter.[*]

Washington, Ga., January 26, 1787.

Hon'd Sir:

I shall now have an opportunity to inform you of my situation here at large, as I think you will be desirous of knowing whatever relates to my circumstances and settlement. I give you as just a description of the place and inhabitants as I am able, and it will be at best but a very poor one.

The Town is new, about 180 miles from Savannah, on the seacoast, and about 50 miles from Augusta, the present seat of Government, and 20 from the Indian Lands. The Inhabitants are very numerous in the Country around us, tho' but a few in the Town plott, but those in the Town very compact. There is a Court House, Jail, and a good Latin and Grammar school.

The land is high and very hilly for this part of the Country; the soil exceeding good. No time in the year but the gardens produce some vegetables. I have never seen snow and seldom a frost in the State. The people in general have gardens this year, and their things come up and look as green and flourishing as in New England in the month of May and June. Our garden will produce three and four crops a year. There is nothing to prevent our having a valuable garden but garden seeds. I was in so great a hurry when I came from Hadley that the garden seeds I so much lotted upon bringing slipt my Memory.

The account I have given you of the place has thus far been good. I wish I could give you as agreeable an account of the Inhabitants of the land. There are a few, and a

_____

[*]Her father at Old Hadley, Mass.

very few, Worthy good people in the Country, near us, but the people in general are the most prophane, blasphemous set of people I ever heard of. They make it a steady practice (if they have money) to come to town every day if possible, and as Mr. Hillhouse is the only person that keeps Liquors, we have the whole throng around us, as many as fifty at a time, take one day with another, and sometimes when any public business is done, which is often, fourteen or sixteen hundred standing so thick that they look like a flock of Blackbirds, and perhaps not one in fifty but what we call fighting drunk. It is impossible for you in your part of the world to conceive what Language is used at such times—the Members of our Gen'l Assembly and Senate as bad as any, or as they stile it, as good as any. They have spent in our cellar for liquor in one day Thirty Pounds Stg., and not a drop carried 1 rod from the store, but sit on a log and swallow it as quick as possible.

It's a good place for business and unless some misfortunes happen to Mr. Hillhouse, he will make money here, but, my ever kind Parent, all the State of Georgia would be no inducement to me to bring my dear little Lambs in this flock of Wolves, as I may properly call many of the inhabitants of this State. I long most ardently to see them and have them with me, if it could be consistent with the duty I owe my children.

Please to give my Duty to Mamma and suitable Regards to all friends. Love and Kisses to my ever dear Ones. Hope their good Conduct may in part pay their kind friends. I am with Gratitude for your kindness to them and me,

Your dutyful daughter,

S. H.

Felix Gilbert to Sarah Hillhouse.

May 12, 1802.

Ten thousand thanks and blessings attend you, best and dearest of women, for the charming memento I received from your hands. Could you have seen with what agitation your packet inscribed with my own name in characters so well known was received, you would never repent your condescension. My heart had suggested the tumultuous delightful Truth—when the beloved Lock met my enraptured eyes. O! that I could describe the Effect; it is impossible. Never before was I mad with love. I tho't the extacies of Lovers, as I have seen them painted, were all fiction, but I defy the most extravagant of them all to have exceeded me. Scarcely have spoken a rational word, or done a sober thing since. As for sleeping, it was too sordid, too vulgar an enjoyment for a mind so elevated to think of. Alternately has the Lock been viewed and pressed to my run mad heart. As the first tumult subsides, I view it (may I tell you all my boldness?) as a pledge irrevocable of your regard. As such it will be my supporter during an absence now truly felt as an Exile—How often will it be removed from its hiding place in my pocket-book! I shall make an animate Being of it. I will speak to it and it shall tell me a thousand things. A small part shall go into a case to be placed next my Heart, but the form in which it came from your dear hand, how sacredly shall it be preserved!

I am hurried and confused by an hundred little necessary importances of preparation. How dull, how fatiguing are they!

I wrote you a few lines yesterday. They shall not be suppressed. I wish you to see my whole heart. You will

18

see it at one period in different views; the principal feelings are the same. How differently affected! Adieu. Heaven's best angels guard and watch over you every moment. O, if possible, grant the favor I ventured to ask! Let me know from your own hands your welfare and happiness, and that you spoke not the dictates of your Heart when you said you felt no regret at the departure of

Your devoted,

F. H. G.

P. S.—I promised you the "Prince of Abyssinia."* He had been mislaid. I have found him and will make him the Bearer of this. I know you will be delighted with the sentiments. Many of them are innate with your own Heart. I send also a "Monody on the Death of Major Andre." You will see in him an instance of Constancy in Love, attended by misfortune in every stage. I know myself his equal in the strength of my attachment. Would I merited equally a return! How foolishly I begin to think and write—I won't another word, except to pray by some means for your name in your own hand—

*Rasselas, by Sam'l Johnson.

Felix Gilbert to Sarah Hillhouse.

20th June 1802.

I hesitate dear Miss Hillhouse, how or whether at all to address you. After my last so foolish and ungrateful I ought to be forever dumb, but I hope you will think a Heart so prone to be its own Tormentor, needs not the additional misery of your displeasure. I feel already its effects in the consciousness that I merit it & have nothing to offer in extenuation. Let me then throw myself at your mercy. Neither my Head nor Heart prompted the sentiments my bewildered imagination then suggested. "Meditation to Madness" may certainly be indulged on subjects the most pleasing. View me in that Light. My mind eternally engaged with your image, is it strange, or unpardonable, that fancy should sometimes darken her sketches and produce the gloomy impressions under which I then labored? Think that I am now at Bethlehem lamenting my folly, where every scene presents to my Heart your image,* and reproaches me with foolish, stupid ingratitude. Throw the mantel of oblivion over my offence, & let me once more live in your smiles. A dear Memento now in my sight suggests the flattering Hope that you are not inexorable, & that you will hear with interest of the pleasure I am deriving from my excursion here. I arrived last Evening, perfectly enraptured with the lovely Country around. I don't know if you ever travelled the present Stage Road from Philadelphia. Surely never were Nature and Art more happily united than for the last 6 miles. I never

*Sarah Hillhouse had attended school at Bethlehem, Pa.

attempt description, but if you will peruse Miss Williams' Alpine descriptions, lessening the rugged towering Alps into gentle rising mountains covered with a teeming Harvest, and the rapid blustering Rhine into the gentle silver Monocacy, you have the Lovely Landscape thro which I passed to River Lehigh. You have often spoken to me of this delicious River on which the rural Moravian Town is situate. How did my Heart swell with almost bursting emotion, while I breathed the pure morning air on its Banks, and reflected that I was treading the ground on which your youthful form once moved. I am just now returned from attending the morning Lecture to the young Ladies. It engaged not my attention. After I had taken the view of their Charms which Gallantry demanded, I closed my Eyes for the purpose of calling up your image and investing you with the Sisters Cap. What a lovely glow it gave your cheeks and how charmingly did your beautiful Hair appear. Like Prometheus I had almost clasped in my arms the idol of my own Creation. Unfortunately it is Sunday, and I have not so good an opportunity of seeing the place and its novelties on this as on another day, and to-morrow I must return to Philad. on my way to New York. Old Dada Thomas is to escort me this afternoon to see the Sisters. Such a Squire & such a Knight have a right to expect adventures. He is a kind old Soul, but they are a mighty quizzical set of folks.

I had the pleasure of spending several Hours with Miss Massey. What a Charming Girl she is. I acknowledge now that she is not handsome but how infinitely more engaging than thousands of mighty pretty people I have seen. Her Mother is loquacious to annoyance, and I should have set her down in my Catalogue of Pests, but that she is one of your admirers. Will you credit that I did not find Miss Massey the two first days I was in the City, because I did not know North from South. Let this be a proof that I am sometimes crazy. I hope the mania will not increase to require Confinement till I return to Georgia; then I am hoping for such Chains, as,— Halt there, Boy, the fit comes again. Stop when you are well; put on your lackadaisical face and spite of the precious memento which, thus I kiss, say you are the repentant, Hopeless,

F. H. G.

Bethlehem, Pa.

Felix Gilbert to Sarah Hillhouse.

New York, July 28, 1802.

I will not, dear Miss Hillhouse, attempt to apologize for my late silence, farther than by declaring that it has originated from a conviction that it must be agreeable to you, after the specimens you have had of my talent in addressing the Lady I love. If ever the world should be favored with my Epistles, St. Preux and Werter will certainly be thrown entirely in the back-ground.

To be serious I am a self-condemned wretch, both when I write and when I am silent, and think myself so undeserving the esteem and confidence you have shown me, that I almost regret sometimes that I ever asked it. I recollect to have asserted to you that I was resolved to lay before you every Emotion of my Heart. I pray you not to believe me. If you saw all its workings since I parted with you, you would perhaps pity, but I much fear you would also despise it. Let me then forbear to speak of it, except to swear that all its best feelings are connected and regulated by Love, the most Ardent, and Esteem, the most respectful, for Miss Hillhouse.

I returned two days since from the Eastward, and found several letters from my friends. I was not vain enough to expect one from you, tho' I did feel some chagrin and disappointment that I did not. I hear you are well and happy. These are cordial tidings. I will not say how much alloyed by the constancy of my friend E. C. I met him as I came on. My eyes recognized a rival. I will not say that my heart dreaded a successful one, tho' I believe I thought he ought to be so. A constancy so long

23

and so tried certainly has claims. His first enquiries were of you, and I doubt not his penetration discovered how little pleasure his earnestness afforded. My correspondents suggest a foundation for a thousand fears from his agreeable qualities and unremitted attentions. Is it wondrous that far absent and self-condemned, I should feel alarm? I will say no more. It is time I had spoken of your Friends.

I was a week in Rhode Island, one day of which I spent with Mrs. W. I dare say you are surprised at that shortness of my stay, and will be grieved to hear that it was because I thought myself an unwelcome guest. Superior to most women as she is, she has her foibles, and I perceived that the sight of even a Friend in an humble habitation was mortifying, and her arrangements for my accommodation partook too much of solicitude to enable me to be at ease. She is about 20 miles from New Port and in a very unpleasant situation. She, however, spends but little of her time there. I delivered your letter and was anxious to learn why you wished me not to bring it, but if there was any particular reason, I must still conjecture. Poor little Betsey was overjoyed to see me! She says she will not go back to Georgia, but insists on loving her Friends there better than those of Rhode Island.

Doctor Hay informs me he looks for a sickly season. I am become so selfish as to be indifferent on the subject further than my friends and above all the Mistress of my Heart are concerned. Heaven shield you!

Maria affected me to tears by her account of Miss Pope's last moments. It is useful to the mind to hear of such examples when engaged in dissipation and business. It has certainly made me a better man and a better Christian since I read it.

I expect to leave this place in a fortnight. I should go immediately on by Savannah, but I should hurt Sister Taylor greatly, having stayed so little time with her as I came on. Great as is my confidence, I can not be at ease under the unopposed address of an insinuating and accomplished rival. He may be more agreeable and more worthy, but he can not love more than I do.

Farewell beloved, angelic girl! Remember that there is an absent, an adoring, tho' sometimes capricious

F. H. G.

Felix Gilbert to Sarah Hillhouse.

Dear Sarah:

I am yet at New York detained by adverse winds. Will our interests ever again be opposite, my sweetest— I hope not, thro' a long life of mutual happiness— At present they are. The same wind which detains me, wafts speedily & safely, I trust, my heart's dearest treasure to her destined port. With this Hope, how cheerfully, with how much real pleasure do I bear the delay in my own setting out. The packet will at any rate go this evening— Altho I shall at setting out be increasing the distance between us, I am anxious to be gone as commencing the route which is to restore me again to your dear society. I wrote you on Sunday and inclosed my Letter to your Mama. I hesitated afterwards whether I was right, and could hardly persuade myself to put it in the office. I am now happy I did. I am sanguine enough to feel secure of her approbation. If I am mistaken, you know whom I shall blame for my false confidence, but I have not much to fear. Altho' I may not possess her entire confidence, I think in *Washington* I may hope for comparative approbation—and having thus (without her consent) made her a party to our engagements, seems to have given them a sanction which renders them more tenderly interesting, more dear to my Heart, for I now consider you as my wife— How cold, how inexpressive is that word, of all the charming ideas it calls up— O my sweetest Sarah, what emotion swells my heart as I anticipate the moment when we acknowledge to the world our interest in each other— In vain would I attempt a delineation of my feelings. Your own I fondly believe comprehends them all in delicious sympathy.

Newport 12th—at Night—I am this moment landed after a pleasant passage— How beautiful was the last night, how deliciously melancholy were my feelings while I sat on deck, my whole soul full of your image. I sigh'd heavily when I tho't how sweetly we should have enjoyed it together— I saw you in imagination pensively viewing the moon's silver image reflected in the smooth sea, and hoped your mind was occupied in sympathy with my own— I became for once romantic and spoke in soft whispers to the dear vision of my imagination. The delusion was too happy to be lasting—painful images succeded—and presented your little Barque contending with angry waves and encountering opposing winds—yourself, sick, weary and desponding— My gloomy forebodings became excessive, and were aided by the dream you mentioned—do not think, my dear angel, that I speak the Language of romance, when I tell you that they pursued the dark prospect, till I saw you buried in a watery grave— It was then and at other moments when anticipating the possibility of such an event, that I most regret my not being with you for I feel most poignantly that to perish with you would be infinitely more desirable than to live without you— I almost fear to submit to your inspection sentiments like these—but you will not suspect me of affecting more than I feel—of duplicity to you, my sweetest, best Girl, I am not capable. Would to Heaven I could lay my whole Heart with all its emotions before you. I think you would be pleased with the inspection— Let me only say now that much as I love and dote on you, my respect, my esteem and veneration for your mind and character equal my Love—are in fact its basis—its best foundation and surety of its unabating fervor and continuance.

My feelings had overpowered me and I was forced to quit my pen. I had on my arrival sent a note to Miss

Mumford inquiring for Mrs. W—— Frederic brought the answer. My anxiety to get on had determined me if she was at Tiverton to decline calling on her—but he seemed so disappointed, and I felt myself that she would be so much hurt if I did not, that I have consented to accompany him tomorrow— We go on foot 9 miles thro the fields, a pretty good walk for a Beau.

(13.) I have just returned from Miss Mumfords. F. is to call in an hour to commence our pedestrian expedition —part of the forenoon has been spent with Mrs. McLaws and Son and Daughter— The old woman was much gratified at meeting a Georgian here in this dullest of all dull places.

Tiverton (14) I have been unfortunate enough to find our Friend from home on a visit 6 miles off— I am truly sorry for this, as it will abridge the short time I had to spend with her—and I cannot lengthen it—my impatience to set my face homeward where so much of felicity and of extacy awaits me increases every moment— F. is gone in pursuit of his mother and has left me with the horrid old Aunt. Having a natural antipathy to old maids, I have in defiance of all gallantry left this old Lady, and am now sitting on a rock, a mile from the House, viewing the loveliest and sublimest scene my eyes ever witnessed. Would to Heaven you were with me. How truly should I then enjoy it—but separated from you, nothing has charms for me—the Sea which forms part of the prospect calls up melancholy ideas with it— Let me dissipate them and bright Hope take their place. Let my mind's eye see you safely landed on Georgia's sandy shores, and rapidly hastening to be restored to the society of loving and beloved Friends—I am going to write to Betsy, and shall give her a faint sketch of the prospect now before me— altho I am so unsuccessful that I hardly ever attempt it— I shall enclose this to her, as the same objection which applied to my directing immediately to you, arises in directing very often *our* Mother. I mean to write very often

—dont be frightened, my next will not be perhaps so long as this. I will try not to be so selfish.

Sunday 15th— I am again in Newport waiting a passage to Providence. From Sister Hay, you will learn particulars of the time I spent with our Friend— She had recd your Letter and written you in answer— I was really sorry to stay so short a time, and felt afraid she would attribute my impatience to the unpleasantness of her situation. Tomorrow night I hope to be in Boston— from thence how joyfully shall I turn my steps toward Georgia. I wish I could sink in the perspective the time which is to be spent in Virginia—heavily will it move altho with a Sister I love and friends I esteem—but worse than dull and insipid to me seems every place where you are not. Think of me sweet beloved Sarah constantly and affection- ately. Never again can you doubt that I am wholly and forever yours.

Your own

F. H. G.

Felix Gilbert to Sarah Gilbert.

My Dear Wife:

I arrived yesterday morning in good health, after a fatiguing ride, having it first very warm and dusty, and then an inundation of rain.

As I feared there is not a single New York packet in Port, and only one small sloop with very bad accommodations bound there, nor is there any prospect of a packet in less than ten days at shortest. Anxious therefore to be on the way and at the same time obedient to your instructions not to trust my precious person in an indifferent vessel, I have taken a berth in the "Agenoria" for Baltimore, a capital vessel and remarkable for fortunate passages. Our accommodations are excellent and our Captain a very clever fellow, so that having some good company, I am in hopes to have a pleasant time, tho' my satisfaction is lessened by the reflection that that route will defer my arrival at New York, and, of course, my time of restoration to the arms of my beloved wife and dear little infant.* I assure you I feel the full force of Col. Willis' observation as to this our first long separation, and am perpetually wishing that you had been my companion. I won't tell you which I think most of, yourself, or our sweet little kitten; indeed I could not tell myself. Heaven guard you both and grant us a happy reunion.

We expect to sail on Sunday, if weather permits, tho' the prospect is at present unfavorable, the weather being cold and thick, with wind strong at N. E. I am to have as companions, Hellyer, B. McKinne, S. Thomas, and old McIver, besides some I don't know. I have an after state-

*Sarah, afterwards Mrs. A. L. Alexander.

room on the same side with that in which you came. The sight of it forcibly recalled some little tender ideas to my mind—you may guess whether I chose that berth from any particular cause.

I saw Wm. Prince yesterday for a few minutes. He is as sanguine as ever and has fallen on new plans of living and teaching, all of which he says are just the thing. I have not seen Grimes. I intended to have called on him last night, but was invited to old Newells just as I was going out, and dreading the interview felt glad of an excuse for delaying it. I mean to call this evening, and shall give you the result by Sherrod who returns tomorrow. Old Mother Twining was at Newell's and entertained me with a history of the astonishing cheap goods she bought in Savannah, so much below what I ever could find, that I mean to propose to her to buy for me on commission.

Mr. Baldwin is here and expects to be in Washington. We lodge in the same room. I have made him promise to visit the widow and fatherless in Washington,—he says I looked as if I repented or was hurt at the expression. I did feel a little choking, but I won't be sorry. Am I not going to see Baltimore, New York, and all the fine places and things? Yes, but I had ten thousand times rather see one kick of our sweet little kitten's foot. O my wife and my dear infant! How superior are the delights you afford to every other. My heart swells at the idea. The prospect of a happy reunion, and of our dear babe's improvement must support this tedious absence.

I comfort myself on the prospect of detention with the hope of a letter from you by Monday's mail. You won't disappoint me I know, and you can have much to communicate. All Maria's little frolics are topics of the best sort. God take you both unto his keeping, fervently prays,

Your affectionate husband,

F. H. G.

I shall write to Brother by Sherrod and send your Mama a New York paper.

Sarah Gilbert to Felix Gilbert.

Fairfield,* May 17, 1806.

I this moment received my dear Husbands letter (if such a few lines can be called letter) from Augusta. I did not mean to complain of the shortness of it. I feel truly grateful that you stole a few minutes out of so short a time to tell me you were so well. May God continue you so! I heard last night that you got off from Augusta Monday evening, a Mr. Thomas from that place was here, introduced by Mr. Cummins. The Girls from the Maj'rs were here with Majr. Long part of the evening, and Mr. Shepherd came at dinner time and is still here, and has had a great to do this morning spruceing himself up—your razors were gone, Billy cannot be spared from the hall before breakfast —and I sent Jack to him to go for one, or a barber. He would not do, or Emanuel would better (by the by Emanuel is quite sick) and is still out. I am writing while the girls are all sleeping, & was up this morning soon as I got a fire, which is very necessary, I don't think it was colder during the winter, with the exception of a few cold spells than it has been here since Thursday night. The wind is exactly ahead here. I am not sorry for that, if there is any vessel in port ready to go, it will detain her till you are ready to go with her. I am very fearful you may be detained there or in Charleston, I am glad you will go to the latter place if obliged to wait.

Poor Mrs. Barkley is doomed to swing—the Governor will not respite. She has asserted I hear, that she never will be hung, it would not be surprising if she was to end her own existence.

*The name of her home at Washington, Ga.

32

They are better at the Maj'rs.

Now, let me tell you something of our darling, she grows sweeter every day and calls almost incessantly *pa pa* and is now at it, she took Mr. Shepherd for you—the girls have been fit to eat her up.

There is a hunting party at Upton today some of the Beaux from town went last night down.

Sunday 18—

Last evening we spent at the doctor's and agreed to go today to "Clarks Station" to hear Mr. Clay preach, but it has rained constantly since morning, however Majr. Long & Frances Casey came over to breakfast on their way, but on our declining they stopped and together with Dr. Casey spent most of the day here. Frances and Mr. Shepherd are still here— Oliver Prince was added to the number this evening but not even the beaux could take my attention off from watching the wind which the middle of the afternoon changed to exact South & perhaps my Gilbert is now off the Bar. I have not patience till tomorrow, when I shall hear more certainly I trust—it is now eleven or very near it. I have taken a minute from sleep, or rather from my pillow, for I don't feel like sleeping, but must not be long for fear of leaving too little room for tomorrow and Frances who sleeps with me, & is now in Mary's room, will be back & laugh at my fondness, as she will call it. Yes here she comes. Good night dear Gilbert.

Monday night 7 o'clock.

I cannot even say thank ye, for the dear favor I received from Savannah this evening until I tell you how sweetly Maria* is dancing by my side. I came in to write half an hour ago but have been so fascinated by her life & charming ways that I was unable to leave her— Mary has hold of her & you never saw such a frollic, nothing she has hitherto done in that way comes up to it in the least—the moment Mary begins to sing after a short rest, her little feet fly with her hands eyes and every feature in unison. Sarah, Bill & Charles are all helping her. After

*Afterward called Sarah.

33

condescending to receive a little entertainment from each, she turns to her delighted Mother for her approbation and caresses, then begins again.

You told me in your dear letter from Savannah that Maria's little frolics are topics of the best sort. I am glad she has put me in spirits for I felt before & indeed do now not a little regret that I am behind but hush! on this subject— I don't think, nor wont write again. You say a great many affectionate things,—my heart traces your own in every line and beats a response to every wish, to every sentiment, but I shall get quite jealous if you *"cant tell which you think most of, me or little kitten."*

Mr. Hay received a letter from Mrs. Taylor this evening she is well but still writes of her disappointment at the Drs going in alone.— I wrote you by Mr. Mathews last week & also by mail, indeed I could write you every hour in the day, and hardly then find time for all I would wish to say, you would not think to see me now with the pen it was the same who two weeks past hated to take it up so very much. Mrs. Hay was here this evening to get me to request you to get for her a small Fender for her Drawing room, it is 2 foot 7 inches from one Jam to tother. She would not trouble you but that it is hard to get one so small & impossible here— She also says if you can get her a piano of low price that is of the plain kind but good she would be glad you would, about 200$ is the extent of price I believe or about that. Perhaps Ann Massey would undertake to choose one.

I have to add to your memorandum also a Universal Gazetteer, Hair Brush—& 1 or 2 yds of India Book Muslin & if you wish me to wear them a fashionable & handsome pair of earrings. I have at last consented to pierce my meat.

Brother & Mary are here. Mary says she dont want to send her love to you any more, I write too often.

God bless my love, good night—Good night.

S. G.

Felix Gilbert to Sarah Gilbert.

New York, June 15, 1806.

My Dear Sarah:

Instead of going to church this morning I stay at home to enjoy the dear pleasure of writing you and of telling you how happy your sweet letter of the 20th has made me,—parental anxiety had been aroused at the thought of our dear babe's indisposition. The failure of your letter on the day expected, when it ought to have reached me, had increased it, and I was full of gloomy apprehension. How sweetly, my dear Girl, have you removed my alarms! How delightedly has my imagination made me a spectator of those enjoyments in the frolics of the sweetest pledge that ever blessed two fond parents. O my Love, how anxiously do I long for the day which shall restore me to those scenes which alone can now give me real happiness! I have labored hard this week past and altho' I never found more difficulty in procuring goods, yet have got thro' the worst part, having made most of my purchases. I have now to ship them and to look out for some small articles not to be had in the regular way. This will occupy me I expect till about Friday next, when I expect to go to New Haven. My stay there will be short, not more than three days. On my return I have a visit to make to Long Island, and by the time that is over I hope the carriage will be in readiness for me to proceed.

I began my business with less spirit than ever I felt before, but in proportion as I advanced I improved and never dispatched more in the same time. My health is very good. I generally go out at 6 in the morning for the purpose of doing odd jobs. After breakfast I go to regular work till dinner, after which smaller affairs again employ me.

I have been only once at the theater, and this because you enjoined me to be careful of my health. I walk on the Battery sometimes. One evening I have spent at Mr. Patricks, one at Clendinings, and one at Mr. Fays. The same particular or singular kind of manner which struck me before, again affects me with regard to those folks, and makes me feel doubtful whether I am welcome or not. Fay has never called on me. I shall go once more, and, if I see no reason to alter my opinion, that will be my last visit. The evening I was there Henry Meigs and wife were present. She is a sweet little woman and plays and sings most divinely. Meigs himself is, I think, on the whole one of the most elegant and agreeable men I ever saw. He has pressed me to call on him and I mean to do so when the throng of business is over. I am generally so fatigued of an evening that I feel but little disposed for company.

I shall attend most particularly to all my dear Sarah's memoranda. The ear rings and sleeve pins are bought. I find a good plain piano forte may be had for 180 dollars. I shall, of course, get one for Nancy Hay, but am at a loss whether to depend on getting one here, or to get Ann to chose it in Philadelphia.

I am surprised to hear that Shepherd is growing such a beau. You don't tell me whether you still think his attentions are designed for our Sister Mary, or whether you think they may be successful or not.

I know my dear Sarah is not serious when she says she is jealous at my doubts whether I love her or Kitten best. These are questions of the heart, impossible to decide; or rather they are not questions at all, for in proportion as I feel all a fond parent feels for such a blessing does my affection glow with increased and with a hallowed fervor for the wife of my heart. Heaven in thus crowning our bliss seems to have approved and sanctioned our union, and to have given a promise of lasting felicity. Yes, my dear Girl, I feel this promise and my confidence in it is great. I never thought nor felt it so much as since I left you. We never know our blessings until we are for a while deprived of them. This separation has shown me how fortunate I have been. May I be able to merit and to communicate all the happiness I feel and enjoy. I look forward with impatience till tomorrow. It will, I trust, bless me with yours of the 26th. I wish I could receive them when at home or alone. They always are delivered me at Clendinings' store when I can not enjoy them as I should in my own room, because I must suppress emotions which are too strong to be shown to others. It is truth, my dear girl, that when you speak of yourself and our dear Maria my eyes always fill with tears. They are sweet delicious drops and those moments are the most happy of my life, but they would appear ridiculous to those who know not their source; for this reason I look very hastily over your letter the first time and defer my full enjoyment till my return home. May your next letter tell me all I could wish to hear of your health and happiness.

I am just called on by some gentlemen. We are going to view the place where Hamilton fell. I must therefore bid you adieu till next Sunday. I will say, God bless you a thousand times. When I don't write it nor speak, I breathe it—for in blessing my dear Sarah, am I completely blessed. Farewell, my dear wife and my sweet babe. O that I could peep in on you for a moment,—the wish affects me too much. Time fly swiftly and bring the blissful moment when I may press you both to my full heart.

F. H. G.

Felix Gilbert to Mrs. Taylor.*

Washington June 12, 1808.

My Dear Sister:

Your tender sympathizing Heart will explain to you
what my emotions must be, at first writing after the heavy
affliction with which it has pleased the Almighty disposer
of us all, to visit me. O my Sister! often within a few
short years have we experienced the ravages of Death
in our near & dear connexions, but compared with what
I now feel, every deprivation seems to have been light—
Half my existence seems lopd off. She whose virtues were
my rule of Life, whose smiles & whose approbation were
my solace & delight is gone never, never to return—. Doctor
Hay has informed you of the rapid progress of the disease,
which snatched her from me. I had for some weeks previous too fully anticipated the catastrophe & had vainly
imagined that the composure & celestial patience she
exhibited, in suffering, with the heavenly assurance she
displayed in her last moments of happiness hereafter had
enabled me to submit with resignation to the Will of
Heaven. My first transports of sorrow were not so bitter—
I could mourn my loss, & in Tears I felt a sweet relief
—viewing her as amongst the blessed above—for such
she surely is if Mortals can anticipate in their last moments
their future destiny—a hope more confident, a composure
more serene was never exhibited, & after the Soul was
fled which animated her loved form never did mortal see
so heavenly a countenance in death— Strange as it may
seem, I could view it with something almost like rapture
—& in the consciousness of her happy exchange of the

*A sister living near Orange Court House, Va.

38

ills of Life for eternal happiness, felt myself for the moment buoyed above the selfishness of Grief— Alas my Sister, this could not last— Every minute, every spot, & every circumstance continually remind me what I possessed & what I have lost—& it seems as if the poignancy of these regrets gain force every day— When I review the three happy years which Heaven granted me in her loved society, when I retrace all those sweet endearing scenes of domestic Happiness, when My Heart acknowledges that whatever of Virtue, or respectability I possess, depended on & was derived from the contemplation of her exalted mind & my desire to be worthy of her, I feel as if every tie was rent asunder, & this whole world were to me a dreary void, in which our happiness only is uncertain & transient, our woe alone certain & permanent.

Thus far I had written last night my beloved Sister, in a moment of deep despondence— I had been yesterday engaged in reading over her dear letters—sweet painful mementos of one of the finest minds & most sincere & affectionate of Hearts— I am often struck with wonder, my Sister, when I reflect on the strength of the attachment I had inspired in a mind so well regulated, a Judgment so clear & discerning— Every line she ever wrote to me proves that her heart was truly devoted to me— O Nancy, how can I support the thought that I am forever bereft of such a Wife, such a Friend! God Almighty grant that the remembrance of her Virtues may keep me worthy of having possessed such a heart, & may conduct me in such a course as to justify the Hope of once more beholding that sweet heavenly face in realms where sorrow cannot come— It is impious perhaps to repine too much, with the assurance I have of her present felicity. A very few hours before her last sigh she told me that altho she had as much to render life desirable as any one who ever quit it, her wish was to go. (Her sufferings had been great, her patience unequalled & heavenly)—her pains, she said, were over & her hope was without fear— She enjoined on me in a solemn manner, to inculcate early, religious impressions on the dear pledge she left me. God grant me the disposition to feel them properly myself—then shall I be able to obey this her dying request— I feel my Nancy that I am wrong in paining your affectionate & already suffering heart by the recital of such mournful ideas—but there is a luxury of grief in dwelling over her last words, & last Scenes of such a Life—I have no one to whom I can pour out my Heart here—. I feel a melancholy consolation in the assurance that you will shed a sympathizing tear with your unhappy Brother. My task is hard & severe—to assume a composure & cheerfulness for the sake of my surrounding friends. How much more severe are my griefs when opportunity is afforded to indulge them—when my mind recals a thousand sweet images of departed bliss— never more to be repeated—but let me no longer dwell on such themes—painfully has your heart been tried my beloved Sister. Death which for a long time seemed to spare our connexions, has of late selected us as his first objects— Three Sisters, a wife & sweet infant have been snatched from me in two short years—such visitations are perhaps intended in mercy by our Father in Heaven to show us the vanity of placing our hopes on such transitory blessings & to lead our minds to that contemplation of Joys which last forever—pray for me my Sister, that I may be enabled rightly to improve them— My sweet little Girl, who now bears her Mother's name, is happy in having her loss supplied by her Grandma—whose fortitude on this trying occasion is truly astonishing— I derive some consolation, when reflecting on my own loss, in the assurance that this darling Child will have in her Grandma, a friend who can so guide & direct her opening mind as to make it resemble as far as Nature permits her sainted Mother— To poor Nancy Hay* no one here can fulfill so necessary a part— She had you know been living with us—& during the short

*Daughter of a deceased sister.

time our travelling so much permitted us to see the effects
of her Aunts example & admonitions, gave the most promising hopes. Poor Girl! her situation is now widely different.
Without a friend to guide & direct her at this critical period,
I feel the most anxious solicitude for her future prospects—
living alone with her Father, who possesses I fear not a
sufficient degree of firmness & Judgment to enable him
to advise her rightly I think her prospects by no means
happy—in addition to which the present state cf society
here amongst those of her age & sex is in my opinion
peculiarly unfavorable— I never have known a time when
pleasure & dissipation seem so entirely to have engrossed
the minds of the young—& when so little attention was
paid to solid & useful acquirements—French, Music, painting, dancing are almost the sole studies—& even these they
acquire in such a very superficial way as to be of no service,
even were they of that sort that could add to usefulness, to
amiability or respectability. I cannot but wish Nancy were
with you— I am sure she would there acquire more that
would render her amiable, useful, respectable & happy in
one year than she ever can here, even if there were no
apprehensions of danger for her, living unprotected as she
is by the care of any elder female— You my Sister, as
well as our departed Maria & Betsy had no education of
this showy superficial sort—yet who were better Wives,
Mothers, Neighbors, friends, than you all? I could wish
if it meets Mr. Taylors approbation that Nancy might live
for a time with you— Her Heart & her Understanding are
excellent— My dear departed Sarah, whose judgment of
character was almost unerring, was very strongly attached
to her. With you, Nancy can learn those domestic Virtues
& accomplishments (for they surely deserve the name better
than a little scraping on a Guittar, or smattering of bad
French) which may contribute to her own happiness &
that of the person with whom she may be destined to pass
her life— If it should meet your approbation & Mr. Taylors,
I wish you would write to the Doctor on the subject— I

41

think he will embrace your offer—& I am certain it will be highly agreeable to Nancy— As to her going on I presume the Doctor or Brother would go with her—unless my dear Sister, you can summon fortitude enough to visit these scenes, now bereft of so many of their beloved Tenants—if you could conclude on paying us a visit, it would be to us a most pleasing consolation—your time could be divided between here & the Doctors—& if you have no convenient way of coming out, I will send in my Carriage for you. I would accompany it myself, but, am confined at home by my building*—in which I had progressed too far to decline, when the Event took place, which would otherwise have induced me to decline it entirely. Brother will set out for Kentucky in 3 or 4 weeks on business— Next Spring I would return with you—as Mr. Taylor could have spared the time to go to Richmond, tell him he will certainly not pretend to excuse himself for want of time to come out here. Write soon & tell us you are coming.

Sister Gibson is well, her little Girl is not so, having had an attack of dysentery some time ago & not entirely recovered. All other Friends are well. I have written you a long letter my dear Sister— I did not intend to have dwelt so much on my own concerns—my object was to write on account of Nancy, but Grief is selfish & since my fatal loss, I have not once unburdened my Heart— I think it feels lighter—this will compensate you for the painful feelings I may have excited. In speaking of her who is now lost to us, in paying to her Virtues their just tribute, in the remembrance of her Love & kindness to me, in acknowledging the influence my attachment for her has had in forming my character, I feel a pleasure which tho melancholy is dear to my Heart— I am certain, as long as I cherish her recollection I shall be a better Man for it, & I hope her happy end will make me a better Christian— God bless you my Sister— Remember me

*The present home at Washington.

affectionately to Mr. Taylor, to Mother & to the Boys—
John has not written me lately, from his last I presume he
may be now in Tennessee. My particular Love to my
namesake, who I hope is a very good Boy.

Yr Afft Brother

F. H. G.

Brother desires his Love to all.

Felix Gilbert to Mrs. Taylor.

Washington 27 May 1813.

My Dear Sister
You have heard from us last about 3 weeks ago by
Nancy Hay—we have since been anxiously expecting one
of your dear letters, it being a long time since we heard
from you. Indeed you have been so good in the forepart
of the Winter, that the long interval since your last gives
us some uneasiness to account for your late silence—. As
we all know that it has not proceeded from your want of
inclination, so we will hope in the Mercy of Providence it
has not arisen from any Misfortune. I presume Nancy
told you I was again contemplating a journey to the Springs,
and I am apprehensive you will have drawn conclusions &
formed Hopes from this circumstance, which are errone-
ous— The truth was I had been persuaded for a few
days to think of a step which I felt at the time to be a
desperate one, and despair alone could have induced me
to the undertaking— I have remained so long in the same
situation without any apparent diminution, or increase of
strength and my pain and suffering so severe that my
fortitude and that submission to the will of my God which
I hoped I had acquired seemed almost entirely to have
deserted me, and I felt tempted to risque almost any thing
that promised either relief or release—. But I have for
two weeks past felt so much worse, as to convince me of
the madness and folly, if not wickedness of the attempt—
I trust also I feel more submission and willingness to leave
the Event in his hands whose are the issues of Life and
of Death, and whose will concerning me can be accomplished in any way his providence may order—and alas,

44

my Sister, every day's Experience convinces me that all I suffer and much more is necessary to subdue this proud, stubborn, rebellious, unbelieving Heart—so much remaining attachment to the things of time and sense, so little spiritual Life, so much coldness, deadness and indifference to divine things, constitutes the general tenor of my feelings for two months past, that I feel awfully afraid I am yet in the gall of bitterness, the Bonds of iniquity— Yet I lament and mourn over these things, and often ask,

"If I am thine, why am I thus"
Blessed be the name of the Lord, however, I can yet see light thro all the gloom and derive some comfort from the Hope that my bodily weakness and distress is in part the cause, for feeble and weak as is my faith and Hope, and dark and confused as are my views, yet I trust I can say and feel, that when lowest and darkest, I would not give it up, for Life, for Health or for a thousand worlds—. At times, when I can see and most deeply feel my own vileness and insufficiency, I cease to look within myself and can then find comfort by reflecting on the free, sovereign, all sufficient Grace of our dear Saviour—but I too soon alas! fall back into what I suppose is the remains of a legal spirit, by looking for something within myself that is to recommend me and finding worse, oh how much worse than nothing, I am again cast almost into the blackness of despair— You have probably felt this and can enter into my situation better than I can explain it.

Sister Gibson has been with me a few days—she looks very thin and has a troublesome cough which as usual she insists is the consumption and is very low spirited—there seems however no reason to believe her fears are just— Brother has had very poor health all winter. I am exceedingly desirous he should go to the Springs—but he seems to find it almost impossible to persuade himself to leave me in my low state. I shall continue however to urge it— and if it pleases the Lord to spare my Life to see him return, shall indulge the hope of seeing Mr. Taylor and you with him—think of it my dear Sir—there is certainly little prospect of my surviving—but my case being a singular one, and my situation so little altered for many months, I may possibly linger a long time. Our friends not mentioned are generally as well as usual. I have received a second letter from our good Mr. Glassell—tell him how grateful I feel for his kind attention— Remember me affectionately to those you know I love—and respectfully to friends and acquaintances generally. May the Lord bless and visit your soul my dear Sister with the consolation of his holy Spirit— and if it be his good pleasure that we meet no more here, may we be united at his right hand, in the world to come, where is fulness of Joy and blessings ever more, is the earnest prayer of your affectionate.

Afflicted Brother

F. H. G.

Sister Gibson bids me add for her, that almost all her hopes of recovery from *her Consumption*, depends on your coming in the fall and begs you and Mr. Taylor will think seriously of it.

Felix Gilbert to David Hillhouse.*

July 1813.

My friend and Brother:—

With a weak and tremulous hand I will try to trace a few lines—should I not succeed you will not, however, doubt how much of interest I feel in the approaching Event. I feel it warmly as the best human assurance of *your* happiness,—I feel it also most soothing and gratifying to my anxious parental feelings, as securing in your amiable partner a second Mother for my dear Child, such a one as my warmest wishes would have chosen. It seems as if in thus securing a successor to our dear mother, should it please Providence to remove her, I have scarcely a wish to form for the dear Orphan. Endowed plentifully with this world's goods, under such friends and protectors, her mind will, I trust, be formed to every Virtue, and with the blessing of God she will, I hope, early imbibe, thro' the examples and instructions of her beloved Aunt, such a knowledge of and love for her God and her Redeemer, as will form a sure foundation for her temporal and eternal felicity.

My dear friend, I scarcely think it possible I should live to greet your return— My pains and suffering are very severe; my debility increases fast; it is not for me to pronounce the time—it is with the Lord. O that I could cease to will or desire, except as he may order!

If he ordains that we may meet no more, receive my last adieu, accompanied with prayers and wishes for yourself and my dear Sister, for such indeed my heart feels her. May the God of all Grace bless you here, and may he by

---

*His wife's brother.

his Holy Spirit working in you both to will and to do, fit you for blessedness hereafter. Farewell, my dear Brother and Sister.

F. H. G.

Don't hurry, I entreat, or travel fast on account of my forebodings— You know how I have already lingered beyond expectation.

Savannah Society in 1818.

Mrs. David Hillhouse† to Her Son David.

Savannah, April 25th, 1818.

My dear Son,

As I calculate on receiving more letters from you than any one else, I will not set you so bad an example as to neglect the opportunity of writing by Mr. Gilbert*, who goes tomorrow. To him you may apply for anecdotes respecting our movements. He has a store. We have been so much in a constant flutter among the butterflys of Savannah, that I begin to feel like one myself. I am now for the first time, even for ten miuntes, since I left Washington, in a room alone and quiet. Before I had finished the last sentence a summons came to the door. A lady had called on us. The ladies in Savannah seem at a loss how to *kill time* and I suppose they expect some amusement from the awkward embarrassment of the *Crackers*. They therefore overload us with civilities, and draw us into parties which they justly think will excite our astonishment. Luxury and extravagance is carried to a greater excess than I ever expected it could have arrived at in America. We hear ladies with families of small children boast of having been out to parties 10 nights in succession until after midnight, and sometimes until 3 o'clock in the morning; and that they had not seen their husbands for a week. You must know that it is not the ton for husband and wife to go

†Mother of Mrs. Gilbert.

*William, brother of Felix.

49

to the same party; the husband toils through the day, to raise money for his wife to spend at night, when he takes charge of the nursery. Mrs. Scarborough lately sent out cards of invitation to five hundred persons. Three hundred attended. Every room in a large house was newly furnished for the occasion, the beds etc sent out; refreshments handed round from garret to cellar through the night to guests, who were mostly standing and "delightfully squeezed to death." How delightful! If I could, I would tell you of some of the wonders we have seen in miniature but fear shall not have time; however I will try to give the details of a dinner given to us at Mr. C——s— At 4 o'clock dinner was announced. At the head of the table was a large flat chicken pie with one fowl only, which the lady of the house informed us was made by one of the best French cooks in America and that it cost four dollars; at the foot of the table, a ham, which Mr. C. informed us cost three times as much as American hams. Fish, oysters, shrimp and crabs were present; a small dish of lettuce in the middle of the table. After feasting half an hour on a real good dinner, the lettuce was dressed with all the airs and graces, displays of fingers, languishment of eyes, bows and simpers, etc etc, by the fair hand of Mrs. M——, mother-in-law of Mr. C., who was dressed in the extreme fashion, (as a turban without border, etc.) a widow belle of sixty odd years standing. This lettuce was the second course. The third course apple dumplin and cheese; then puffs in great variety. After these things glass wash bowls were placed before each guest. The ablution was begun by Mrs. C's washing her hands; Mr. C. next washed face and hands, with many a hearty scrubbing. We followed as far as to wet our fingers and wipe them on napkins put on each plate, when we sat down. After the servants had wiped the table, (all the cloths having been previously removed,) a fresh supply of wines and olives were brought forward. At every new decanter a fresh recommendation of its delicacy, with its price, was given us, which varied from 4 to

2.75 dollars pr bottle;—in short, (after so long a detail,) our plates were changed 7 times and wine glasses five. From this you may well suppose we were all tipsey; however after all the parade, not one glass was drank, except by Mr. C. and Mr. Cranston, the Episcopalian clergyman of this place, who were the only gentlemen present. What a waste of money in a man that will not or cannot pay a debt of one dollar; and what a waste of paper and time in noticing such nonsense.

I have now removed from a boarding house to Mr. Early's where Mrs Griffin does not accompany us. I shall therefore for the future decline going any more; how I have stood it thus long is a matter of wonder to myself. This evening we are invited to Mr. Howard's for the second time. The first we were engaged at Mr. McHenry's, where we were at an evening party when the second fire broke out, which consumed one whole square with the exemption of one house. Had the wind been high and set a different direction, most of the town must have gone, as the water failed and everything so dry. * * *

Pray write before I leave Savannah, which I fear will not be soon as no vessel is in port for New York. Mary (Aunt Shepherd) has lost her spirits and looks all the time as if at a funeral. I shall write again to some of you while here, if I can have leasure, which is uncertain, for never was my time less at my command. This morning I go to Dr. Kollock's meeting and in the afternoon to the Episcopal church, where we are invited. None go without.

Affectionately your

MOTHER.

Sarah Gilbert to Adam Alexander.*

Washington, April 8, 1822.

I have been consulting my letter book to see how long it has been since I wrote to you and find it is not quite four weeks. This is rather sooner than I meant to write, but as I am indebted to you for two letters I will not defer it any longer. And first I must reproach you for the unkind and unjust suspicions expressed in your answer to my last, that my own change of feeling and doubts of your honor prompted my insisting on your promise to inform me of any change in your inclinations. I think you can not seriously believe this. It is not necessary nor proper that I should tell you now all the reasons which influenced me to make this request, but the principal one was my knowledge of the unhappiness of a marriage where the affections of both parties are not placed on each other, and also of the mutability of human affections. Now I have your promise, I am entirely satisfied, and you must not again accuse me of want of trust in you. I think I have given you sufficient evidence to the contrary of this.

I am glad you have so favorable an opinion of me as to think you may anticipate happiness in a union with me, but after all we must not expect to be made happy by any change of external circumstances. I hope I shall make it my endeavor to be everything you wish or expect, but we know that we need not look for happiness to anything but religion. With that we may be happy in any circumstances; without it we can be in none. I hope we

*Written during their engagement.

both possess this indispensable requisite and that the grace of God may endow each of us with such qualities as to render us both useful and agreeable companions to each other.

I received your present safely by Dr. Simmons, a young gentleman belonging in Elbert County. I felt very foolish, I assure you, until he mentioned that Mr. Holmes gave them to him. I thank you very much and shall not value them the less because I had them before, but I fear you will think me anxious for such a trifle not to wait a little while, but you may as well learn my faults now. I was very much pleased with Percival's poems. I think those contained in the present number far superior to those he has published before, and I also liked your taste in marking several pieces.

I have heard nothing new from New Haven lately except the marriage of old Mr. Stebbins, the West Haven minister whom you saw the day you went after me (not the one who catechised you so closely) to Miss Steers, grandmother by marriage to this Prof. Fitch. A youthful couple! Why did you not tell me the name of the student who requested an introduction to H. L. Staples? I think she must be quite a belle by all accounts. I do not think she has refused Foote, or had not when she wrote me last, but I am confident she will do it if he offers himself. She deserves a better husband than he would make. Toombs is courting a Miss Dubois in Lincoln County. I believe it is very doubtful what will be the issue of his suit. He told a friend of mine that you and himself were not on good terms when he left New Haven having had a "falling out." If it is not a *great secret* I shall take the liberty of enquiring the occasion of it some time or other.

I am very sorry to hear that your mother has declined coming up the country this Summer as we had anticipated a great deal of pleasure in a visit from her. I hope, however, that Louisa will come. I should think your aunt might take the journey, however, if your mother can not come.

I am glad that you study hard as I do not like *lazy men* though I bid fair to be an exceedingly lazy woman, and I dare say it is for your own happiness and comfort to exert yourself considerably. However, I think you will not get through under two years from the time of commencing.

The weather is very warm here and has been for sometime. I suppose it is still more so in Savannah.

I am most heartily ashamed of my production, but I am so warm and my hand trembles so much that I find it difficult to write and you must learn to excuse. Write as often as you can and I will endeavour to write once a month to you until you come to Washington. Do burn this.

S. H. G.

The next time you build castles in the air I wish you would write me a description of the materials, etc.

Sarah to Adam Alexander.

Washington, Jany. 25, 1824.

If the weather is in Sunbury as it is here today, I expect my dear husband is quietly seated by the fire in comfortable *confab* with mother and aunt instead of bending his course Midway-ward (if I may make a word for my own accommodation). I like to fancy you to myself enjoying yourself at your old home, and mother and aunt as much pleased as yourself, and should like to join the party as I flatter myself my company would be some small addition in *your* eyes, so effectually has the little god blinded them. While you have been enjoying yourself in Sunbury as I suppose, your poor *rib* has had a desperate fit of the hysterics. Grandmamma was here Friday, and as I was sitting after dinner sewing and talking as usual, a thought came suddenly across my mind, and my eyes filled up before I could finish my sentence. I went to the window but it would not do. I ran out to the kitchen and gave Fielding and Melinda a terrible scold—but even that would not answer. I came back and sat down to play "Away with Melancholy" but scarcely touched the first note when I bellowed out to grandmamma's infinite astonishment, who had just come in the drawing room to hear the *tune* and a most melodious one it was. "Well child," she said, after waiting in vain for the storm to subside, "you might as well take it out at once and get over it." So I marched upstairs and stayed until the fountain was completely emptied, washed my face, which always looks uncommonly rosy and pretty after a good cry (you must know I took a peep as I passed the glass) and came down to see grandma off. The fit lasted the whole of the evening, but the patient was better next morning and has continued so ever since.

I received your letter on Wednesday evening and am hoping for another today. I have stayed at home the whole of this week except returning two or three calls. Miss Martha Burno stayed with me until Thursday when she was sent for to stay with young Mrs. Toombs who has been unfortunate in becoming the mother of a stillborn infant.

I have been quite unwell for a day or two but feel better to-day.

Joseph Maxwell drank tea with us Sunday evening and seemed much disappointed at finding you absent. I asked him to stay for some days, but he declined and went on the next morning in the stage.

Alexander Pope has lost his little boy this week with a violent sore throat. These are quite prevalent about. Do my husband, if you have one, attend to it and use means to cure it.

Uncle* and myself have exchanged fewer words since you went away than in any similar space of time before. He has been very much entertained with the German theater and reads constantly, and I spend my evenings in knitting, reeling, winding, and, when my eyes admit of it, reading. The pack of cards is stationary where you left it.

Uncle says you must try to get some seed of the Brazilian cotton from Mr. Wilkins. I told him that it was too late now to mention it as you will receive this letter after your return from Sunbury, but he said you might have an opportunity of getting some in Savannah.

I hope this is our last separation for some time at least, my dear husband, for I feel already as if it had been a very long one. I think I shall overwhelm you with a torrent of words when you come back, for not-

*William Gilbert.

56

withstanding my long letters I have a mighty budget of talk accumulated now for you which will doubtless enlarge daily. Do you not wonder when you open my letters what wonderful event can occasion such long ones?

Ever your own,

SARAH A.

Sarah to Adam Alexander.

New Haven, July 25, 1828.

My dear husband:—

I was strongly tempted to commence a letter to you the day after you went away but concluded it was too foolish for a wife of five years standing. Since then I have been going out so much that I have not had an opportunity of writing at leisure. All things have gone their usual course, however. Sarah* has found me full employment whenever I have been at home, between coaxing and punishing. I made strong resolutions of patience and forbearance with regard to her, and I think I have got along better with her in consequence, but it is a constant trial. I have to call up every moment the most serious recollections of my responsibility and the importance of the present period to her future welfare. I hope that by gentle means and constant attention to prevent the occasion of anger and irritation, she may in time be cured of her unhappy propensities. I made also some other good resolutions with regard to the disposition of my time,— you will guess at once that I allude to my novel reading propensities. I am very sensible that it is to me a criminal indulgence for I have not self-command enough to read with moderation and merely for relaxation, and I hope to be enabled in future to resist the temptation and devote my time to such reading as may help to qualify me for the discharge of my duties as a mother. Do you think it inconsistent with this resolution to amuse my evenings in

*Her second child.

58

that way during your absence? I felt so lonely and sorrowful without you in the evening that I have allowed myself this kind of reading at night but without spending a moment upon it in the day.

Mrs. Whitney sent me some books on education which have interested me very much. That subject is her hobby and I was glad to have an opportunity of benefitting by her judgment.

I have paid most of my visits and spent one afternoon with Mrs. Taylor. Mrs. Herrmann came to see me the day after you left. She is lively and pleasant, but speaks very lightly of everything connected with the subject of religion.

I have received no letters or papers since you left. Richard comes up occasionally to enquire if I am furnished with all I want, and except the want of your company I am as pleasantly situated as need be. I hope you will remain long enough at the Springs* to reap all the benefit of the water, even though you should have become tired.

Write me often and let me know your plan as to prolonging your journey. Love to Louisa if there. "Think of me oft."

Yours ever,

S. H. A.

*Saratoga.

Early Recollections

Of Harriet B. Cumming.

My earliest recollections are of my perfect devotion to my little Sister Sarah, two years older than myself. I was about three to four years old; she, five or six. Memory is very clear as to how we spent our days.

Directly after breakfast we took our little baskets with our lunch and went into the grove to the cemetery lot, where were four or five graves: our grandparents, a little sister of mother's, and Uncle Gilbert's. By the latter we always knelt down to pray—the inscription on the tomb was, "These all died in faith"—and we felt that unless we were Christians and "died in faith" we could not be buried in that graveyard, but would have to be put outside in the grove. Our devotions ended, we left the graveyard and played all the morning around under the trees,—made doll houses, played with feathers for ladies, broken bits of china and glass, and such dolls as we had.

In the afternoon we had another religious exercise to close the day. At the foot of the hill on which the house stood was a little stream, and on the other side of that rose another small hill, prettily wooded, and divided from the wagon road by a worm fence. Towards sunset we two little ones always went down the hill, crossed the branch and went up on the other side. That was "Meditation Ground." Sarah helped me up to the top rail in one fence corner, and she took the one next to it, and we each sat in our corner to "meditate" on the sins of the day and say our prayers. Sister Lou found us out and then she used to come after us and, while we sat on the fence, would stoop in the corners and cry like a cat, bark like a dog, or crow like a cock, thereby much disturbing our meditations. Sarah tried remonstrances on the impiety of such conduct, but in vain, till our complaints had to be carried to head-quarters, when sister was forbidden to go down the hill at all in the afternoon. Cliff was her favorite, while Sarah and I were never separated.

Occasionally as we played in the grove we would be terrified by seeing two or three Indians come thro' the gate and go towards the house. They came to sell beads and moccasins, but we were dreadfully afraid of them tho' they were perfectly harmless. That was about the time of the trouble with the Cherokee Indians in upper Georgia.

H. V. C.

Sarah Alexander, Jr.* to Louisa Alexander.

Savannah, August 11, 1832.

My Dear Sister:—

I have not written to you since I have been down here, and that certainly is a long time, but I have not had a good chance before this.

We are all very well and enjoy good health. I wish to know how all are at home. What do you study and how do you improve? How is brother and Cousin Felixina's little babe?

I intend now to tell you of the delightful celebration we had on the Fourth of July by the Sabbath school children. In the morning at 8 o'clock all the children of the different Sabbath Schools met under the trees and marched to the Independent Church, where they commenced the exercises by the little Infant school children singing a hymn. Hatty was among them. They carried a little blue banner. On one side was written in letters of gold "Suffer little children to come unto me," and on the other side "God is love." The hymn was composed by Mr. Baker; it began,

> "Why are people so gay,
>   Why sounds the stirring drum?
> It is our country's natal day,
>   The Fourth of July has come."

*Aged six years.

The little children sat on a stage erected in the middle aisle before the pulpit. The other children sat in the pews, which were as full as they could hold. Each teacher carried their class. Our school was the largest, and our banner was a beautiful blue silk, and on one side was painted a Bible with "Search the Scriptures" in letters of gold. In the evening we had the best part of it, for then we marched to the Academy yard, where there was a table as long as you ever saw spread with cakes of every kind, and sugar plums and fruit. Our school wore white frocks and blue sashes. I enjoyed myself very much, but Harriet said she did not have enough for she only had three slices of cake. She says I must give her love to you all. Give my love to father and mother and tell them I am sorry to say that I have not quite yet conquered my disposition, but I am trying very hard, and Aunty says I have behaved better lately and she is in hopes that before long I will quite overcome it. You must give my love to Cliff and kiss her and little brother for me.

Mrs. Bowen says I must beg mother to save her some of her best cherry seeds. She wants them to plant at Fair Lawn. I see Livvy and Martha Bowen every day. They live near the School-house. Hatty has taken William Bowen for sweetheart and he sends her honey and sweet potatoes and kisses her.

I am studying grammar and like it very well. I got a ticket for good behavior from Mr. Williams, and Hatty got a book for good behavior at Infant school from Mr. White.

Aunty says I must give her love to you, Father and Mother, and tell them that she would have put a postscript to this letter but she was busy boiling preserves. She says you must kiss the little children for her, and says that she will be much disappointed if she does not receive a letter from Mother tomorrow.

I hope you will answer this letter soon for I will be glad to hear from you. Give my love to Aunty Shepherd.

I hope Cousin Ann has got well. I and Hatty send our love to Cynthia*.

I have no more to say, but remain,

Affectionately yours,

S. R. A.

P. S. Grandma and Aunt Van Yeveren send love to all.

*Mammy Cynthia was the beloved friend and servant of the family.

Sarah Alexander, Jr. to Her Father and Mother.

Savannah, Sept. 21, 1833.

My Dear Father and Mother:—

I would have written to you last week, but was unwell with a bad cold and cough, and the day after Aunty wrote her last letter I had a little fever and Aunty thought it best to send for Dr. Waring, and he said my sickness was caused by my cold. He gave me two teaspoonfuls of oil three times, and Aunty said I took them very well indeed, but I am quite well now. The only thing I made a fuss about was because he would let me have nothing to eat, and I made this poetry on him.

> Oh Doctor! Oh Doctor! you are very cruel,
> To say "give her only gum-water and gruel."

> You give me oil most every day,
> You give me too much oil I say.
> I do not like your starving plan,
> You ugly great long-legged man.

Aunty says that Mr. Mills from the Hospital brought her two hyacinth roots for you, and he refused to receive any pay for them.

Mrs. Bowen has been very sick out at Fair Lawn, but now is much better. Aunty has not been out there for a long time as one of the horses is sick and Uncle sent him in the country.

Miss Preston, the sister of Mr. Preston, is dead. She was afraid to remain in town and went to spend the Summer with Mrs. Blodgett on the Island. She had a very bad fall from a horse and was never well after. When they brought her up to town she was so low that she died a few hours after she came.

I have nothing new to tell about my studies as they are just the same as they were when I wrote you last, but I am still very much pleased with school. I have been reading some of Mrs. Opie's Tales, and one of Miss Edgeworth's, "Madame de Fleury," which I was very much pleased with.

Aunt Van Yeveren has made us a Morrice board, and sister and I know how to play the game. We are very fond of it and it amuses us very much. I forgot to tell you that Mr. Williams has put us in his Botany class, and we like it better than being in a class by ourselves.

Give my love to Harriett and Cliff and tell them I wish to see them very much. Kiss Willy for me also. Sister sends her love to you both and says kiss the children for her. Aunty sends a great deal of love to you all. Give my love to all my relations and tell all the servants howdye for me. Grandmother and Aunt Van Yeveren send their love to you, and say you must kiss the children for them.

Please to write to me soon for it gives me great pleasure to hear from you.

I remain, dear Father and Mother,
Your affectionate daughter,
S. R. A.

P. S.

I composed a small piece of poetry on Mount Sinai which I will copy for you.

When on Sinai's top I see
God in majesty descend,
There does Moses bend the knee,
And the Lord his ear doth lend.

2.

There does Moses kneel and pray,
    Oh Lord! forgive our sin
Which we commit both night and day,
    And cleanse our hearts within.

Sarah* to Adam Alexander.

Madison Springs, Ga., Aug. 13, 1837.

My dear husband:—

By Mr. Wingfield I received a bundle of papers together with the agreeable intelligence that all were well at home. He could also inform me that you arrived home in safety, though he had not seen you.

The ladies here are all much interrupted this morning by the non-arrival of the mail last night, and the statement of the stage-driver that he can no longer bring it, as the postoffice here is discontinued, and he can not wait in Danielsville to have the mail opened, so that letters can not be received here before Tuesday night, unless they can send from here to Danielsville for them, which Mr. Collier says he will not do, and perhaps can not. When you write to me by mail, pay the postage and I will send to the postmaster there, and ask him to send my letters by persons passing. I should be miserable if I could not hear constantly from home. I think a great deal of my dear children, and feel a great deal at being separated from them, though I think sometimes I must appear an indifferent mother to remain so long absent from them. Nothing but the hope of being enabled to be more useful in my family in the possession of a greater degree of health and strength, would reconcile me to it, and sometimes I doubt, whether even under the circumstances, I am justified in doing it.

*"I wish I could exhibit one of her letters as an epitome of her neat, dainty and perfect personality, and to show how she perpetually scanned her whole horizon for new duties as astronomers do the skies for new comets. The warm spontaneous flow of word and sentiment was no less admirable than its outward expression. It was the simple natural story of daily life, a life devoted to the good and happiness of husband, children, friends, neighbors, servants and the poor."

E. P. ALEXANDER.

SARAH HILLHOUSE ALEXANDER
(*b*. October 23, 1805 at Washington, Georgia)
Copy of an oil portrait painted by Jocelyn of New Haven, Connecticut, in 1828, about five years after Sarah's marriage to A. L. Alexander.

No one upon earth, without experiencing it, can ever know how the sense of my own unfitness and incapacity to discharge the duties of a mother, weighs upon my spirits. *Nothing*, my beloved, but your unwearying affection and kindness makes life desirable to me, for I can not feel that I am of any other use in life than to minister to your happiness, as I know I do, notwithstanding all my infirmities, physical and mental. I do not write thus to elicit from you your partial appreciation of me, for I know full well how far beyond my deserts you value me, but that you may understand in some degree the painful feelings which sometimes weigh upon my mind and depress my spirits. You have fully answered all the demands, reasonable and unreasonable, I have made upon your sympathy and forbearance, and have made me, as far as you could do, a happy wife, and I can only grieve that I have not made better return, but, my dear husband, I have given you the whole of my heart, so far as created beings are concerned, and have ever felt and appreciated your devoted love, and I can not reproach myself with having neglected to study your wishes and strive to make you happy. I hardly know how I have fallen into this strain, for it was not in my mind when I took up the pen, and I have gone on almost insensibly to myself. It seems to me sometimes that I can write as fast as I can talk, for I certainly do not stop to collect ideas, tho' I might write better if I did so probably.

I wish we could have some religious service today, but there is none to perform it, and there hardly seems any to wish it. These public places know no Sabbath, except as an interruption to the dancing. I hope you have Sabbath school at home for the children and regular family worship. I sometimes fear we are not sufficiently punctual in that particular. Do, my beloved, try to be cheerful and pleasant, and do not allow yourself to feel gloomy or *look* so, because your good for nothing wife is not there. For mother's sake and the children's sake and mine have patience with all, and make our home pleasant for its inmates. I feel as if people must be led to think how little worthy such an effect is the cause, when my absence can make you silent and reserved, who are usually so animated and cheerful. You must be a more attentive father to make up to our children the deficiencies of their mother.

The house continues full. There are still more than can sit at the first table, though there are a great many gone away. Mrs. C. has not got into a very good humor yet. The "Spy" was not sent with my papers. Have the numbers taken care of and sent, if you please. I have become quite intimate with the *Alabama curiosities*. The mother was an acquaintance of my mother and seems very fond of me, and is really a very intelligent, lady-like woman. Uncle Hillhouse knows them. Write me how he comes on selling out, and how Carry and her beau got on. Aunt S. thinks him good and clever, but *not smart*.

Love to all the dear children and mother. I send some old newspapers knowing they are often wanted, and the phrenological report, and two dresses to be done up and sent back by you or anybody else who comes first.

God bless you, my dearest, prays your

SARAH.

ADAM LEOPOLD ALEXANDER
(b. January 29, 1803 at Sunbury, Georgia.
Married Sarah Hillhouse Gilbert, April 29, 1823)
Copy of an oil portrait painted by Jocelyn of New Haven,
Connecticut, in 1828.

Adam Alexander to His Daughter Louisa.

Saratoga Springs, Aug. 31, 1841.

Though I have yet received no letter from you, my dear Louisa, I still feel assured that you have written to me, and much do I wish that your letter and others that I am *sure have been* written to me were in hand, as I have heard nothing from home, since mother's letter of the 12th inst. When I rose this morning from my bed, it was with the determination of devoting the fore part of the day to you and your Aunt in Savannah, but I have never had less control over my own time than through this past month, and though I have neglected none of my correspondents, for fear they would neglect me and thus punish me more than I can them, still it has in almost every instance been accomplished with much inconvenience to myself, and I fear, therefore, with but little satisfaction to them—for my letters are written literally not only "currente calamo," but "currente animo."

I have been occupied the whole morning with Dr. Taylor, first in riding out a few miles to try a horse which is the third one we have looked at with a view to purchase —for in purchasing the Doctor will have a *pet* as well as a horse, which makes him as fastidious almost as if he was choosing a wife— Then we had two long games at nine pins, and concluded with a most refreshing bath. I find in him the most pleasing as well as profitable companion, having so many points of sympathy, to dwell on which affords us mutual pleasure. He has in him a rare union of heart and head, which endears him to me, as well as inspires me with a reverence for his mighty intellect. We sat together last evening in the piazza from 7 until 12

71

o'clock at night, touching now on facts which called forth thoughts, then on thoughts which reminded us of facts; on anecdotes leading to reflection, and reflections producing more anecdotes, while the hours passed by unheeded as the waters of a river in their endless course. Were it "the witching hour of night" and not the "garish light of day" by which I write, I would take upon myself the pains of materializing our spiritual feast, both your pleasure and improvement, but the hour suits not the theme. Yet methinks we both rose from that interview with the feeling that the *age* of a cultivated mind is even *more luxurious* than its youth; that nothing is a source of greater happiness to ourselves, or more attractive perhaps to others, than a genuine and ripened imagination that knows its own powers and imparts its treasures with frankness and fearlessness; and that these thoughts, these reminiscences, these intellectual acquirements, though they die with us, are like ourselves, dead only *to this world*. If they are what they ought to be, they are treasures which we lay up for Heaven. That which is of the earth—our wealth, our rank, our honor, and all other earthly and perishable things die with us, while nothing that is worth retaining can be lost. Affections well placed and dutifully cherished, friendships happily formed and faithfully maintained,—these will accompany us into another and better state of existence, as surely as the soul will retain its identity and its consciousness— (Interrupted).

The mail for the day has arrived, my daughter, but brought me no forwarded letters from N. Haven, so I will remain here a day longer still hoping that I will hear from my family. I did intend returning to Troy tomorrow, for I miss Carry's lively company and find it very difficult to supply the loss of a lady's society. Dr. Taylor says nobody has so good a right as we have to feel unhappy when away from our wives, because he knows no one "who leaves such good ones"—a discovery which I long ago made for myself. Among the ladies here I have not made a single acquaintance, though it would be easy enough to do so, for this place, like most other watering places, might with equal propriety be called a fishing place, being much frequented by female anglers, who are in quest of such prey; the elder for their daughters, the younger for themselves. But my observation leads me to think it is dangerous sport, since the fair piscatrix is not more likely to catch a salmon or a trout, than she is to be caught by a shark. On the other hand it is equally amusing to see the many gentlemen, both old and young, who are *trying* to *run* in love. I use the word "run" as appropriate to express a thing that is not accidental. To run in love is as when one runs in debt; it is done willfully, intentionally, and generally (as it is done here) rashly, foolishly, ridiculously, ruinously. To *fall* in love is a very different thing. I always *fell* in love, just as I would fall down stairs, and so does every one who *falls* in love. It is an accident— something which he neither intended, nor foresaw, nor apprehended—and the circumstances are such as can leave no room for censure, however unfortunate it may prove in the end. To set about *seeking* a partner for life is like seeking one's fortune, and the probability of finding a good one, in such a search, is less, though poor enough, heaven knows, in both cases; and it is equally unwise for one to run in love, because he or she is determined to marry, instead of marrying because they are in love. I am not thinking of any one particular person in making these remarks, and tell you so lest you should think, or Miss Brackett,* that I have Miss P— in my mind.

Though I received no letter "from home" as I told you, I did receive a letter, and oh! such an one, as you, and the young ladies at Mrs. Colley's would *give your eyes to see*. Tis lying by my side with its fair superscription so elegantly done, and postpaid, and well may it bear that motto (though it does not) that peacockish motto "I can

*Governess to the older girls of the family.

73

a tale unfold." It is the best *discovery* I have made for years. "O the mystery of this wonderful history" says Southey, and an older person than he has said that "a question not to be asked is a question not to be answered," so you need not ask me, Lou, nor you Sally, nor you, young ladies, though after this I shall never look at—at—at—one of you without a smile. I intend showing Mother the letter, and would show it to Miss B. but I know she could not keep it, and the attempt would kill her and I would be accessory to her death, which heaven forbid. Now you must not even speak of this to any one out of the family, except the young ladies at Mrs. C—'s and then be patient, and be ignorant.

I wrote your mother so long a letter yesterday that I have nothing to add about the incidents of my travel, or my plans for the future. On Thursday I shall certainly leave this place and Dr. Taylor will go with me, as far at least as N. Y. on our way to Boston, and him I will request to forward me to B. such letters as may be in N. Haven.

The end of all my writing will have been accomplished when you know that I have remembered those, who I please myself with believing, both remember and pray for me. If I can find the time to write a few lines to Hatty and Clifford I shall feel that my labors of this sort are nearly accomplished, for hereafter I shall write shorter letters and at longer intervals. Indeed, I shall have but little time to spare after tomorrow.

Give my love to those that you think love me enough to value it, and believe me to remain as ever,

Your affectionate father,

A. L. A.

No time or patience to read over.

Sarah Alexander to Her Daughter Harriet.

Savannah, Dec. 18, 1841.

My dear Hatty:—

Father enjoined it upon me in his last letter not to write again to any of you, as he considers himself entitled to all the productions of my pen, and I certainly feel considerably flattered by the value he seems to attach to such poor affairs; but as I had previously penned a promise to answer your letter, I hope he will not consider himself aggrieved by my compliance with it, especially as I do not intend to write him any *less*, but only this much *more*. I wrote him on Thursday which I hope will reach him on Monday, and I will write again on Thursday, when I shall be able to say more definitely on what day I will leave here. This will depend, of course, on the departure of the boats.

It has turned very cold within these two days and we are all shivering over the fire morning and night, though it is pleasant enough in the middle of the day. Christmas is coming on apace, and I suppose excites the usual degree of expectation among the juvenile portion of the community. Porter has ascertained to his satisfaction, by numerous enquiries, that Savannah forms one of the stopping places in St. Nicholas' annual peregrination, and is anxiously considering which of his stockings will form the most capacious reservoir for the gifts of his bounty, which he calculates knows no limits, but the size of the receptacle. Aunt went out this morning and returned with a mysterious looking box, which I suspect is the result of some concert of action between herself and his saint-

75

ship, and mother commissioned me, in one of my morning rambles to purchase her a pretty picture book—but time will unfold all these mysteries. Meantime Porter is very well contented and makes numerous calculations as to the potentiality of nine coppers which he has collected, in the way of providing a suitable present for every member of the family on his return home. I hope you will all have a pleasant Christmas, though what will be the ingredients to constitute the *especial* agreeableness of the occasion, I can not conjecture, as I have generaly found it anything else than a *merry* time. I hope, however, you and Cliff. will try and afford such assistance to the servants as you can, that they may have the full enjoyment of the time, which coming so seldom to them is especially valuable.

I am very glad to hear that you have adhered to your plans for the vacation, and been diligent in practicing, and at work. I am very anxious to have you all grow up with a proper estimate of the value of time, and the habit of disposing of it systematically. I do not wish you to feel yourself debarred from recreation and innocent amusement, for they are proper and necessary, but you should regulate the time devoted to them by *principle*, not *impulse*.

I begin to feel very strong drawings towards home, and am getting almost tired of my holiday, though I find no lack of employment, in the way of little jobs of work, varied by plenty of visiting, which must be done. I hope to be with you by the beginning of the New Year, that we may enter upon it together.

Have you heard that Georgia Nichol has made a profession of religion? She united with the church the 1st Sabbath I was here, and is I believe the youngest member.

Tell Sarah I received her letter yesterday, and her apologies were quite unnecessary, as I found all her communications quite interesting. Love to her and Cliff. whose note I received safely, but can not consent to her sleeping arrangements. Love to Felix. Mary Lucia seemed quite pleased with the notes, etc., your sister brought her. Porter says I must give his love to you all and to Cynthia. Remember me also to her. Much love to dear father, and tell him I shall have a sheet full ready for him in a day or two, unless he comes down in the Ivanhoe tomorrow, in conformity to Sarah and Cynthia's advice. I am called off to company. Kiss Charlie and Hillhouse for me.

God bless you, my dear daughter, prays,

Your affectionate MOTHER.

Sarah Alexander to Her Daughter Harriet.*

Home, August 26, 1843.

For three days, my dear Hatty, I have been striving to commence a letter to you, thinking that by writing at leisure I might make a letter more interesting to you; but mail day has arrived and I have got the whole letter to write, and even since I began have had nearly a half hour's interruption with an altercation between my two young hopefuls, Charlie and Hillhouse. Sarah's absence makes a great difference in my leisure, as I have now no assistance in the household department; indeed, I was hardly sensible how much she did relieve me until since she has gone. I look forward to your return with the expectation of finding you a very efficient substitute, or alternate with her. How often I have thanked the kind Providence which gave us daughters first rather than sons, for how great comfort I have already found in them, both as companions and helpers! Whenever I find myself in feeble health and think I may be removed from my family, it is an inexpressible satisfaction to think that they are so capable to supply my place to the younger ones.

Your father received your letter on Monday and seemed much pleased with it. I must not forget to tell you how much we all admired the very neat appearance of the last I received from you; it was well written, beyond what we supposed your ability. I have felt much grieved and troubled at different times at finding that you felt the privations to which you are subjected so much, yet I want you always to write just as you feel and not

*Then at school with Miss Dwight at Northampton, Mass.

keep back anything from us, for I should be constantly uneasy to think you did so. I know how to make allowance for your discontent, but have ever believed it would be temporary, for I have that confidence in Miss D. which will not permit me to doubt either her good judgment or her substantial kindness, and I am sure your own desires for self-improvement will lead you to appreciate her efforts to do you good. If you will only give no place to your besetting sin of disparaging and lightly esteeming those whom you should look up to with respect and reverence, I have no fears but you will answer all our expectations for you, which are neither few nor small.

I sent you by Mr. Cleveland yesterday a note and a pair of mitts which I knit for you. He is only going to New York but I asked him to give them to Mr. Parmelee to send to you, so if any one you know should happen to go there you might send for them to No. 10 Pine St. I did not think them worth sending, but as I had knit them for you and had nothing else to send, you will receive them I know as a token of my thoughtfulness of you.

Your sister continues quite feeble and unwell. I hardly know how to give you as good an idea as I suppose you desire to have of her actual state, but she is certainly no better it seems to me than she was when you went away, and I think worse in some respects. The cold she took in her attempt to go to the Springs put her completely back, and though she is very good and submissive in the use of remedies, she can not learn to be prudent. Her spirits are not good and I shall be glad when S. and your aunt come, especially on her account. I expect them about the middle of September, and sister will stay with us a month I expect, and probably Lou will go down with her, as the climate of Savannah is so much milder than ours. Josephine is coming back, too, to spend sometime. We have had a great deal of company this summer, and it is just now the quietest time we have had since May. I feel the want of it for I have become worn out with the excitement of company, though I enjoy it for the time.

My visit to the Springs was pleasant though short, but I was much disappointed at not being able to go to see Miss Patsy. Sarah writes that she enjoys herself very much. They are going to Clarkesville, Dahlonega, etc. etc. Cliff is going on much in the old way. Sarah Colley and she stick very close together, and have many walks, rides, and visits together. She seems most at a loss in the evenings, and generally amuses herself with Minnie who is really very good company. She has been often unwell (the babe) and looks very delicate, but is lively and playful, and we think looks very sweet sitting alone upon the floor with her little play things about her.

Charlie has entered Martha Dyson's seminary of polite literature, located in Mr. Hunt's old house, and is in a fair way of learning his letters in the course of time. Hillhouse is under a course of discipline to break down his proud spirit, which seems likely to succeed very well, though it takes strong measures to produce any effect. Charlie asked me last night if Adam and Eve were buried in our graveyard. Will and Edward are going to Mr. Scudder and we hope will do very well. If he proves as good a teacher as your father expects, he will not think of sending Felix away.

There is no news among us. Cliff writes you everything about school, I suppose. She says she now has a folio in progress for you.

I am sorry to hear Miss Brackett's mother is in such poor health. Give my love to her and tell her I postponed writing to her after hearing she had had so many letters from the family. All send love. Cynthia talks and thinks a great deal about you. I wish we could have gotten the fruit ready to send you by Mr. Cleveland for I fear opportunities will be scarce. My time and paper are both pretty well run out. Some of these times I think I shall try a folio but I think the others will interest you more as I deal so much in advice.   Do you not wish me to write one letter without any?

Have you ever seen Miss Abby Clark or her niece, Catherine Phillips?

God bless you my dear child.

MOTHER.

Adam Alexander to His Daughter Harriet.

Washington, Oct. 3, 1843.

My dear Child:—

This is a very busy day with me being our Sale day, and yesterday was our election for Governor and Representatives, still I thought I would write you a line, fearing lest the engagements of the family might cause them to forget you, or if not as bad as that, at least, neglect you for a short time.

We have had so much company through the whole summer, that home has been but little of a home to me, except the short hour that mother and I always will have before retiring to rest. I sigh for the *quiet* of home, and wish that I could for a short season, at least, enjoy the seclusion of the sweet room, such as you have described our dear Miss Brackett's to be, and her sweet and quiet society.

You must not think, however, that you are forgotten amid the engagements of present friends, for I keep and always must keep a quiet half hour or more every evening sacred to the memory of absent friends and to you, my child, and I vainly wish that I could exchange faces and voices here for those that are gone, alas for me, and shall be absent for weary months to come. How sad it is that in this ever changing world we can not keep permanently with us the friends and the circumstances they make around us, and which we so much love and would never change but for others in which these are still actors, but in nearer and dearer relationships. Yet if we could, we would be satisfied to make it our eternal rest, which it never was designed to be.

82

Georgia Sneeds' wedding has given an air of gaiety to our place quite unusual, it being the occasion of a good many young people visiting us, and which is you know the signal for parties and other amusements. These things occurring with our election, disturb our usual quiet and add to your mother's cares.

When will we ever be rid of the confusion that girls introduce into a family? For the first time in my life I begin to feel the inconvenience of girls, who every night introduce into our quiet family circle some face, which looks so ugly that you feel that the owner has abused the privilege that all gentlemen have of being as ugly as they please, and who have lost all hopes of immortality, by not having lived at the time Pope wrote his "Dunciad," —"Oh Heavens! was I ever such!" I often ask. Mr. Bryan is now here and at our house day and night, and often comes to me at Bank, and actually I made him assist me the other day in counting cash to keep his tongue still.

We continue in health much as generally. Mother's health is not so good as it was in the Spring. She seems more feeble and has almost constant headache. I am thinking of going out to the Chattahoochee with her in the barouche on a visit of a week or two to our friends in that region, with the hope that the journey will restore her. I think she will recover again when she has less care on her mind than she now has. Your sister Lou is, I think, better. The Doctor's remedies begin now to show their effects. Her cough is much better. Indeed, I have not heard her cough for two weeks. She looks too some better, but yet how changed from what she once was! I shall keep her at home until some time after your Aunt goes to Savannah, that the Doctor may have more time to pursue his plan and use his remedies. He thinks she ought not to go as soon as your Aunt does, which will be about the 10th or 12th inst.

On the 12th our Presbytery meets here and that will bring more trouble, after which we hope for rest.

Mr. Petrie has bought Benton's house and is now living there.

Give my love to my sister when you see her, and tell her I received her paper, sent me on the 25th ult. and am very thankful to her for it. I think of her for days after receiving from her the slightest token that she still remembers me. May God bless you both. Give my love too to Sarah Sneed whose friends are all well and whose bride-sister looks very lovely and behaves with great propriety. Tell her I think she has gained a fine brother-in-law. What is dear Lizzie Whitney doing and why does she not get married? I saw the marriage of that Angel in Easthampton (Clarissa Wright) in the "Gazette."

Love to the Whitneys and believe me ever

Your affectionate father,

A. L. A.

P. S. You ask in one of your letters what you shall be allowed for pocket money. I am sure, my child, that my sister will allow you what is proper, and even what is liberal, which I requested her to do. I wish you to have enough, of which she can be judge.

Harriet Alexander* to Her Sister Clifford.

Boarding House—Sept. 4th.
Wed. eve 1844.

I went over just now, dark as it is, to the Sem., dearest Puss, to get my materials for writing, that I might begin you a good long letter, and in my desk I found a nice little bowl of fine plums, great rarities and delicacies with us. It is the third or fourth little gift I have had from different persons, lately, and I assure you they are more acceptable and more tokens of friendship and goodwill, than you living in the midst of such abundance can well imagine. I have likewise had the extra luxury today of a pear, a reward for being in order in my room. Thus has the day been one of remarkable pleasure. Its hours are fast passing away, and I am improving them to begin a letter which I promise myself shall be a great pleasure to me. Situated as I am here, it is the delight of my life to write to one to whom I can open my whole heart with its now accumulated store of petty joys and griefs. There has been much happening with and around us since I last wrote—and I have longed to write to you several times and tell you all about it. But I thought I should accomplish my business better, to finish one thing before I began another, and I have had a good many little jobs of work to do, lately. In addition to these *necessary* things, I have assumed the very *unnecessary* job of reading a novel, Deerbrook, which I had heard the good folks at home talk a good deal about. This was completed this afternoon and tho' I found the book very interesting, I was very glad at heart when I

*Aged sixteen.

85

could lay it down, for I am always dissatisfied with myself when I am foolish enough to indulge in novel-reading. This is the first that I have read since I have been here, I believe, except—Miss Bremer's—and I think I am much better without them. I shall give them up entirely for the next few years of my life, unless I alter my present mode of thinking. And Cliff darling, you may expect me to try very hard to induce *you* too to give up both novels and these common newspaper stories. We will find a plenty to read together that will be useful as well as pleasant. But Deerbrook has lead me into a sermon that I meant to have reserved till we meet. I have other and sadder things to write of—things that oppress me, even while my heart is so happy in the hope that day after tomorrow will bring dear Father to me. Since I wrote you last, sickness and death have been among us. Two of our number have gone to their long home. Kate Smith and Lizzie Plant, within two weeks of each other, we have followed to the grave. Lizzie had been declining for two or three months, so that her death was not so unexpected a blow. Just seventeen, and so beautiful, it seemed sad to see her the victim of Consumption. She is the fourth daughter of just that age that her parents have lost. There was a bunch of white flowers on her coffin, and to them was pinned the mourner's verse "The Lord gave and the Lord hath taken away, Blessed be the name of the Lord." Up stairs was a miniature of her, taken about two months before, and a few words under it, addressed to her schoolmates, comparing her as she was there, and in her coffin, and using her death as a warning to us. Six of us acted as pall-bearers, and dressed in white, held the ends of the pall as the body was carried to the graveyard. This is not generally done, and the novelty of the situation made it unpleasant to us. Pall-bearer at a funeral! It made me feel dreadfully afterward, tho' at the time I didn't care so much as the rest. Poor Lizzie was so sadly changed after death, that no one would have recognized her—and a stranger would have taken her for a woman of thirty. Sallie seemed to feel *her* death very much—for she still loved Lizzie, tho' they were not so intimate as they had been. I could not feel her death as I did Kate Smith's. I have written you sometimes about her, but cannot tell you on paper how very intimate we were, and how many things, joys and sorrows, she was my only companion in. This is the first time since I have been old enough to feel, that Death has taken away any one on whom I had set my heart. I never realize what a blessed lot has been ours, until I see here so many happy homes invaded, and so many hearts left desolate. In thinking of our own family, the words that Father used to use in prayer sometimes come very often to me—"May the *goodness* of God lead us to repentance." Prosperity hardens us, I have often heard men say—but placed in such circumstances as we have lately been in our school, it softens my heart more and fills it with more love to God to think of his *mercies* to us than I can conceive of in affliction. Kate was an only daughter, and oh! it seemed to me, as tho' the parents' hearts must rebel that their only delight should be taken from them. She died too without hope—and this makes the cup seem more bitter.

Friday morn. If you think of me today at Home, dear Cliff, I know that it is as of a perfectly happy being; and so perhaps I should be. But there is a foreboding at my heart, a fear amounting almost to a certainty that Father will not come today. My anticipations of happiness have been so great, that now I am sure they will be disappointed. Oh Cliff! I *cannot* believe that after so long an absence I am again to see him! Yet I think of it all the time without ceasing. I have finished all the little jobs that I can do myself, and therefore I must be idle, which gives me more time to think. Study is out of the question. I have not done much of it lately, and now I do less and less every day. There is a feeling of self-dissatisfaction which troubles me, and the fear too, that

Father will be dissatisfied. I shall long to know his thoughts and whether he will be disappointed in me. I will not write any more. I think it makes my heart heavier. If Father does not come, I will write again this evening. I don't believe I shall want to talk with you till I am out of suspense. Besides, if he *should* come, I shall want *all* my room, to answer the letter from you that I am anticipating—and to tell you of our meeting.

Saturday noon. He *did* come, dearest, and had you heard the scream of joy with which I welcomed him, you would have felt assured of my happiness. It was late, after tea, and just as we were moving back for prayers; so late that I had given up all hope of seeing him. When they called me and told me he had come, I couldn't stir, and when Miss D. told me to go to him, I only turned crimson and looked at her. But when I *did* go! Poor Father was almost knocked out of the door by the ponderous mass of flesh which was so violently thrown upon him, and almost deafened by the yell with which I sprung at him. I cannot write or think of it without laughing, for it really was a sight and scene worthy of a painter. We sat a while and talked, and then went to walk. I mus'nt forget to tell you however, that I never *dreamed* of asking Father to come in. I stood by him, perfectly satisfied, and never once thought of asking him to enter the door from which I had thrown him in my overwhelming caresses. He staid all the evening with me, saw Sallie and Miss Dwight. He did'nt come until late this morning, about eleven, and then went over to the Sem. and heard Sallie's Virgil class. He has gone now to Mr. Whitney's for a while, and I am to meet him there this afternoon—so I must close now, or rather soon, for he wants my letter to go as soon as it can. He has begun a long letter to Mother but does'nt know that he shall have time to finish it—so I am to send my letter without waiting to finish it. You may perceive, my dearest, that this was intended for a folio—but as Father wants me to hurry, I have separated my sheets.

Perhaps, after all, a folio, written so close as this, would have been too long, even for you. Thank you for your long letter, and "the box" too, tho' as yet I have'nt seen it. Father brought me yours and Sister's notes last night, but the rest I have'nt seen or any of the things sent with them. *Thanks to all* for what they have been kind enough to write and send, tho' as yet I enjoy them only in anticipation. But Cliff dearest I am not so happy as I thought I should be. I know that Father is disappointed in me. Instead of the tall girl whom he expected to see resembling somewhat her well-favored Sisters, out hopped a short fat Dutch girl, and with an Indian yell, saluted his "ears polite." I read it in his face, (for I watch every look to read his thoughts) that he is disappointed, that he feels that I shall be the Leah among his Rachels—*the black sheep*. Ah Cliff this does make me feel a little sad. I write it to you, just as I would write in my journal; for you are my second self. How delightful it will be, when at length I can have some one to whom to tell every thought! I have read your letter over twice, and shall probably consign it to the flames in mercy to you. I cannot tell you now more about it. But I shall see you soon—I can only say, *I am sorry—I am sorry*. I know how you feel, and can well imagine your happiness. But I do not rejoice with you—could even wish you less happy. Do not blame me for want of sympathy, my dearest, but believe that 'tis pure love for you that dictates what I write. You may doubtless imagine my surprise in reading what you had to communicate.

I am weary, darling, and must stop now. Father is coming in a few minutes to call on me, with Mr. and Mrs. Stoddard and Miss Habersham, all from Savannah. I dread a call from any one, and especially from perfect strangers. Goodbye for the present. Mary Cooley sends love. I dont believe you can imagine what sort of a girl she is. You could'nt imagine anybody so queer as she is. You'd like her I think.

Monday noon. Father is coming this morning to take my patchwork letter down to the office for me, so I must finish soon. I went home with him (at least "Home," according to the definition "And what is Home and where, but with the loving") from Church yesterday afternoon, and spent all the rest of the afternoon and evening with him. I cannot tell you how much I have enjoyed it. We sat in his room and talked over all that our hearts were interested in and travelled home in tho't. After tea we walked in the piazza and talked to Mrs. Stoddard and Miss Habersham, whom I find very agreeable. Then Papa and I went to walk, and walked a very long time, and talked of "Mother, Home and Heaven." He seemed almost Home-sick in his longing for Mother and "his baby." Says I must give a great deal of love to Mother and tell her he thinks of her a great deal and misses her every step he takes. He told me that he was not disappointed in me—that he was glad that he had sent me here. Cliff dearest, he spoke too of you and told me all that I wanted to know of you that *could* be learned from him. I have had your miniature with me, since Saturday, and I love to talk to you, even *there*. It is very like life, and very pretty. I have enjoyed the society of my three sisters! I have seen since I wrote last, all the notes and letters, and little bundles, and would now return thanks for all. The box is beautiful and *very sweet*. Thanks for all. Tell Mother the pin will do me good all my life thro', for Miss Dwight has engraved a verse on it for me. I showed it to her and she said "Oh dear parents! precious parents! 'Honor thy Father and thy Mother.'" I can never look at it now without thinking of it. Thank Emma and Mary West for me. I don't know whether I shall write either of them again, tho' I may if I find time.

Oh Cliff! I am growing so impatient to return! so anxious to see you all again. Home does seem now the very happiest and loveliest spot on the face of the earth—

a perfect paradise, angels and all. Betty must indeed be an addition to this latter class. I have quite a curiosity to see her, for from accounts she must be a natural curiosity. I am glad to hear that Cora is improving so much. Why didn't she write to me? And Cynthia too? I certainly expected to hear from her by Father. Give much love to her—tell her that in my tho'ts of Home I never forget her. Tell her I'm a great deal better girl than I used to be. Oh I must'nt forget to tell you that Father thinks my hair has lost a good deal of its fiery hue and is quite passable in comparison with what it was. This you may be sure is a comfort to the soul of your Sister, tho' you little dream of the many unhappy hours caused by the fact of my hair's being so intensely and unaccountably ugly. I wonder if Sister Lou remembers a scene in her room one noon, preceding an evening when Mother was going to have company! If she does she knows something of my feelings on that subject. I used to be a very silly girl and care a great deal about what people thought of me and my looks. But I don't care quite so much now as I once did. I cannot say that I am perfectly contented, but—I'm resigned— Sallie sends her love, or much love, or something, and says she will answer your questions when she comes Home. Beware how you let her know the extent of your knowledge of her concerns! She would not thank me much. Oh Cliff, you don't know how much I shall have to talk over with you when we are together again! I grow so impatient when I think of the time! I've got a good deal to take out of your little head that has no business to be there, and a great deal to put there that ought to be there. You don't know what a good older sister I'm going to make! Well, well! if my talks are all as long as my letters——

Do some of you good folks write to me again soon! Dont think that because I have a "living epistle" that I dont want any other. The living epistle can't tell me what's going on now. I am sure that I deserve letters to the very last minute—for I have been a good correspondent. This is comforting to me, if it isn't to you. Write soon.

Ever

Your aff.

HATTIE.

Verses by Sarah Alexander, Jr.

How sweet the music of the spheres
   Will be to us above!
Melodious to our listening ears
   The praises of His love.

Nor shall our tongues be silent there,
   And only others sing,
We too shall praise Immanuel's name
   Our Saviour and our King.

What tho' my voice be songless here,
   And tuneless be my praise
The wonders of the heavenly world
   Shall call forth angel lays.

Then speed the time when I shall be
   A saint in worlds above;
When I shall hear celestial songs,
   And praise the God of love.

S. G. A.

Sarah Alexander to Her Daughter Harriet.

Savannah, Feb. 19, 1846.

My dear Hattie:—

This stormy day assures us of a quiet forenoon, and
I have sat down to improve it as well as I can for your
benefit, that I may be sure of time to fill up my sheet as
I need not mail it until tomorrow to reach you on Tuesday.
Your letter came on Tuesday, and I assure you afforded
me much pleasure, which I shared with those around me
by reading it to them. I delivered Cliff's epitome of an
epistle to her uncle who received it with a kiss in token
of his pleasure. Sallie was here and took your letter and
read it, while Lou braided her "shining tresses" and bound
them with a wreath for a wedding party at the Owens'.
The young people are enjoying quite a lively time just now
in the bridal parties given to Caroline Nichol. Another
comes off tonight at Mrs. Waldburg's, and what will father
say if I tell that I had entertained a serious thought of
going, if the weather had been fine? You will all think me
demented surely, but many *old ladies* are going, and I have
been so much urged, and then I have some curiosity to
see how these things are carried on in the gay world, to
see my own daughters in company, and last, not least,
they have most delightful music with harps and violins,
which is a great attraction to me, and Mr. Sorrel was to
be my gallant if I went,—a safe one surely, is he not?
However, the weather puts it out of the question, and perhaps I should not have told you that such an idea had ever
entered my mind, only to show you now what must be
the difference in my health and spirits since you saw me;

94

but you must not tell it out of the family, lest my character should suffer.

I must tell you how pretty Lou looked the evening of the Owens' party, and how proud I felt of my two daughters who I knew had so many fine qualities, besides their good looks to recommend them. Lou says her companions tell her I must be her step-mother, so you may infer, if you please, that I am considered quite juvenile in my appearance, and Lou says she is making capital out of my good looks (on your father's principle), so she cultivates my curls and adjusts my caps, etc. with the utmost care.

A pleasant interruption—Sandy with a precious letter from father. Tell him it deserves more than I can say in reply, but it brought tears to my eyes and must have its response addressed to him. I am sorry the mails are so uncertain and so much time is lost in the transmission of letters. I have not failed to write twice in every week, yet it seems there are sometimes considerable intervals in the receipt of my letters. I hope I am thankful for the great mercies we are enjoying; my own improving health and that of my dear ones at home. Truly our Heavenly Father is gracious beyond our powers of gratitude or expression, and I do desire most earnestly to devote to His service and the good of my family the renewed strength and ability He may please to bestow upon me. My heart is much with you all, though you must not suppose I am at all restless or dissatisfied, for my time passes very pleasantly and I enjoy much in being so constantly with Lou and Sarah;* the latter especially, from whom we are to be so much separated for the future. What do you think of her saying she does not expect to revisit home until this Spring twelve month? She does say so and assigns as a reason that Mr. L. will be detained here all the summer by his partner's absence and she will not

*Married to A. R. Lawton.

go without him. I say nothing, because if the choice is between her parents and her husband her own heart must decide. I do not forget, my dear H—, to be thankful that I have you to supply her place to me, and that you not only occupy the position, but fulfil the duties of a daughter, and I am sure your best recompense would be found in knowing how my heart rests upon you in its hopes and expectations for the future. My dear Cliff, too, I know as she grows older and has less to occupy her in the improvement of her mind will stand ready to be a comfort and help to her parents, so that I need not say for many years yet, I hope, "my house is left unto me desolate."

Sarah and her family, consisting at present of her husband and William* who is here on a visit, dined with us yesterday, and she sent us word this morning that as Mr. L. and William were going to dine out, she would come over again to dinner. It rains so however that I hardly think she will get here. I fear it is another sleet storm with you for it is quite cold. I am daily struck with sister's unwearied kindness to Sarah, which is shown in so many ways that I know not how to enumerate them. They dine or drink tea here once or twice in every week, and sister seldom has anything nice upon her table without sending her some of it. She is blessed indeed in having such kind friends and in living so near them. I must tell you something of our dinner at Mr. Sorrel's on Monday, though I shall reserve the details for Cynthia's entertainment some morning when we are "washing up." We went about 4 o'clock, sat down to dinner at half past 5, and did not rise under 2 hours, the candles being lighted before the dessert was brought on. Then we sat in the parlor about an hour when tea and coffee and sponge cake was handed, after which we returned home about 9 o'clock.

*William, brother of A. R. Lawton.

96

I feel no temptation as yet to introduce Savannah fashions into our Washington modes of living, though I am always amused with seeing the different customs among different people.

Tell Cliff Lucy seems to think very hardly of her not writing to her. Mrs. S.' children reminded me so much in some respects of my own that it quite made me homesick for a little while.

Your affectionate,

MOTHER.

Sarah Alexander to Her Daughter Harriet.

Rowland's Springs,
June 26, 1846.

My dear Hattie :—

I conclude I am already indebted to you for the letter you promised to write today, so though I shall not receive it for some days, I acknowledge the debt and hasten to repay it. If you could see me as I am seated to write, you would say "well mother has certainly found her Arcadia now"—and so it is. Just fancy me seated by the open window of a nice large log cabin, of which your father and I are sole occupants. From the window runs back a steep little hill, at the foot of which runs a clear little stream in which the ducks are swimming all day long; and on the opposite side facing said window rises another declivity prettily wooded, with abundance of rocks scattered about. Down a short distance from our cabin winds the same clear stream, across which are two beautiful springs of sulphur and chalybeate water, running from large rocks, and close by stands a bathing house and spring house. Above us in different positions, scattered about a large enclosure, stand five or six cabins similar to our own; and a large framed house is raised and covered in, and the sound of hammers is going all the day, in token of the spirit of improvement possessing the proprietor. But you will wonder where is this sylvan retreat and how we found our way to it. It was by a most trivial accident, as it seemed, that we heard of it, just after I had sent off my letter to Cliff from Marietta, and we set off for it without even knowing we should find the means of getting here. It is situated six miles from the railroad, in amongst the Altona hills, and has only been settled two years. The proprietor, Col. Rowland, is a wealthy man, and plants on the Etowah river, some miles distant, and only occupies this place in the summer. It is certainly the most charming place for my wants that I have ever seen in my life. The nights and mornings are cool enough for blankets and fires; the water delightful for drinking and bathing; the fare as good as could be desired, and everything as clean and comfortable as possible. The family are very kind and quite agreeable people, and there is very little company besides ourselves. I have taken a shower bath today, and feel as if a month's stay here would almost make me young again. If I were fixed for it I would certainly remain, and let your father return without me, but neither the wardrobe I have along, nor my home arrangements would admit of my doing so. I have grieved a dozen times that you and Cliff were not with me to enjoy the delightful ride we had yesterday on the Railroad, with the fine mountain scenery. Lou, I know, does not like traveling, but you two would enjoy it highly I am sure, and I hope you may be able to come up this Summer sometime. I never enjoyed traveling on a Railroad so much in my life, and we were fortunate in meeting the daughters of Col. Rowland in the cars, and as a conveyance was sent for them, they gave us seats, though we had to leave our baggage and could not get it till today. Your father is as well pleased as myself, and we both should like to spend sometime here if we could. As it is, we shall probably stay here till Monday or Tuesday and then go up the road and across to Rome one day, and back to Marietta the next, and stop there one or two days as we may have occasion, but shall not be home certainly before Saturday. The only alloy to my enjoyment is the fact of our not being able to hear from home here. They have a piano, and plenty of books and periodicals and papers.

Saturday Morning— I find I shall have but a few moments to finish my letter in season to go to-day, and I don't know how long it will take to reach you. I have just returned from a pleasant walk through the woods. Oh I do long for you girls to be here and enjoy it with me! There is something so bracing in the air and water that it makes me feel quite *new*. Tell Cynthia I wish she was here with me. She would get strong again directly. I have a very nice mulatto woman to wait upon me—the kindest creature imaginable.

Much love to all. How does Lou get on with her charge, and Cliff with housekeeping, and how does the little pet do without papa and mama? Kiss her till you are tired for me and tell her I want to see her very bad, and I love her very much. She must not forget to pray for her father and mother. I long to hear how the good work goes on among you. Remember me to the servants, and tell my dear little boys I hope to hear a good account of them when I get home. Father sends love— In haste,

Yours very affectionately,

S. H. A.

I will write again if an opportunity offers.

Sarah Alexander to Her Daughter Harriet.

New York, 1847 (?).

It would have been expecting too much of me, dear Hattie, to have left your weighty packet to Cliff unopened till her arrival, knowing as I did, that it must contain so much of which I wished to hear, so I opened and opened and opened till I came to "entre nous," and there I stopped and respected the motto most sacredly. I read the rest of the letter with great pleasure and interest, and enjoyed it I am sure as much as Cliff will. I have thought much of some parts of it since, and felt as if I might reply to it in a way which perhaps may bring some comfort to your heart in those moments of depression of which you speak. I do not consider those frames of feeling as mere ebullitions of sentiment and folly, my dear daughter, and I can sympathize with you in them fully, while I am persuaded that there is much of wrong and mistaken feeling connected with them. I too, dear H—, have felt that sense of distaste for the common and ignoble occupations of life and care for the physical wants of a family, which take up so much time and thought. I fancied myself made for higher and nobler pursuits, and as if my strength and energies, moral and intellectual, might be worthy a higher sphere of action, and fancied how much good I might do to myself and others, could I escape from this drudgery of life. Are not these your feelings sometimes when you can not secure to your self a moment of that time which you value and would improve? Well, my dear child, just remember at these times *who* it is that marks out for us our sphere of duty and action in life. Your parents and others whose influence controls it are but instruments in

His hand, who sees the end from the beginning and knows far better than our united wisdom can teach us, what will best secure your *highest* good. These petty cares and anxieties, these trials of your patience and temper, are doubtless just the discipline He sees that you need to subdue your natural infirmities and exercise the Christian graces in which you may be deficient, and fear not that in this school of discipline you will be divested of anything which can adorn the female character. Only walk by faith, dear child; endure as seeing Him who is invisible—Him who pities our weaknesses and bears our infirmities, and who despises not those little sorrows which seem light to those who are not called to bear them. If your daily routine of duty is blessed by communion with God and the light of a Saviour's love, it will be sweet to you however humble. The consciousness of living for Christ can make a life of toil and suffering easy to be borne, as many can testify, and how should it add pleasure to one still crowned with many blessings. For while I would not underrate your trials, for I can enter into them I am sure, most fully, I would have you remember how much that is pleasant is mingled with them. How many young persons have to exert all their powers for the service of their families, in ways far more trying to the health and the spirits, in occupations of much more unpleasant kind, and without those pleasures and enjoyments which can afford you abundant recreation and refreshment! You have the pleasure, too, of knowing how materially you contribute to the comfort and happiness of your parents and the highest good of those entrusted to your care, and are establishing for yourself in their hearts a lasting claim upon their love and gratitude. While you may be deprived of the privilege of storing your mind with such knowledge as you would like to acquire, still your intellectual powers will improve and develop themselves, while your character is maturing in its most valuable points by the continual effort of self-discipline to which you are called. Take comfort then, my dear child, and do not indulge the feeling that your best interests are suffering in the course of duty which at present devolves upon you. Cultivate a cheerful temper, and seek continually for that grace to help, which women in domestic life, I think, often need as much in kind, if not in degree, as martyrs at the stake. I hope these efforts may not be required of you for any length of time, but remember if you are God's child, you are on a pilgrimage of trial and effort, and if released from one sphere of duty, another awaits you, perhaps equally trying. For so must our lives pass, not in living for ourselves, but for Him who made and redeemed us, and it is only the continual struggles of *self will* which make the Christian's course so painful and difficult. Could we only acquiesce as entirely as we should in our Heavenly Father's appointments for us, any course of life would seem pleasant with Heaven at the end of it. But I fear I have wearied you with my long sermon. I have preached one if I have not heard one (it is showery), and I hope it may do my own heart good to recall these truths, for I, too, my dear child, have many rebellious struggles, when I feel that I would like to choose my own way and mark out my own course of life. But I bless His Hand who has led me so far, though often by a way I knew not and liked not, and I trust now the prevailing feeling of my heart is one of submission to His will, and perfect reliance on His grace to strengthen, and His guidance to conduct me in all the paths of life.

You must not suppose your letter to Cliff expressed all these feelings I have supposed to pass through your heart. Mine gave a key which I thought opened yours and I have written accordingly. May God bless you with His abundant grace and strengthen your heart and keep you happy in His love, and may the sympathy of our hearts in the sorrows and trials of the Christian's pilgrimage add strength to the ties of nature and affection, which shall be a bond of everlasting love and confidence, when the relation of mother and child has ceased to subsist.

It is a great comfort to me to know that Porter is kept at home, and I hope he will improve his time. Still this must be but a temporary arrangement, and I do wish your father could see it best to send him on to me and let me place him either with Miss B— or Lucy Clark.

I saw Julia Goodrich in N. H. and she talked much about you and seems to wish much to see you. She is engaged to a young man named Hill from Boston; so is Emily Jones to somebody else. Emily Fowler is coming to N. Haven with her father to live. The servants at Mrs. Hillhouse's all enquired about you.

You must send me H. Goddard's directions before I go to Boston. Remember me kindly to Sara, Morotto, and Mary; to Maria, Caroline, Charles, and Harry; and, indeed, any of them who enquire about me.

Love to Cynthia and tell her to send me particular word about her health. What of Cora since I came away?

Adieu, yours affectionately,

MOTHER.

P. S. Love to Mr. and Mrs. Petrie, Ella, and Matilda, Mrs. Toombs the Doctor, etc. etc. I hope you don't forget to show some little attentions to Sally Smith. How is Mrs. Mayo coming on?

Plantation Life.

Harriet Cumming to Her Niece.

Baltimore, 1908.

You have asked me, Dearie, to tell you what I can recall of the Old Plantation days and ways in the Long Ago. Some part of it is vivid and imperishable. Some has waxed faint as the years have gone on. But I will do what I can for you, remembering that the days are at hand when there will be few left to tell what life was under conditions so different from all that we know now.

Well, to begin, there were always two very busy times in each year: the times when the summer and the winter clothes were to be provided for the servants at the plantation. First, the sheep were to be shorn; then the wool washed and sent to the factory where the jeans for the outer garments was woven. It was usually of a dark gray color. When the great rolls came home, the work in the house commenced. Every living creature on the place sent a garment of each kind that they wore as a pattern for size, etc.—the men, coats, pataloons, shirts, vests, etc.; the women and children, down to the youngest baby, a garment of each kind worn and the name of the wearer pinned on each garment. In one of the outhouses a room was set aside and everything pertaining to the work was piled neatly in there, each family's belongings to itself. Mother employed a white woman who understood such work (Mrs. Floyd by name) to help her, and for weeks they worked all day long at a big table, cutting out the garments. When we were old enough we girls helped in rolling up the garments, marking, etc. So many garments of each kind were cut out for each person, male and female, old and young, and in each bundle were put the buttons and thread for the making, and the name of the person for whom it was intended. As the bundles were made ready they were piled in the work-room, each family to itself, and were given out to the seamstresses to be made as fast as convenient. At one time they used to give the wife and mother of each family the clothes to make for her own people, but mother found that they made them so badly and spoiled them so often that she gave that up, and had everything made and given out ready for wear, only leaving the mothers and wives to do the mending as it became necessary. It kept busy needles going all the year.

So much for the clothing of those for whom we were responsible to Him who placed us in charge of them.

But there was another side of our duty that was harder to look after; that was the teaching—the effort to make something more of them than convenient servants for ourselves. On Sunday afternoon the young children all came from the plantation, and mother had Sunday school for them in the dining-room. She taught them the Commandments, hymns, and a simple Catechism, the same that the children of the house were taught. There was a colored Sunday school in our church, and I had a class of half-grown ones there. As they out-grew mother's class, they went to the Sabbath Schools of the different churches preferred. We taught any of them to read and write that were ambitious to learn. Cora always had her lesson hours when I undressed and dressed, night and morning, she being my special little maid by her own request. She could read and write quite comfortably, tho' she never got so far as Andrew did when he went to "Marse Charley" to beg him to teach him now to use a "Rajer-racter" which he had bought. (Which being interpreted meant a "Ready Reckoner" used by the Banks for computing interest, etc.) Cora was the one who immortalized herself when about eight years old. I was teaching her to say her prayers, night and morning, and one petition was "make Cora a good girl!" She commenced the sentence, then stopped, turned her head around and said, "Miss Hattie, if I say Cora, God won't know who I mean, 'cause my name's Corinthia Ann Ball Mary Wilkerson Weems Jones." Mitchell was added to the list, years afterward when she married. She went with me to Savannah when I was married and lived with me till long after I had grandchildren, loving all that belonged to me, depending on me in every emergency, and was as real a part of my family as our old "mammy" was of my mother's household.

You ask about the feeding of the plantation hands. Every family had a house of its own. The big woodpile was common to all. About the provisions, I am not very clear, that part being altogether in masculine hands. But as well as I recollect, the meat, meal, salt, molasses, and such things were given out every month from the smoke-house and storeroom, according to the size of the family. Every man had his "patch," and they raised potatoes, peas, cabbages, or corn and cotton as they chose. They all had some money from selling poultry, cotton, etc., or taking in a little washing and they could easily supply such little extras as they chose. They had some fruit trees and father planted fig trees for them in the fence corners around the quarters.

The Doctor for the plantation was employed by the year. The price was agreed upon in January. If there was much sickness, it was his misfortune; if little, father was the loser. He was sent for whenever needed, and went to the patient, either in the yard or at the plantation. Then he came to the house and gave his directions, and one of us weighed or measured the medicines and saw that they were sent with all directions not left with the patient by the Doctor himself. All ordinary medicines were bought by the quantity and kept in the "physic-closet" which was as well known a part of the house as the dining-room itself.

I only remember one white overseer on the place. Usually one of the oldest or most reliable hands was foreman and directed the work, coming up to the house on Saturday night to report what was done and take orders for the next week's work.

Alongside of our own burying-ground under the shade of the dear old trees in the Grove is another enclosure where the dead among our servants were buried. But there was one exception made. Our old and well-loved "Mammy Cynthia" who nursed us all and loved us as her own, was buried by mother's side, with a white marble stone to mark her resting place, and "Well done, good and faithful servant" as her epitaph. Mammy's mother had belonged to mother's grandmother, and "mammy" had been born in the same yard where she lived and died. She was about mother's age and they had grown up together. I suppose mother was *the* love of "mammy's" life. She had never married and always spoke of us as "my childun." She had authority over us and mother always left her at the helm when she went from home. Mother had no ability to follow us around, but "mammy" was omnipresent, and we felt, omniscient too. We could hide nothing from her, and many a time our hearts quaked when we saw that lithe figure stepping over the wet grass in the orchard, skirts held high, and pace set unerringly to the fence corner where we had made a nest and hidden our choicest horse-apples to ripen in the sun.

After we were all married and gone from home her happiest times were when we came to pay a visit there, bringing our lambs with us. She was a magpie for hoarding and many a quaint old-timed garment she brought forth to show the children, and gave them some old relics that are still held in great esteem among them.

I have the photos you sent Tom. I think "mammy"

"Mammy Cynthy"

Cynthia Peters. Born in Washington, Georgia. Originally owned by
the Gilbert family, she grew up as a child with Sarah Hillhouse
Alexander. Reproduced from a daguerreotype taken probably about
1850.

will go in the book, tho' to suit my memory the head hand-kerchief ought to be piled higher on the head. I remember her best that way, as she sat trotting my first born baby boy on her knees. My mother-in-law said "Cynthia, don't trot that baby so, you'll addle all his brains." A moment's pause, then in clear tones: "I done nussed ten chi.dun. I ain't seen no fools 'mong um yet," and the trotting was resumed. That picture is clear in my mind, and the hand-kerchief is piled high in the back.

In her last days she had a marked case of aphasia, using all sorts of unintelligible words unconscicusly to herself. I have asked her how she felt and been told that she "had a keel missle dole in a bassle," that "her nor hollered her reeling round the nabe and she walked bocker shuffer," etc. At my last visit to her cottage she bade me not tell her goodbye, that she could'nt talk to me and her bread was bitter in her mouth because I was going away. As I drove away from the house she was on the lawn, leaning on her stick, a boy's straw hat on, over her high head-handkerchief, watching with sad eyes for the last glimpse of us. This world was poorer for all of us and ours when that faithful heart was stilled.

Goodnight, sweet child. It is almost midnight. You will be sorry that you ever asked me to write you this letter when you find that there is no end to the flood that I can let loose upon you. A garrulous auld grannie is hard to muzzle when you start her on topics such as these. Words flow apace, for you open the gates of the Lang Syne Land where the aged dwell, finding the present the "fleeting show" and the real life all there in the shadows of the past.

Lovingly,

GRANNIE.

The Building of the "Cottage."

From Sarah Alexander to David Hillhouse.

Washington, Oct. 8, 1848.

My dear Uncle:—

I have felt very much troubled at hearing thro' Mr.
Henry that you were sick again in Augusta. We expected
you, according to your promise, early in September to join
our family circle, and I feared then you might be detained
by sickness somewhere, but your message by Mr. Semmes
made me easy on that score. I regret much that you did
not come up, as I think you might have escaped this attack
here, or, at least, have been more comfortable here. You
must never indulge the morbid feeling that you are not an
object of interest and affection to any, because of your
isolated position, which I fear you sometimes do, and
therefore keep aloof from your relatives. Be assured, my
dear Uncle, that though I am surrounded by many who
have the first claim on my thoughts and feelings, you are
never forgotten, or thought of with indifference. The
memories of early life are linked with you and your care
and kindness in my orphan state, and I have never ceased
to look up to you with that respect and love which was
then inspired in my heart. You are still to me the same
kind Uncle I always loved, and ever since you have adopted
your present wandering and unsettled mode of life, I have
wished again and again that you would accept a home with
us, and allow me to supply to you in age and sickness
the cares of a daughter. Now it seems to me the time
has come when you must yourself feel that it would better

suit your state of health to have a settled home and be with friends, than to change from one hotel to another, ever among comparative strangers. Will you not then make up your mind to come and live with us, making only such occasional journeys as your health or inclination may prompt?

You are aware that we have but one spare room with a fireplace, which we must hold in readiness for the visits of distant friends and children, and therefore I could not offer you comfortable accommodations in the house, but my plan is this: For you to have put up near the house a single room for yourself, furnish yourself with a good servant to attend upon you, keep fire, etc., and take your meals and spend as much of your time as you see fit with us, and consider yourself one of our family. You could in this way be as retired as you please, and yet be with those who love and care for you. I am not writing mere sentiment, my dear Uncle, but plain feeling, which I hope will find a response in your own breast. I do feel distressed to think of you as sick and alone in a public house. Mr. A. would go down and see you, if he thought he could be of any service to you, but we think it so much better for you to come up to us. As soon as this attack is past and you are able to ride, do come, and then we can talk over these plans and arrange them I hope. You had better not come by Railroad and stage, but hire a carriage and come by easy stages, which will not fatigue you.

Mr. A. will probably have to go to Augusta about the 24th with Louisa, who will then be returning to Savannah, but I hope you will be able to come before that time. Aunt Shepperd stayed with us till the 24th of September, and was disappointed at not seeing you. She will be in Milledgeville till sometime in November and then go down to Stuart.

My health is poor since my confinement, but I have

a healthy and thriving little daughter,* who has yet no better name than *Dot*, being we consider the full stop or period to our patriarchal family. Felix left us two weeks ago for N. Haven again, having grown and improved greatly, we thought. Sarah has had a delightful trip to the North, and improved greatly in health and appearance, as well as her child, and I presume they are now at home again, as they were to come out in the new steamer for Savannah.

I will not ask you to write if you do not feel like it, but send word through Mr. Henry or Dr. Willis, who are often writing, how you are and whether you will come up.

My husband desires me to say that he concurs in my wishes and most earnestly invites you, not only to come and see us, but to come and make your home with us.

Believe me as ever most truly,

Your affectionate niece,

S. H. A.

Washington, Oct. 9, 1848.

Dear Captain:—

The plan which my wife suggests, by which you can secure the comforts of a home for yourself, with and among your true friends, is one, which after much consultation together, we have thought the best. I hope you will seriously think of it, and finally agree with us. You may select any spot in the Grove and build on it such a house as will suit you, furnish yourself with a good body servant, whom you had better *purchase* at once, (such a boy as the one who waited on you when I saw you in Augusta) eat your meals with us, to which you shall be more than welcome, and be with us and among us as much as you please, and alone to yourself when you prefer it. I think this plan will secure you *comfort* effectually. You will have the privacy and *liberty* of your own home, convenience without trouble, proximity to

*Alice Alexander.

your friends when you are sick, and as *much*, or little of their company when well, as you find agreeable. Don't imagine now that there are any objections to this plan, for there *can* be none. Such an house as you will need, will cost you furnished and complete about $350.00 or $400.00, and a good servant about $900.00 or $1000 more, all of which you can easily spare, when it will secure you the comforts and *respectability* (I may add) of a good home. We are sorry indeed to see you wandering about without a place you can call home. Come then and make yours with us, on the terms proposed and you are welcome.

Sincerely your friend,

A. L. A.

Adam Alexander to his Wife.

———

Savannah, Feby. 23, 1849.

My beloved Wife:—

I received your dear letter of the 19th last night, and I well knew before it came how full it would be of anxieties felt for us while traveling during the late bitterly cold days. It was indeed cold, but we felt it less severely while actually upon the road than when housed. The cars were all well warmed, and the steamer that brought us from Charleston was as pleasant quarters as is our own fireside. It was in fact a glass house, affording fine views in every direction, and not at all like the river boats with their little windows of 10x12 inches. I never had a more delightful trip than that from Charleston, and one of its greatest pleasures was to see Brackett's* extravagant delight and wonder at the new views she then for the first time saw. It was milder at sea than on land, and she was never tired at looking over the boat at the rushing waters and the track of foam we left behind us. She saw all she wished to see but some whales. It was too bitter cold while in Charleston to let her leave the room, which I regretted, but I felt too anxious about her to venture the least.

I can't tell you how pleased she seems with everything. You can better imagine it. Corinne is her daily companion and they are enough for each other. Yesterday (being Washington's birthday) we had all the military companies out, and it was a great delight to her and all. Hilly looks very well indeed, and for the first time in his life hangs

*Marion Brackett Alexander.

about me a great deal. He comes into my room early each morning and talks to me while I am dressing. Next week I carry him with us to the Plantation, where he is most anxious to go. As yet I have said nothing about Brackett's remaining here and with whom, but I know that will be easily arranged. Yesterday we had a pleasant family party at Sally's to dinner, and in the evening Cliff went to a Polka party at Mrs. Sorrell's (I say *Mrs.* because *Mr.* hates them and will have nothing to do with them, and even leaves the room whenever Lucy stands up for such a dance) at which not only the daughter but the mother danced. I saw Cliff when she was dressed for the evening and it would have done you good to see anything so really beautiful as she was. I expect she is by far the *most* beautiful girl in this City. She is accordingly very much admired, but not for her beauty only, for she is intelligent and amiable and above all perfectly unaffected. This is one of the most attractive points in a young girl's character. She is never troubled about what others will think, and, least of all, what they will think about her. Lou did not go to Mrs. Sorrell's because of a bad cold, and we thought she ought not to expose herself at night. She is well enough to go about at day and is not otherwise sick. Sister looks well I think and seems to enjoy her usual health, and I can not see that any changes have passed over our old Aunt.* They all express a great desire to see you, and if you were but here I should want nothing more. But I can not at any time enough forget the absent ones, to enjoy perfectly the pleasant society of those present. I suppose all your fears about us must have been relieved yesterday by a note from Mr. Henry who enquired for you by telegraph if we had arrived, that he might write you by mail. I enclose you his note and also one I sent to Porter from Augusta the day I was detained there, that you may see how these things are done. I yesterday saw

*Mrs. Van Yeveren.

Mr. Hutchinson who called to see me, but have not seen the rest of his family. We seem to be great favorites in his house.

Your letter has afforded me great relief by letting me know how well you and Hatty get along with Dot in Cynthia's absence. It will serve to make me easier in my absence to know that it brings no further inconvenience than such as is always felt, and I hope ever will be, when separated from each other.

I shall mail this letter to-day, but I do not know when it will leave here. I will speak to Mr. Schley about the mail. Brackett is by me and sends you much love and a kiss and says she wants to see you very much. All unite in love to you, Hatty, and all. Remember me to Mr. Wright and believe me, dearest wife, ever

Your affectionate husband,

A. L. A.

Harriet to Clifford Alexander

Tuesday, April 3rd 1849.

Hattie* is gone, and poor Papa has a headache, and I—ah! dear Puss—I am disconsolate—"feeling full" as Major would say. So I betake myself to you for comfort and sympathy. Poor Hattie! it was a sorrowful thing to see her go out to make her own way alone in the world, and my heart did ache for her. "She left a large circle of friends and acquaintances to mourn her loss," as the obituaries always say—for I never knew any stranger who made so universally favorable an impression. Everybody who saw her, admired and liked her. At home they have all been kinder to her than I can tell you—as kind as even *I* wanted to have them—and their kindness to her moved the deep foundations of my heart. She is a girl that is not easily moved herself, but this morning when Father prayed long and earnestly for her in family worship, she was completely overcome, and we both had such a crying spell that we could'nt make our appearance at the breakfast table. Father engaged Macon's services to escort her to Union Point, where she is to meet Mr. Pope (Cousin Ed's neighbor) and finish her journey under his guardianship. She hated to leave *us*, worse than she did to leave home—for she says she never enjoyed three weeks so much in her life. Mammy is more enthusiastic in her praises of Hattie than I ever heard her before, except when Cousin Mary is her theme. Indeed, her generous donations this morning to all with whom she had had anything to do, will cause her memory to be embalmed in the minds of all. By the way, what on earth did you all do to Mammy

*Hattie Goddard, a school friend.

when she was in S., to make her so good-humored. I never saw her so uniformly cheerful and pleased, as she has been since her return home. Indeed I have'nt heard her scold a single time, tho' she has certainly had as much provocation as she used to have.

Thursday. I wish you could see the authoritative air that Dr. S—— asumes in his intercourse with me since his return. For example, when he came here the other day, I had on a sack—and shortly after he had seated himself, he remarked to me that "there was *one* thing that he was going to lay his veto upon, from the beginning —that was, if it did'nt interfere *too much* with me, and that was that *he must forbid* my wearing those sacks." He said they would do well enough to keep house in, but he did beg me not to wear them for anything else! That's giving me a touch of the matrimonial, with a vengeance— hey? Likewise he reproved me for my manner towards R. M. W.—said he heard I had been flirting with Mr. W. and that "if *he* had been here, that would'nt have happened." He told Hattie the other evening, right before my face, that I always disliked gentlemen who paid me any attention, and that he knew *he* had paid me as much as anybody had! We both pronounced that a cool announcement. I just remember that he told me that he wrote Sister Lou a letter, from Carolina! It must have been a rare production, judging from the self-complacent accounts that he gives of his visit in Carolina. Now I've got something beautiful to tell you about Cousin C——. That individual presented herself here today, and almost immediately after taking her seat told Mother that she wished to explain a speech that she made, and at which she understood that I had taken so great umbrage, that I had declared that I never would come to see her again. You remember the speech dont you? about your being the only good-looking Alexander that ever she saw. She says she only said that she thought you prettier than me—and that she must take the liberty of remarking that she had

heard many others express the same opinion! Hurrah!
Puss, a quarrel about our relative claims to beauty. Mother
begged leave to assure Cousin Caroline that nobody was
more willing to uphold your claims to the superiority than
I, and remarked that I always thought myself very like
her—i. e. our dear Cousin— She did'nt say it in quite that
connection however, as that would have hit the nail on the
head too palpably.

Friday night. I sat all the morning with Sallie Sneed,
and this afternoon with "good Mrs. Brown." Dr. Andrews
came in while I was there, and made some such charac-
teristic remarks that I can't forbear repeating them—
'specially as some of them tended much to the soothing
of my wounded vanity. "Well, Miss Hattie," was his
opening remark, "so you've come to see my Aunt Sally
—now let's hear what you think of her." It was rather
a poser—but he pushed the point, till I did'nt know what
to say next, when he suddenly broke off by remarking to
Mrs. Brown that I was looking very handsome this afternoon (I had on the *green* dress, wh. accounts for it!)
Indeed he thought that I was growing handsomer, and
for his part he thought that I was prettier than you—tho'
you were generally esteemed a beauty. Said he just was
telling Fred Ball the other day how much prettier he
thought me than you (Ah ha! *Miss*) On the whole
he said, "Miss Lou was his beauty"—then he went on
to praise Marion &c. You may judge that I was completely
non-plussed and could only turn red and look silly—for
everything was rattled out in such a volley, that there was
nothing for anybody to say, till he got thro'. If it had
been anybody but Dr. Andrews, I should have thought it
quite an insult to be talked to in that way—but as it was,
I only laughed and thought I'd tell it to you, to keep
you from pluming yourself on what Cousin Caroline said.
I have heard all the family discussed to-day, for on the
way home from prayer-meeting this evening, Russell opened
upon the subject of Father's merits—and for *once* grew

almost enthusiastic. He says he never knew a man anywhere that seemed to him so perfect in all parts of his
character, and who was so complete a model of what a
gentleman should be. He compared him to Mr. Toombs
and Gov. Gilmer—they being both great men—and pointed
out where his superiority over each lay, until I trod the
earth more proudly at the thought that I was the daughter
of such a man. I fairly loved Mr. Wright while he talked.

H.

Old Days in Wilkes County*

Our ancestors came here from Old Hadley in Massachusetts. Washington was then not more than an Indian fort. My great grandfather, Mr. David Hillhouse, edited a paper which was one of the first published in Georgia. It was called "The Monitor," and a copy is now at the Library. After his death his wife continued editing the paper. It was unusual in those days in this part of the country to see a woman who could write. The customers in his store often asked him to bring his wife in to see her write.

The court-house was built of logs and when the jury retired, they retired to an old log at the back of the courthouse and sat there. My uncle told me that they used to give balls in the court-house, and this is the way they would call out the figures: "Gentlemen, lead out your partners. Them that's got on shoes and stockings will dance the cotillion; them that's got on shoes and no stockings will dance the Virginy reel; them that's got on nairy shoes nor stockings will dance the scamper-down."

My mother's mother died when she was an infant, and she was raised by her grandmother, Mrs. David Hillhouse. Her father, Mr. Gilbert, was one of the Broad River settlers who came from Virginia. An account of this Colony is given in Gov. Gilmer's book "Georgians."

My mother was educated in New Haven, Conn., and there met my father who had come to Yale College from Sunbury, Ga. They married in 1823, in the house that now belongs to Mr. Gabe Toombs, opposite the Presbyterian

*Anecdotes told by Mary Clifford Hull, to her grandchildren and called by her the "Family Chestnut Tree."

church. All their ten children were born and raised in this place. There were no public schools in those days, and good private schools were few and far between, so when my father's four oldest children, who were girls, were old enough to begin their education, he went on to East Hampton in Massachusetts and brought back a teacher, and built a little school-house in the grove where she took a limited number of scholars. That was in 1835. There were no railroads in Georgia then, so my father went down to Augusta in his own carriage to meet the teacher and bring her here. Her name was Miss Brackett and she stayed here eight years, and proved to be such an exceptionally fine woman and good teacher, and the pressure was so great, that my father had to agree to have her take a school. The citizens subscribed and built a large Seminary here. They sent on North for more teachers, and at one time had over a hundred scholars who came from Alabama, Carolina, and all over Georgia. Miss Brackett taught me to read. I was not quite five years old when she came, and I commenced my education with her.

Miss Brackett stayed here until my father's oldest daughters had finished their education. Then his boys came on, and he did the same thing for them. He went on to East Hampton and brought out a teacher* and built a little school-house in the grove. Afterwards he proved a very good teacher and my father agreed to let him take a large school; so he taught in what was the town Academy.

I grew up here leading a very quiet sort of life. People did not travel then, nor move about as they do now, but stayed at home, generally Summer and Winter. In those days we all went to school morning and afternoon both, and went all Summer long, and nobody thought of this being any hardship. We had June for a vacation and school began again in July. People did not require as much change and amusement as they do now, and dress was much simpler. Women never wore hats in those days;

---

*Mr. Russell Wright, mentioned in preceding letter.

they wore bonnets, and instead of having three or four in one season, we had one for three or four seasons. If we had a nice velvet or silk bonnet in Winter, when Summer came we put it away carefully, and the next Winter we hauled it out and wore it again just as it was.

When we were small children our father had a cottage at Madison Springs, some little distance from Athens, and every Summer wagons were sent up loaded with household furniture, bedding, etc., and the family went up in carriages and buggies to spend the Summer there, returning the same way in the Fall. All the traveling was done by stage coaches, or by private conveyance.

Postage was from 18 to 25 cents, and you paid for what you got and not for what you wrote. If your letter was one sheet and as big as a table cloth, you paid single postage, but if two sheets as big as your hand, you paid double postage. Therefore people often wrote on foolscap and folio sheets. There were no envelopes, and folding a letter was quite a complicated affair. When children were taught how to write letters, they were carefully taught how to fold them as well. They were sealed sometimes with a thick red wafer, about the size of a dime, which you had to soften in your mouth, and when they used sealing wax they had little glass seals with mottoes and designs engraved upon them. I remember one that had a quill pen on it, and the motto was, "I came from a goose;" another had a turtle engraved upon it and the motto was, "Always at home." When postage was reduced to 10 cents, we all thought it very cheap.

Before my day and before the gin was invented, cotton was all picked out by hand. They would load a wagon and send it on to New York. About three weeks after the wagon of cotton had left my grandfather would leave on horseback, and would pass the wagon somewhere in Maryland or Virginia. I have seen many of the letters that he wrote home to his wife from those journeys, telling where he overtook the wagon, and how the mules and negroes were. He would reach New York ahead of the wagon, and be there to receive it. He would sell the cotton and then load the wagon up with supplies of different kinds to be sent home to his family.

The people did not dress as much in those days as they do now, and there were no such things as patterns to be bought. There were not so many magazines published, and newspapers never had anything about fashions. So the only way that people had to see anything new was to see somebody wear it, and country people and people who lived in small places like this might be several years behind. If you saw any new fashion and wanted it, you borrowed the garment and looked at it and copied it. The teachers in the school were all from the North, and they went home in the vacations. When they came back they brought the latest fashions, and everybody was eager to see them.

There were no Express companies in those days, and the only way you could get anything brought you from a distance was by a friend—you might get him or her to bring it in a trunk.

It took, in those days, about five or six days to go to New York. Part of the way was by railroad, part by stage, and part by water. There were no checks for your baggage and wherever you changed you had to go and see your baggage transferred from one railroad to another, or from one stage to another. There were no sleeping cars, and if you traveled at night, you had to sit up all night, so ladies could not travel alone then as they do now.

There were no such things as canned goods in those days. Neither could you buy preserves or dried fruit as you do now in the stores. You either had to make it or do without. So all Summer long preserving, pickling, peeling, and drying fruit, would be carried on, and it was one of the burdens of housekeeping.

Nobody ever heard of dinners being served in courses; the soups, meats, and vegetables were all served on the table at once. So you, at least, had the advantage of seeing what was there and taking your choice of what you wanted, as you can not do when they are served in courses. The table for company was always set with two table-cloths, and when they were through with the soup, meats, etc., the upper table-cloth was removed, and then the dessert was brought on. The under table-cloth was for that. We never saw ice in those days, and the desserts were a great variety of puddings, pies, preserves, syllabub, custards, and cakes. There was always a small darkey to brush flies with a peacock fly-brush.

Miss Bremer, the Swedish authoress, visited friends of mine in Savannah, and she requested them to have the fly-brush dispensed with because it made her so nervous. She would often get up and walk around the table to help herself because she could not bear the servants, and would not let them wait on her.

When we were young ladies (my sisters and myself) we always spent the Winters in Savannah with our aunt, and it would take from two to five days to get there, according to the way we went. Sometimes we took a steamer at Augusta on the river and that took three days. Sometimes we went by stage from Augusta to Millen and then took the railroad.

I went once from here to Lincoln county to the wedding of a friend. We went by private conveyance the day before the wedding. On the wedding day we set the table in the morning soon after breakfast, and I counted sixty large iced cakes which they had provided. Cake, meat, biscuit, fruit, and everything was piled up on one long table all at once, and after the table was loaded down, there were at least eighteen or twenty large and beautifully dressed cakes not touched. I wondered why they had provided so many, but afterwards I found out, for every single soul who came expected to take home a good supply of cake.

The wedding was to be at eight o'clock in the

evening and the company commenced assembling about three o'clock, many coming with babies and children. They came in and sat in a solemn row all around the room from three till eight, putting the children down in the middle of the floor to play. It was more like a prayer-meeting than a wedding, for no one said anything to anybody. Candles were put in tin sconces all around the wall, and about dusk in the evening the lady and gentleman of the house came in, got up on chairs, and lit the candles. The men did not come into the house at all, but collected in the yard, where they had fires built on raised stands. The young men on the porch looked at the girls, but did not come in, nor have anything to do with them.

The bride and bridesmaids were dressed about two hours before the ceremony, and about a half hour after the ceremony was over, they were all invited to supper. After supper a few of the braver young men ventured in where the young ladies were, and tried to persuade and coax others to join them. Three of them went out and took hold of one very bashful fellow and brought him in, kicking and struggling, and introduced him to some of the girls. The minute they let him go, he turned and rushed out as fast as he could possibly go.

Many of the company stayed all night and the bed-rooms and floors were covered with pallets where the women and children were packed in like sardines in a box.

I think the climate here has changed and grown colder than it was when I was young, for we used to wear silk mantillas, or crape shawls, all winter long. The first blanket shawl I ever saw was one that one of the teachers brought from the North. My mother's criticism was, "It is very nice, but there would not be three days in the winter when it would be cold enough to wear it." The undershirts and drawers that everybody wears now were unknown then and when they were first brought out they were considered things for invalids and very delicate people.

The first fur I ever saw in my life was when I was about fourteen years old. A cousin of ours* from New Haven came to spend the winter and the first Sunday she went to church with her fur collar and muff, she caused such an excitement that all the little boys and girls had to be constantly thumped, and jerked, and reduced to order by violent means.

Fire-crackers and fireworks were very scarce and very expensive, and for weeks before Christmas my brothers spent all their spare time gathering reeds from the cane brakes to let them dry for bonfires on Christmas morning. They would pop and make as much noise as a fire-cracker. We always got up at the first crack of day on Christmas morning, and after getting the stockings which Santa Claus had filled, we went out with the boys to make the bonfires. When my faith in Santa Claus was just beginning to waver, it was strengthened and confirmed for several years by receiving a note in my stocking from Santa Claus. He told me he would have brought us more candy, but coming from a neighbor's, over the Seminary, his reindeer had run against a lightning rod and torn a hole in his pack and spilt some of his candy. We all rushed to the Seminary as hard as we could go, and sure enough, at the foot of the lightning rod was a great lot of sugar plums and candy. This steadied my wavering faith for a year or two longer.

My father had a great way of doing little things like that. At one time he thought one of my brothers was more interested in his hunting and traps than he was in his studies, so one day when he came in late to dinner, father said, "Where have you been, my son?" Porter replied that he had been in the woods to look at his traps.

Father said, "Did you catch anything?"

"No, sir."

"Why, was'nt your trap down?"

*Miss Hillhouse.

"Yes, sir, it was down, but there was'nt anything in it but a Davies' Arithmetic." He was a very matter-of-fact youth and took it as quietly as though it was the most natural thing in the world to catch a Davies' Arithmetic in a trap in the woods.

When I was a young school girl, it was the fashion for most of us to be very sentimental. We all had "secret sorrows" and "broken hearts," and longed to fly away and be at rest, and "the gathering storms were wild and woeful like our own souls." I had a blank book full of the most sentimental poetry which I had copied in it. One night I left it down stairs, where my father got hold of it. In the back of it, in a very pinched-up school-girl hand, I had written, "Heaven hath no broken hearts." The next morning when I got it my father had imitated my writing, and filled it out and this is the way it read:

> "Heaven hath no broken hearts nor heads,
> There, no one limps on wooden pegs.
> There, Mary Barnett and Miss Cliff
> With shoulders straight and backs so stiff,
> Purged from all dross, and freed from sins
> Hold up their heads and in their chins."

Mary Barnett was a playmate, who like myself, had a habit of walking with her head stuck out in front of her, and my father was always telling us to hold them up.

Sunday schools in those days were very different from what they are now. We went very little to Sunday school; mother taught us at home. My brother Porter came out from Sunday School one afternoon and said, "he did'nt think Heaven was no such a great place nohow, but, however, if ma wanted him to, he would try and get there, but he never could go out anywhere without getting all stuck up, because the Bible said it flowed with milk and honey." He had such a hatred to milk that he never would eat anything that even looked as though it had milk in it. So that description of the Heavenly Kingdom was particularly uninviting to him. One day when he had been sick in bed all day, I was in his room late in the afternoon, and asked what he had been doing all day. He said he had been "thinking," and I asked him what he had been thinking about. He said, "Thinking about God, and how hard I could butt."

The day my sister Sarah was four years old she walked into the room where my father was and said, "Father, I am four years old today and I have'nt yet triumphed over the fear of death."

In one of the Sunday School lessons my mother was talking to my brothers about telling the truth always. She asked Charlie if he knew the meaning of a lie. Charlie said "yes," and mother asked him to tell her what a lie was. Charlie said, "Yes'm, I know what's a lie. When me and Porter and Mose goes up in the grove to play, and Porter and Mose tells me to go to the house and fetch a old tin pan, and I says 'no;' cause I was afraid they would run away and hide, and they said 'no,' they declared they won't, and I goes and gets the old tin pan and when I gets back, I don't see Porter and Mose nowhere and I gets scared and begin to cry, and Porter and Mose jumps up from behind a old hollow log and says, 'Jinuary fool, Jinuary fool,' that's a lie."

My old black mammy was very particular with the children about their table manners, and very much mortified if they did anything that was not good manners. One day at the table she asked Charlie if he would have some okra, and he said, "No thank you, I don't eat okra it looks too much like horse slobber." Mammy almost fainted away at his saying such a thing at the table.

One day Charlie came to mother and said, "Mother, do you think this is fair? Me and Hilly has a crop together, and every day when I come from school I goes there and works in the crop, and Hilly he won't work a bit. Sometimes he say he got the headache, and sometimes he say he got the backache, and sometimes he say he ain't got the right hoe, and we offers him every hoe we got, and nairy hoe ain't the right hoe. Now do you think this is fair?"

Hilly had very curly hair, and one day I met him when it looked pretty tumbled, and I said, "Hilly, when was the last time you had your hair brushed?" His answer was, "It ain't been the last time yet since before my head was begun to be stopped combing."

He was very fond of wading in the duck trough, and used to get wet up to his waist, so mother told him she would punish him if he did it again. A few days after he came in to ask for something to eat, and mother saw he was wet up to his waist. She said, "Why Hilly, what have you been doing to get so wet?" He looked very much agitated for a minute, and then said, "I was just walking by the duck trough and my breeches went in."

Alexander H. Stephens was a poor boy in Crawfordville, helped by Mr. Webster, who was the Presbyterian minister at that time. Mr. Webster taught a class of boys, and Mr. Stephens lived at his house and went to school to him with the other boys. When Mr. Webster died, the Presbyterian church undertook to educate Mr. Stephens, and he lived around in the different members' houses for a year at a time. He lived one year at my father's house, when he was a small boy. After he became a member of Congress and a distinguished man, he was often in Washington on law business with different courts, etc., and always came to visit us at this house. One day one of the children rushed into the dining room and said to my old mammy, "Mammy, mammy, Mr. Stephens is coming. He is at the front gate now." Mammy drew herself up to her full height and putting on all her dignity, she said, "Well, chile, en what if he is. I shan't make no 'miration! Alex. Stephens has done stood byarfoot in dis yer yard and gimme imperence too often."

When the colored women at the plantation were sick

for any length of time, and could'nt get in to church, mother would send us down to the plantation to read to them. On one such occasion a woman who had been sick for a long time was talking to me about her two sons, Solomon and Jerry. She said, "Now Miss Cliff, Solomon is kind of a senseless chile, an always was. Jerry is a very study boy. I dessay he has a great deal of badness all to hisself, as most study people has, but he was always a study boy." From that day I have never heard of a "steady boy" but I think of Kitty's remark, founded on a long and wide experience with boys.

In those days it was safe for children to roam all through the woods, and we would spend our Saturdays wading in the branches, gathering wild flowers, building dams, etc., and never thought of there being any danger. One day my sister Hattie and I concluded that we would paint our faces with pokeberries, and come and scare our mother, who would think we were Indians. We succeeded beyond our utmost expectations, for when mother saw us she thought it was blood on our faces, and she screamed and fell down in a faint. Father and all of the servants came running to see what was the matter, and Hattie and I were glad to run away and hide in the most secluded corner that we could find, not hankering for an interview with father just at that minute.

My mother was a dear lover of flowers and always had some on her work-table by her. If she could not have any flowers, she would have a vase of green. She used to go in the garden every day in the season and cut lavender flowers, dry them, and sew them up in little bags, to put in amongst the sheets and towels. So the smell of lavender is always associated with her in my mind.

Some of the darkies had a great idea of fancy names, and the mother of one of ours named her children (some of them) as follows: Dosia Ann Darthula; Benedicta Henrietta LaFayette; and Corinthia Ann Ball Mary

Wilkerson Weems. One of the boys was Mortimer Hoskins, and one was Solon Lycurgus Cicero, but Solon did not long survive his name. He died in infancy.

M. C. H.

HARRIET VIRGINIA CUMMING (*b*. April 24, 1828) and
LOUISA FREDERIKA GILMER (*b*. June 9, 1824) ·
From a daguerreotype taken by Carey about 1848.

Harriet to Clifford Alexander

Savannah, Dec. 1849.

My ever precious Puss. Sitting by your side "cheek touching cheek" I date my letter and write this first sentence. Tarry we now till we see what the next will be.

Dec. 4th Tuesday. Far "away from Home and thee, Mary," thinking of you, yearning for you, and reproaching myself that I am where I am, I write this next. Yes, yes—I feel a pang in the midst of every joy when I think of my home and remember that it is all enjoyed at your expense. I'm not going to write of this now tho', considering that there are other things of which to write that will be more cheering in their effect upon you, than the homesick yearnings of a child absent from such a home as mine. I am going to write you a real *feminine* letter, full of nothing but dress, fashions, gossip and chit-chat. So all those masculines that dont relish such frippery must stand aside and let us have it all our own way. Well, imagine me then seated in Sister's room by the window, stopping of course to look out ever and anon as some bird of gayer plumage than ordinary flits by. Mrs. Lawton was the last that flitted, looking so spruce and trim that I did'nt at first recognize her. Imagine me likewise—dont look at the picture. I dont look *quite* so stylish yet—but imagine me feeling as stuck up as you *can* imagine in all the glorious uncomfortableness of a bran new dress with a standing collar to it, and a turn-down over it almost in my mouth, a knot of red ribbon on my chin, by way of fastening to my collar, and a perched-up looking tight body, buttoned up in front. My puffs have'nt expanded yet, so the cup of misery is not yet full. To increase my comfort and delight I am but about two-thirds relieved from such a cold as rarely falls to the lot of mortals. Where I got it, I dont know—but I began to cough the day I left Charleston, and in twenty-four hours afterwards, I could scarcely speak so as to be heard.

So far I have seen more of Miss Washington* than of anybody else, and paid her more visits—I'm going to make a scrap-bag of my letter, and send you pieces of my. dresses, some ribbons &c. This is a good place to begin to tell you about the fashions but I've work to do, and must wait till the time comes for another entry. I'm going to make a journalising sort of letter of it.

Wednesday morning. Feeling much more comfortable this morning arrayed in my beloved seven-pence calico, I take up my sheet again to have another little chat with you. Now I'm going to tell you all the things I have been buying for my winter wardrobe. I send you scraps of the only new dresses that you have'nt seen. I had to give up my pet idea of a raw-silk, because I couldnt find a nice and pretty one—so I got the blue mousseline de laine instead— Everything is made plain waist and trimmed with velvet and buttons. The silk had to be low-necked, but in place of capes to such dresses, they have another waist, made plain, very close in the throat and buttoned in the front with silver buttons. The sleeves are sewed in the low-necked waist and the other is worn *over* it, just as a cape would be. Miss W. says she has'nt made a cape this season. So much for dresses— They are generally made with standing collars, but they wear turn-downs over them. Either are fashionable this winter much to my joy. My mantilla, or rather *sack*, is a blue and gold silk, with a row of embroidery round it; very pretty, and Mr. Hodgson says, quite *Parisian*. I dont know what you'll say to my bonnet, but it is a green drawn

*The dressmaker.

silk, lined with white drawn satin, and a tab of bright flowers. It is tho't very pretty and becoming. I was horrified at first at the idea of anything so gay, but was assured that if I wore a cherry-colored merino, a lemon shawl, and an orange bonnet, I should only be fashionable, and by no means conspicuous. And it is the fact. I have seen several ladies dressed pretty much in that style. The most brilliant red dresses like what we saw at Mr. Clevelands, and red shawls, are all the rage—with yellow bonnets. I send you a little scrap of one of Sister Lou's yellow neck-ribbons, to give you an idea of what is worn. The brocaded ribbon is a scrap of the trimming on my straw bonnet. It is lined with cherry and has bright flower tabs. The bonnet that came out for Sister Lou was so small that she could'nt get it on. So Mr. H. made her send it back and order another like it, but larger. It came on Monday, and was rather small for *me*, so you may know what it would be for her. She was in despair but Uncle relieved her by taking it for one of his nieces, and she has got one from Mrs. Beaulard. It is a very pretty white silk, with small feathers on each side—looks neat and simple—and is much prettier than the one from N. York. Now I have given you such another chapter of fashions as you never read before. Nobody would listen to it but you and Mother—but if I was in your place, I think I'd like to know how you were dressed—so I've told you everything that could help you to an idea. I've got a lot of other things to say to you, but as there is no reason why I should'nt write as long a letter as I choose, I shant endeavor to restrain myself. You were a dear child to write me such a long letter and so soon—and I thank you for it. Guess who was spending the evening with us, and kept me from reading your letter for two or three hours! You give up? Well, it was Edgar Dawson!

He is here for the winter, reading physic with Dr. Bullock—and as he brought a letter of introduction to

Uncle, I have a fair chance of making his lordship's acquaintance. We discoursed long and eloquently of you, and he told me to tell you that he had a beautiful (interrupted— Goodbye for the present) Thursday morning. He had a beautiful *calf* at home named Mary Clifford. Illustrious girl! Two white babies, two black ones, a dog and a calf named after you! I *do* think Edgar rather sort-o'-ish good looking—and found him very chatty. *Your* hero has'nt made his appearance yet, and it is surmised that he is out of town. Joe hasn't arroven yet—but he's got a cousin here, the one from Prussia, that is one of the prettiest girls I have seen—and I'm dreadfully afraid she'll throw me in the shade and blast my precious hopes and expectations. My "sister Kitty" looks so improved in colors, that I did'nt know her, and have been passing her in the streets without recognizing her in the least. Miss Joe has a little boy of four or five days old, weighing eleven pounds, and Sister's daily visits to her interfere somewhat with our walks. She has a good many calls &c to occupy her in the evening—and sometimes Aunt Lou and Sister Sallie are busy too. So I take Minny for a companion and we entertain each other. I do feel so thankful that she is here. It seems like a part of home—and I never tire of having her with me. I think her wonderfully improved. She has color in her cheeks and looks much plumper and healthier in every way. Aunt Lou dresses her very prettily, and I really find myself *struck* with her appearance at times. I have been with her to dancing school and think her quite expert, considering how short a time she has been there. She is devoted to me so far, and wants to go everywhere with me. I am glad to take her, glad to do anything for her. So far I have been too unwell to settle down into a regular life—but I am sure that I shall be able to spend my time much more profitably than ever before when I was here. The next few days I am to spend with Sister Sarah.

Mr. L. has gone to Milledgeville and I am to do what I can towards supplying his place.

Fondly, lovingly yours,

H.

Corinne always speaks of Father as "her putty danpa, what aint got no beard." Aunt has got one of the prettiest silks for you that ever your eyes lit upon. I send you a scrap of mine. Minny sends special love to Mammy and begs Hilly to write to her soon. She contemplates an epistle to Mother.

Adam Alexander to His Daughter, Marion.

Washington, Ga., April 22, 1850.

My dear daughter:

I received your pretty little note, and was pleased to think you cared enough for me to write so long a letter. I hope you will learn this summer when you return home and attend school at the Seminary to write for yourself, which you can do in a short time, if you will apply yourself. I often think when I look over at the children playing in the Seminary yard, how much greater interest I shall feel in their sports when you are one of them, and I am sure you will feel much happier to go to school with so many young companions, than if you were alone in your studies and your plays. They have more than sixty girls now in the Seminary, but among them all I don't think there will be a better girl in deportment or in scholarship than little Marion Brackett. It will be pleasant times to have you home again and once more to have you meet me when I am returning home from bank. I often think of you at such times for though Dot sometimes comes to meet me at the gate, she does not come as regularly as you used to do.

I was sorry to hear that poor Ponto died. He was a very pretty dog. But I have a very pretty dog for you which I reserved from among Letty's puppies expressly for you, and I never saw a prettier puppy, or a livelier one. He is as black as a raven with white and red breast and feet and we call him "Mr. Toots," but that is not of the least consequence for he is a very sensible dog. I was walking yesterday in the yard and they showed me one of the chickens you left at home, now a motherly hen

138

with a brood of young chickens at her side. Your house*
looks very lonely indeed, though the flowers are growing
prettily in the yard. Sometimes I open the door to look
in upon your children, but they seem to have forgotten
me. They now so seldom see me. I read in the papers
the other day that in England they make dolls that can
say "mama" and "papa" as plainly as anybody can. One
man only can make them and he sells them for $30.00.
When I go to England I will bring one of them for you.

O how you will be delighted to see your dear little
sister Dot! She is as beautiful as anything you ever saw,—
But my paper is ended and so must my letter.

Your affectionate father,

A. L. A.

*The old play house in the yard.

Sarah Alexander to Her Daughter, Harriet.

Washington, Ga., Nov. 22, 1850.
Friday.

My dear Hattie:—

So many extra communications have been made of late that I thought it unnecessary to write at the time I had promised, and now that I have sat down to my writing desk, I fear that it will only be to inflict a very dull epistle upon you, for I have been so shut up since you went away that the current of my ideas runs very sluggishly. I think I have not had more than three visitors during the time, and have ridden out but twice. This week has been one of bad weather—cold and rainy, and there is yet no glimpse of sunshine to cheer us. I have been afraid to venture out, even to the kitchen or store-room, and Sally has been outdoors housekeeper "pro tem." By dint of sending her as many times as there were bowls to be filled, she succeeded very well, besides getting exercise and fresh air. You know she can not carry two ideas at a time. My business, since you left, when I have been well enough to do anything, has been cutting our negroes clothes, and my amusement, watching and admiring Dot in all the varieties of her humor. She has been pretty constantly in the house, owing to the cold weather and a cold she has, and she seems to have a decided preference for my society, which is often more flattering than convenient, as she wishes to take part in all my employments. However, she is certainly a very good child and easily amused. This morning she sat by me, while Caro was gone to her breakfast, in a little chair with a picture book propped open before her on another, and set to music all the marvellous tales contained therein, introducing sundry airs, sacred and profane, to diversify the strain, and entertained both herself and me quite agreeably. She speaks of you all sometimes, but does not seem to miss Marion as I thought she would. Her desire for tales is quite insatiable, and as I unluckily told her one I can no longer plead inability, and I am called on to repeat that four or five times daily, after which she regularly walks off with her head on one side in offended majesty because I refuse to tell some more. One day after lying in one of Sarah's sort-of ruminating moods a long time, she raised her head and informed us all "she did'nt like *tab lantuns*." Her distaste, however, does not include "pudden pie" as she calls for it every day and is always affronted if none is to be had. But fie on me for filling up a page with such a little body, though she is the dearest and sweetest of all the little curly pates in the world!

Last night was the meeting of the newly organized Demosthenian club in the Wright Institute, and we had some of the incipient orators to tea to spend the night. The boys are deeply interested in it, and judging by the thunders of applause which reached our ears, even through the closed doors and windows, they must have enjoyed specimens of eloquence of no common stamp. Tom West was one of the visitors, and this reminds me to tell you that Mary was married last week to a young lawyer in Newnan, by name Wilcoxon, and has gone there to live. Charlie is the happiest fellow you ever saw in the prospect of going to Savannah and I doubt whether he will anticipate a greater fulness of delight in his own wedding, than he does in his sister's.* The fireworks came safely and were most joyfully received. Hilly sat down in the fullness of his gratitude to write you a letter, and was sadly mortified to find last night that it had not yet gone—indeed, he had begun to look for an answer. Tuesday's mail brought us your welcome letter. We felt not a little concern to hear

*Louisa Alexander's to Mr. Gilmer.

of Marion's sickness in Augusta, while I hope we realized more fully than ever the comfort of daily and hourly dependence upon an over-ruling Providence. Poor little one! She is a frail and delicate flower, and I never dare to look forward to aught but *Heaven* for her, but how much nobler and more joyful a prospect than all the earth can give. I only used the expression in reference to any expectations of comfort *we* might build on the continuance of her life.

S. H. A.

Clifford Alexander to Her Mother.

Washington Jan. 30th 1851.
Thursday Night.

While I am beginning this letter my dearest Mother, I imagine you all in the parlor at Uncle's most probably feasting on the one Hattie despatched Tuesday. I hope it may meet with no delays, for when you get Father's, of last Saturday, and hear that we had not reached home, I well know how anxious you will be to hear something more about it. I hope Wallace got to Savannah the same night the letter did, and that he told you of the unaccountable manner in which we were whisked off to Crawfordville. Knowing us to be safe in that delectable settlement, you will easily imagine the rest, and why we were not home to breakfast. Hattie wrote so much at length, that she doubtless told you all about our journey—our haps and mishaps, our pleasures and our pains, and everything in short that there was to tell. So there is nothing left for me to add, even on that never-ending and inexhaustible theme—Wallace's and Joe's devotion—unless, indeed, I chronicle my own private feelings on the occasion, and tell you what a dreadful thing it is to be always the *one too many* —the black sheep of a crowd—for in such a light I was evidently regarded by both the gentlemen who escorted us up the river. As I observed to Felix, in a long letter I sent him today, I never will travel again with *two* of Hattie's admirers, and none of my own, but hereafter I shall always insist on having one at least of the party devoted to my interests and society. There being just "us four and no more," of course we always had to go by *twos*—"a feller and a gal, and a gal and a feller,"

143

so of course for decency's sake one had to be with me. Now Wallace was so obstreperous, that he wouldn't even take turns staying with me, but followed Hattie round like a tame and faithful kitten—a *very faithful kitten indeed* —so you may imagine what a benefit poor Joe had of my sweet society. And I will do him the justice to say, in the words of the Nipper, "that *I never* see such a self sacrificing young man in all my life before." He did his best to hide his emotion and swallow down his disappointment, and tho' I have seen young men livelier and more vivacious than he was, yet still he was quite as cheerful as could have been expected under the circumstances. I did all I could to relieve him by keeping very much in the State room and reading most vigorously in the ladies cabin—for all jesting aside it was not a very agreeable feeling to know that a gentleman was making a virtue of necessity, and keeping company with you, while he was all the time mentally consigning you to the lowest depths. As for staying all together, that was impossible, for which ever one got hold of Hattie *always would* take her off in a corner, all to himself as if she was an apple he intended to eat, and was afraid the other would ask for a piece. They were very selfish with her, but you never saw such generous fellows as they became, as soon as thrown in my society—willing not only to share it with anybody else, but to give it up entirely on the smallest provocation. The pearls of my conversation were cast before swine that week, if they never were before, and they immediately turned again to rend Hattie. I lacked however for no kindness or attention from either of them—no one could have been kinder than they were, and I used to go to sleep every night thinking what a good and great thing it was to have popular Sisters. I don't know a better, except to be popular yourself. When I think of all Wallace's kindness to us I feel quite oppressed with the debt of gratitude I owe him, and I don't know what return I can make unless by giving my full and free consent to have him and Hattie complete the good work they have begun, and do all that is in their hearts. Joe did his best too, and tell Aunt Lou, that I didn't have the heart to do anything to spite such a martyr, in my own behalf, as he evidently was, particularly as I had to spite him so much involuntarily. As the Rev. Mr. Baker would say, "I love those dear young men," and hope I may some day have it in my power to return some of the favors I have received at their hands. I was quite shocked a little while ago, on taking up the paper to see the marriage of Lieut. Alexander—not that I had any, expectations in that quarter myself—no indeed; tho' you may not believe me it is so—but I had heard Miss Bolton was "little and old," which begot a prejudice in my mind, and I never could bring myself to consent to it—so they needn't expect to be prosperous and happy. Not to change the subject too suddenly, I would mention that I took the housekeeping on Monday, and have managed to get something for dinner every day *this* week, without any extraordinary amount of scuffling and scraping. The times will come however, I expect, that will put me up to all I know, and as necessity is the mother of invention, I shouldn't wonder if Cynthia and I invented some new kind of meat before you come home. There are no more boys and men here than usual, but somehow, there are so few women to counteract the effect of them, that their number seems doubled, and I feel as tho' I was catering for an army. Uncle H.* is well and about again. We have been having such disagreeable weather since we came home, that even the Pettuses haven't been to see us. Today the thermometer was at 20—and too cold to live with any comfort or pleasure. I am very regular about exercise and my only difficulty is I can't get enough. Hattie can't go fast or far, and when I'm alone I'm afraid to go much beyond the plantation, which is no walk for such a pedestrian as I am. Alice is the greatest pleasure to me imagin-

*David Hillhouse.

145

able—she seems very fond of us indeed. I am trying to teach her to say her prayers every night, but I don't think she is naturally of a devotional turn of mind, for I always have to give her the most *minute* account of how Corinne and Louisa say theirs and also to make the narrative as affecting as possible, before I can get her religious zeal up to the turning point. Corinne seems to be at once a model and a warning to her, for they have one bad habit in common, and whenever I see Dot do it, I say "Oh Frizzle don't do so"—and she stops directly, and her whole face brightens up, as she says "Toween does dat, and what do her Mama say"—then I repeat Sister Sallie's grave reproof, wh. has great effect.

C.

Clifford Alexander to Her Mother.

Prudence, my Dearest Mother forbids me to begin this letter tonight for I have been reading, writing and sewing, so industriously, ever since I came home, that my eyes have failed me more than they have done in years before. Even in the day, I often have to lay aside my book or my work, to rest them for a moment or I cannot see at all. But I am in no condition to listen, or rather to yield to prudence's voice for this is my best chance for writing, between this and Saturday, and this letter must go then. Tomorrow Lou is coming to take dinner and spend the day with us, and I have had the fatted gobler (*not* Major Roland, but another of the same sort) killed in her honor. I may have tomorrow evening, but cant count upon it, as it is high time M—— was paying one of his periodical visits here, and we live in nightly dread of his appearance. Whenever the young men come here in the evening, (which is *delightfully seldom*) Father stands it like a martyr-hero —he never flinches (tho' you can see the iron has entered his soul) until the clock strikes *nine* — But that is a death-knell to his fortitude—it acts like a clap of thunder on a bowl of milk—and curdles all the milk of human kindness in his heart. Mercy how sour he looks—and how long he yawns and how "vig'rously" he winds up his watch, and how loud he locks all the doors—and how restlessly he walks from the sitting room to the water pail, and then back into his seat with the most agitated expression and with what determination he resumes his seat, as if to let them know he *would* sit them out, even if they stayed till *ten o'clock*, and he died in the attempt.

When we are alone, he considers nine o'clock *ridiculously early*, but just let "a dear young man" be about and it alters the case entirely—then to be up after nine is worse than for ghosts to be abroad after daylight.

Macon and Dr. Hanson came together one night and were so unfortunate as stay until ten, notwithstanding all the alarming symptoms father betrayed during the last hour. After they had all been gone thro' and still no move to go, Father planted himself right in the midst of us and prepared to listen to the conversation. Once, just as I was in the midst of a very innocent remark to the Dr. I looked up and caught Father's eyes—and mercy what a look! He contracted his whole face into one withering frown and shook his head at me most violently. The words froze on my palsied tongue—all my senses and my self possession retired abashed—my eyes stared, my under jaw dropped, and I just stopped short in the midst of the sentence, to gaze in mute surprise at father—quite unconscious as to what he was frowning at, but supposing that I had been uttering profane and treasonable sentiments at least. I discovered afterwards on inquiry however, that he tho't I was making myself too chatty and agreeable and detaining the Dr. whom he declared to be *"a perfect Ass,"* unnecessarily. Oh how they did catch it after they did go. Macon was nothing but "a good natured fool," and it is unnecessary to repeat the verdict on poor Dr. Hanson. He never has forgiven the Dr. and would doubtless glower at him again if he had another chance. He told us distinctly the other day that he intended to be very sour to anybody who came to see us, and intimated yesterday that we had better try and see which of us could get married first, as he didn't intend the other one should at all.

You cant imagine how perfectly delighted we were to see Lou Toombs—and with what greedy ears we have listened to every item of information concerning our Savannah friends. It is well she has a willing tongue, or our curiosity would never be satisfied. We liked the dresses she bro't very much indeed. The barege de laines are lovely, and I am also particularly pleased with my colored morning dress. I feel as tho' I'd never finish all my work. Uncle H. left on Tuesday for Augusta, Marietta, Columbus and all about. Father will have Mercer to do *useful* work for three weeks! I read a love letter for Maria* today in which the ardent swain told her she was "the apple of his eye—the orange of his heart, and the pineapple juice of his soul." Dont let Marion hear that, do, or she'll come home and tell that I *peached.*

You dont know dear Mother how *pained* I was when I came home, to hear that you had issued the death warrant of all my pets—my dear Puddle Ducks—Charlemagne, Randolph Whitehead, Peter the Great, Napoleon Bonaparte, Julia Toombs and Matilda Maxwell have been successively decapitated, ignominiously stuffed with bread and butter and barbarously devoured. But when it came to Edgar and Hattie, I couldn't stand that, and said they *must* be spared. I think it would be a real piece of barbarity to kill that couple. I couldn't permit such a deed of darkness. So Hattie and Edgar still thrive, and come every morning for their ration of cornbread. Wallace and Emma are still alive too.

I have been reading the Life of John Randolph and was extremely interested in it, as well as much instructed thereby. I'm going next to turn my attention to Stephens Hist. of Georgia. But I believe his name is spelt Stevens. Mr. Stephens sent me his likeness by Lou Toombs, an excellent one.

I think a summer in Savannah would be very pleasant —tho' the truth is, I think anything is pleasant there. I think Aunt Lou and Sister very unkind not to sympathize with the disaster of my tucking comb. It was a severe loss to me, I assure you, and I haven't fared near so well since, as I have nothing else that'll keep my hair up.

*One of the servants.

Mat Brooks sits up a little now, but cannot move her arm at all. I leave the rest of this paper to fill tomorrow, hoping I shall be able to chronicle the arrival of one of your welcome missives.

Saturday. We are all right *sick* with disappointments today, for we had no mail from Augusta at all—only the one from above. Tuesday seems as far off, when I look forward to it, as the next century. It goes particularly hard with Father, as he was quite sick all night, with one of those head- and eye-aches, and looking forward to your letter as a sovereign balm for all his woes. Give my best love to *all, all, all*. Please send me a scrap of that morning dress, for cording. Father says quit letting the girls have all the pretty dresses you get.

Ever your most aff. child.
C.

WILLIAM FELIX ALEXANDER (*b.* May 7, 1832)
From a daguerreotype.

A Yale Smoker in 1851.

Felix Alexander to His Father.

Yale, June 19, 1851.

My dear Father:—

As these are stirring and interesting times about college I shall endeavor to write you this morning an account which will bring back somewhat the days in which you took your A. B., though I am interrupted every few minutes to write in the autograph books of my classmates, now rapidly departing.

Since I last wrote you we have finished our "biennial examinations," been through the exercises of presentation day, and been released from all attendance upon college exercises. Some of the professors told me yesterday that our class had passed the best examination ever known in this institution, and displayed an extent and accuracy of information very creditable. High complimenting from such sources.

Yesterday we were assembled in one of the recitation rooms and headed by some of the Faculty marched to one of the lecture rooms where the body of the Faculty and invited strangers were assembled for the ceremony of presentation for degrees of such as had passed a satisfactory examination. The Senior tutor first read to the Faculty, in Latin, the names of the future A. B.s. Prof. Kingsley then in a Latin speech recommended us to the President, and then gave us an address also in Latin. His is the old style of Latin, and it was interesting to hear it rolled out with so much earnestness from so venerable looking a scholar, one whose hairs were silvered with so many years.

Our beloved President then arose, and after recommending us to the members of the Faculty as very worthy men,— though he termed us "nudes, informes, indoctique" when we entered college,—he made us a parting address. It was most beautifully written, and his Latin certainly ran more easily, if less majestically, than Prof. K's. We were then formally invited to partake with the Faculty of a collation, which invitation we, of course, accepted. All official connection between us having ceased, there was no longer any restraint and all were on terms of heartfelt friendship and cordiality. For much as we may rail at our professors, we certainly do reverence and love them. I have had few pleasanter hours than was that dinner hour. The whole class then adjourned to the front part of the college green, and there seated in a ring on the grass begun our afternoon festivities. A hundred long pipes and a box of smoking tobacco were provided and then every Senior, whether he had ever before inhaled the weed or not, took his pipe, filled and smoked our solemn class smoke, which buries in oblivion all society, sectional and personal animosities and unites us as brothers ere we part. Then we had the violins, etc., in the centre and sung all the songs endeared to us by the associations of past years, and those that had been written especially for the occasion. Then there were any number of ridiculous speeches, songs, burlesques on certain members of the Faculty who are "burlesquible," etc. etc. Then forming into a long procession, each man with his pipe refilled and relighted, we marched out by Divinity College, honoring it with three cheers; and with our band leading ran down Elm to Church Sts. at full speed, and then marched slowly down Church and Chapel to the Postoffice; cheering this we marched back, smoking all in silence, to Pres. Day, cheered him and had a speech. Then returning to college we finished by marching through each entry of the buildings, cheering the buildings and the Professors within them. Once more seated on the grass, more speeches were pro-

posed to occupy the hour until we should sing our parting
ode and go to prayers for the last time. And now the
feelings of sadness for a time suppressed, began to show
forth. The speeches became more serious, more affectionate, and the last one of the class spoke of our classmate
who died but a month ago, and a touching speech he made.
Then he sung a parting ode which had been written by
one of the class—a beautiful, feelingly expressive farewell,
and ere 'twas finished there were few dry eyes, though all
the college stood by looking on. It left us with a sad
realization of how soon we must part. I could but think
how like life that afternoon had been; beginning with
happy rejoicings, ending in farewells and tears.

I have just finished writing in Estabrooks' book my
farewell, and 'twas the saddest I have yet written. He
leaves tomorrow and will only return for a day or two
for Commencement.

Our appointments came out this morning and I send
you enclosed a list which will tell you about them. You
see I stand sixth—a prouder eminence that I ever dared
hope when a Freshman, with my preparation, I entered
these walls.

I shall renew my laboratory studies now uninter-
ruptedly.

I suppose that Hattie showed you the pecuniary part
of my letter to her. I shall have to ask you to send me
$50.00 or $100.00 more, for which I will render a satisfactory account on my return home.

Mrs. Wm. Hillhouse still wastes away and I think
she can live but a very few weeks. Please give warmest
love to my dear mother and all others at home, and ever
think of me as
   Your most affectionate son,
          W.

Sarah Alexander to Her Daughter Harriet.

My dear Hattie:—

I expected by this time to have been in your debt for a letter, but as this is not the case I must bestow this upon you as a matter of grace, or rather a payment in advance for the letter which, I am sure, will be shortly forthcoming. I was quite anxious for last night's mail, hoping to hear by it of your safe arrival at home, but instead of that I was only informed that you were heard of on the Railroad, bound to parts unknown, and had not arrived in W——. Some of the family suggested an elopement, as you were in such suspicious company, but I relied on Cliff and Uncle H. to prevent that, so "I am afloat" on the sea of conjecture, but trusting Providence that you did reach home in safety sometime during Saturday, and I dare say in time to get a good scolding, which you richly deserved for causing your father so much uneasiness and trouble. I shall feel quite impatient for the Thursday's mail to explain proceedings. I have conjectured that Uncle H. found you some other protector and concluded to come on down here to see Mr. L. as he was disappointed in his going to Augusta.

I am writing in Lou's room which I find the only convenient place, having no table in my own room, and here she comes with a very complaining look and tone, says she has a very strange pain and chilliness come over her. I have dosed her with camphor and hot flannel and hope she will feel better soon, but she looks so badly to me, and has done so ever since I came down, that I feel constantly anxious about her. I hope nothing is going to happen to prevent the success of Sarah's grand dinner, so long talked of, which is to come off tomorrow. The discussions as to who should constitute the company have been numerous and animated. Some were too dull, some too trifling, some too young, others too old,—and a happy combination of all the necessary qualities for an agreeable dinner party seemed hard to find in the persons of nine out of the 16,000 individuals composing this City. Never before did I appreciate the importance of a *judicious selection*, till I sat, an amazed listener, to hear the merits (and demerits, too, I am sorry to say) of all the members of upper-tendom discussed and descanted upon. I suppose you will desire to know who have been chosen as the élite, after all this deliberation. Fourteen is the number to compose this august assemblage, of whom L. T. and the two Maries, G. & L. constitute five. In addition are Mr. and Mrs. Lamar, Mr. and Mrs. Wm. Law, Jas. Bullock, Dr. Arnold, John Owens (Mr. and Mrs. Sorrel declined; Mary Owens ditto; M. Cummings pre-engaged) and two more yet to be selected. Maj. P., sister, and myself declined to be churned up in this cream of society, and she and I propose to play the useful, instead of the agreeable, on the occasion by officiating in the kitchen and pantry. I am quite amused with seeing the excitement of S. and Mr. L. on the occasion, never having before understood how great an affair is a *big dinner*. As I shall be quite busy over there tomorrow, I must write most of my letter today, besides going out to pay some calls which have accumulated on me considerably, as the weather prevented me from paying any last week.

Saturday night we went over to hear the Hungarian minstrels but they proved to be Yankee humbugs, and their ball music was much nearer the ridiculous than the melodious.

Sunday was so pleasant a day that I went to the Ind. Church for the first time, and heard an Agent of the Am.

S. S. Union. After church Sister and I walked out to the Park and sat on a bench a long time, resting and enjoying the mild air. The weather continues delightful and as warm as April.

Mr. Gilmer had to go to Cockspur today and wished to take Lou and myself, but she had promised to make Sarah's jelly today and it could not be deferred, so we postponed the pleasure of the trip down the River, which I expect to enjoy highly. I have been feeling remarkably well for three days past and have scarcely coughed at all. I think I may venture to dismiss my Doctor, if I continue so well. Yesterday I dined at Sarah's and we rode out in the afternoon. I suppose Lou T. told you she moved up into the attic and she seems to like it very much. I think she misses you girls very much, and she seems to look forward anxiously to the time of going home. You know she does not care much for any of the girls, though she walks with some one or other of them every day, but she forms no intimacies.

On Thursday the Levy's give a grand ball which Lou and Mr. G. will attend, but none of the others. Mary Cooper S—— has gone to Baltimore to spend some time I hear. I have met the Elliotts twice since you left and they always enquire about you. Leila says she almost cried her eyes out the day you went away.

Wednesday, 1 o'clock—Have just returned from Sarah's where I have been washing up, etc. preparatory to the grand affair of today. Miss Cass and Capt. Miller make up the company, and this reminds me to enclose you one of the said lady's cards as a specimen of the latest style.

*Sandy** is to give a cotillion party tomorrow night with some of his companions, so I can see some dancing, though I can not go to Mrs. Levy's ball to which I received an invitation; also to a party at G. B. Cumming's tonight.

Love to the boys and tell Charlie I liked his letter

*The butler.

and thought it very well written and will answer it as soon as I can, and Lou says she will certainly answer Hilly's. I wish you could see Mr. G. nursing and waiting upon Lou. Kiss my darling pet for me. Love to Cynthia and with any imaginable quantity for yourself and Cliff, I remain,

Your affectionate mother,

S. H. A.

P. S.

Tell your father I feel quite melted with the recollection that I have written two letters home since I wrote to him—but all the rest shall be his.

Clifford Alexander to Her Mother.

My Dearest Mother:—

Father insinuated today that I needn't write you one of my *interminable* letters, but a mere line to tell you all were well. He would rest "in pace" if he knew how barren of ideas I am at present, tho' I shouldn't be at all afraid to inflict my six cents worth of matter upon you if I had it in hands, for being from home I am sure you would be interested in it all. Everything has moved on very quietly and very smoothly since you left, and dinner being over for today and provided for tomorrow, I feel like saying to my soul "take thine ease and be merry." Charlie made very small of what I provided yesterday, but as his actions and his words didn't agree I treated his aspersion with silent contempt. And speaking of such things reminds me to tell you that it is reported in town we all had to sit up with Ed Saturday night when he killed that turkey, and we have had quite a laugh at him about it. Will got home yesterday to dinner, and we were delighted to hear you had stood the journey to Augusta so well, and met such pleasant company down. I had a note from Cousin Lizzie yesterday, saying she had heard from the Dr.* who was very sick in Charleston, saying the River was so low you couldn't go down that way, and he had written to you to come on there, and so we were afraid you would have to go that way after all. I am very anxious indeed about the Dr. for Sister's letter made me see more than ever how important time is to him.

*Dr. Robertson, the family physician.

Today I am pleasing myself with the tho't of the meeting in Savannah, and that in your pleasure there, you will forget all your regrets, anxieties and misgivings about leaving home. We have had another cool change in the weather, and I am glad you have missed it—no frost, tho' we feared it. I have found plenty to do, and no time to be lonesome. I remembered my promise to be very prudent, and have been rewarded amply. My face didn't swell any more than when you saw me, and hasn't given me a moment's pain. It is on the wane at present, and in the course of two or three days it will I think resume its former delicate and beautiful proportions. My mumps is such a good kind that Cora, Lou and Mary are trying to take it from me, but haven't succeeded as yet. The girls have been very good about coming to see me. Mary and Cora came Monday afternoon and sat a little while, and yesterday directly after dinner they came again with their work, to sit a long time. Before long I had a reinforcement in Lizzie Barnett, and Jennie Lamar followed hard after. This morning Lou came over, and concluded to stay to dinner, and she just left with her most Aff. a little while ago. So you see I am quite popular, and haven't wanted for company. Tomorrow night Cora and Mary and Lou are all going to stay with me, which breaking in on my quiet routine, will seem like quite a *spree*. Next week Cora is coming to stay some with me, so you see the programme is as pleasant as the performance already past, and you will not be troubled for fear of my being lonely. So far father has gotten along famously—has been as harmless as a dove, and quite bright too. The first evening he solaced himself with a visit to Mr. Toombs, and last night he was so desperately sleepy that he couldn't do anything but read the Youths Companion, and then go to bed before nine o'clock. He has fixed up two or three Eolian harps in his room, and so he has what under some circumstances is considered very delightful, "music to fill up the pauses and nobody very near." Ally* I *see* very often, tho' she spends most of the time out doors with *"Collene."* She seems to have a disinclination to her books, and hasn't said a lesson since you left. The boys you would find just where you left them. Porter is up early and late after another Gobbler, and I wish him better luck than he has had so far, with all my heart. Mary Ann continues to do well, and I keep her on low diet as you directed. She liked Oliver the best of all the names proposed for her child, so Oliver is his name.

I hear nothing more of the scarlet fever, and am in hopes it is not going to spread. Mr. Wright had a complimentary ticket to the concert for himself and Lady, and I was invited to act in that capacity, (positively for one evening only, understand) but was enabled by the mumps to decline. When any of the girls over at Mrs. Pelots have the mumps, Mr. Thayer doesn't go to the table, but he and Miss Peet take their meals in the parlor! I am surprised to find myself on the fourth page, and wonder what I have filled the others with. Do please when you come home bring some nice thin ruled letter paper, the size of this sheet. I'll leave the rest for tomorrow.

Porter begged me last night to tell him to whom Sister Hattie was engaged. I feigned the blankest astonishment but it wouldn't do. He said he had known it for two weeks from something he heard you and father say about writing to Sav. on that private business. He pressed me so close there was no getting around it, so I tho't the best way to shut his mouth and ensure his never thinking of it again would be to tell him at once. He received it calmly. These boys of yours are getting so smart you will have to "mind your eye," and weigh well all your words before you speak them.

"Oh Goodness, gracious me!" (as Mr. Riell would say) if here aint a half bushel of papers from "good Mrs. Brown," and a message to send her "the rest with the story in them." What am I to do! (Later.) I have hunted and

*Alice, the youngest sister.

hunted, but not a paper can I find. I wrote her a note and told her I would ask you about them—so do be sure and tell me in what secret place the precious deposit has been made.

Thursday. I didn't get anything in the mail this morning and feel blue for the first time in consequence. Father said he had nothing particular to say except particular love. Give mine to each and all. Tell Hattie I'm living in the tho't of the nice long letter I'm going to get from her Saturday. Next to that I'm living on the tho't of how I shall revile and persecute poor Emma when she comes. I suppose Father will write by Saturdays mail tho' I haven't heard him say so. I am looking for your first letter to me with anxiety, for I know already how interesting it is going to be.

Your most aff. child

M. C. A.

Harriet Alexander to Her Mother.

Home Dec. 10th '52. Friday P. M.

Ally has gone down-stairs to say her lesson to Father, and I improve the brief pause in the play of Reese and Cozart, to begin my letter, dear Mother, to you. After I am once fairly started, I can play and write at the same time, without difficulty—but it bothers me to collect my ideas in the beginning, with that ceaseless strain ringing in my ears. Ally almost lives in my room now-a-days—and if I write a letter, it can scarcely avoid telling of her and her plays. We are having weather worthy of the time of Noah and the Ark—have had scarcely a half dozen clear days in three weeks—and from present appearances we wont have many more of them, just now. So, blessed are those that can find their amusements and pleasures within doors. Ally and I belong to that happy number—and I believe we get along about as well as if the sun shone all the time.

Sam Barnett made a descent upon me this morning, and passed a couple of hours that *I* tho't pleasant and I think *he* did too. I always appreciate Sam's visits as a special compliment—it being so little the custom here for married men to show such attentions to anybody. Emma has spent a day with me this week, too—and one day we went visiting together. So it has been quite a dissipated week with me.

I feel chatty this afternoon, Mother dear—chatty after the fashion of women—and I mean just to gossip along, not heeding whether I interest anybody but you. I know you'll like to hear all the trifling things I can tell about home and home-folks. I was reminded to say this, because I was just about to commence to tell you about our visiting expediton. We went to see Mrs. Lipham, as you requested me to do—found the old lady in all the excitement of breaking up, and moved to tears when she talked of it. She was to have gone yesterday—but the weather has detained her. She gave me a pretty cactus, to remember her by, and two roses out of her garden. One of them, which I will point out to Mammy, you must call *mine*. Then, as a still more valuable legacy, the old lady bequeathed me a venerable dish, the fellow, I believe, to an old fruit-dish that you had, about which she told me a long history. I dare say that you know it better than I do tho'.

After we came home, Dot was giving Father an account of our expedition, and she said that while we were at Mrs. L's, "an old, old lady came in—older than anybody in the room—but she had on a mighty pretty bonnet!" That old female was Mary Cosart! but I dont wonder that Ally tho't she looked old, in the very dressy white satin bonnet that she wears. Mary is still the heroine of all the plays wherewith Ally beguiles her time—but since then, I notice that she always plays that she's a thousand years old. By the way, she has discovered a new disease which plays the very mischief among all her children and friends. Every day a half-dozen of them are suddenly attacked with "spare-ribs," and it always proves fatal. Since I have heard of it, I have become uneasy about you and Sister Sallie—fearing that that's what's the matter with both of you! I am sure I saw symptoms of it in both of you before you left home—and according to Ally, nobody ever recovers from it. There is no describing to you the enjoyment and entertainment that the new "crying baby" furnishes. I have heard marvellous accounts of how she was walking in the garden and found that dear little creature "crying in the weeping bed, just born"— and I expect to hear her tell it down-stairs, before she's many days older.

Despite the rain, Father has bought his hogs today —and if Monday should prove favorable weather, the slaughter is to commence. It will be a relief to have it over—but my inexperience dreads it. We miss James very much, already, about the lot. Father has taken Tom from the kitchen, to supply his place—and it throws us all into some confusion. I wish we could have finished with the meat before he went away. There's not a great deal of work in the kitchen, now-a-days, for I dont think it necessary to feed my bears on delicacies. Corn-beef and steak are the chief of their diet for dinner and breakfast —and as for tea-time, they consider that coffee makes up to them for all privations in other things. Applaud me, that I pour out coffee for them all, every evening, and yet scarcely ever drink it myself! And it is from principle too; not because it hurts me a bit—or, at least, I dont *see* that it hurts me. I thought it might make you easier in your mind, to hear that I did'nt use it at night. Father seems to thrive on it, remarkably—and I'm sure he isn't kept awake by it, as he frequently goes to sleep before we finish reading aloud to him. I am stopping every few lines, to fasten and unfasten some of young Sarah Alexander's numerous riggins—for Dot thinks "she ought to take the air some," and for that purpose, she had reduced her to a cutty sack. Cruel airing, in such weather.

Did I tell you that Dutch Nisbet had sent me two such nice books? Blithedale Romance and Sir Thomas Moore's Household—with another *Platonic* message! I was glad of the books—but Mrs. Calloway and Bell put me dreadfully to the blush when they gave them to me. Has Father told you about Mr. Livingston's application to him for his type and history? Isn't it a pity that both he and Uncle should refuse to immortalize the family!

I have been scribbling away at a great rate, dear Mother, and have written you a great deal of trash, I dare say—but you wont find fault when I say that it is a relief to a solitary female, to write trash, when I have'nt anybody to talk it to. I write so many letters, that they furnish a safety-valve for all my notions, thoughts and ideas. I have just finished one to Lisa Bowen, to thank her for the books she sent me, and another to Leila, who has been thinking it very hard that she had to write me a second letter to get me to answer the first, wh. first I never received. I enclosed a note to Mrs. E., and referred her to you, for information as to my arrangements and the reasons for them.

Dot says "tell Ma that Nanny Hutchinson has broke my child's head." Poor little Nanny! I wish I could see her again. Now she says, "Play you said, 'Mary, what's the matter with your throat'"—I say it—"Glands swollen"— is the reply, and she walks off singing to her baby. She says "She dont think she'd make noise enough to disturb Major Porter, if she was in Savannah—for she dont sing much now—her husband has never opened his eyes since he had the spare-ribs." I fill too much of my letters with the child's sayings and doings—but they seem so funny, that it is an irresistible temptation to write it as she says it. It is growing so dark that I can scarcely see to write —tho' it is'nt much after four o'clock. I was thinking yesterday, how very different days seem, according as they are divided à la low-country or up-country. My mornings begin about half past six o'clock—but the whole day seems short, when dinner comes so early. I am never at a loss for pleasant employment—and often wish that I could piece out the days with a couple of extra hours. When I get the blues, I float them off in a good shower of tears, and then I feel better. Goodbye now, till morning. We may hear from some of you then, and I'll want a little space for additions.

Saturday morning. After ten o'clock and the stage has'nt come in—so I will have to finish my letter without waiting for it. Have you ever received the first one I wrote you to Sav.? and has Sallie received a bit of a note that I wrote her nearly two weeks ago? There is no regularity in the mails yet. I had a letter from Leila on Thursday that had been twelve days on the way. We have'nt heard a word from Cliff since Uncle took her to Troy. Tell Aunt Loulie that Father has questioned me once or twice about Cliff's return home—but I always say that I dont know anything about it and that she (Aunt Lou) will tell us when we hear from her. She and Uncle must take that matter in hand, for Father feels that he must gratify them in whatever wish they express in regard to her, since they have been so kind to her. Give a great deal of love to both of them, for me—and tell them that I love them more and more, when I think of Cliff. I am sorry to hear that Sister Lou has been sick. A little sickness goes a long way towards worsting her.

Dot is back again—and as all the babies slept in my room last night, they are all ready to begin with today. She went down-stairs yesterday afternoon, and I was just congratulating myself on her having gone to play with Father, when I heard a lumbering at my door, and looking round I saw Sallie loaded with a bedstead, cradle, basket of clothes and two more babies. I knew my fate then—and submitted quietly. I have given her the corner by my bed, to stow away her goods, and hereafter I suppose I am to take care of the innocents at night. "Mr. Cosart was took with spare-ribs just as I was going to Church," she says—"play you burst into tears—and before the bell stopped, he was done dead. He was a mighty good Christian—but I'm sorry for his body and his family." I am afraid that even you will think I quote her sayings too much—but oh! Mother, they do sound so funny as she says them.

Thank Ed, when you see him again for his letter that I received four days ago, and tell him I will reply to it as soon as I find a bit of time. And give much love to dear Minny. Tell her I miss her sadly, when Sabbath evening comes.

We have a little sunshine today, as a novelty, and the weather is colder too—so we may hope to kill,* next

* Kill hogs.

week. When will you and Aunt Loulie make your visit to Liberty? Miss Mary Minton, Rosa Pelot and Georgia Ficklen are going down next week (via Charleston) to make Laura Jones a visit. Maybe you'll see them.

I'll keep my letter open as late as I dare, to see if the mail will come—but will scarcely have time to make additions, after reading any letters that come. Father will probably write on Tuesday.

With love to each and all, ever your affectionate child
H.

"Mammy Cynthia."[*]

WRITTEN BY MARY CLIFFORD HULL.

Mammy Cynthia grew up with our Mother, and when Mother married she went with her as her maid. She nursed all the ten children, and was as faithful and devoted as tho' they were her own. She always had the youngest one, sometimes the two youngest in her room at night, our Mother being all her life more or less of an invalid. When there were no more babies to be nursed, Father built her a cottage in the yard and there she lived and died.

She was a strict disciplinarian, and much observation and experience combined to strengthen her faith in the doctrine of original sin, and also in the virtue and efficacy of Solomon's prescriptions therefor. She had an eagle eye for deviations from the path of rectitude and virtue; and a strict sense of her responsibility for the great trust and confidence reposed in her, made her impervious to corruption and as faithful to report as she was quick to see the sins of our youth. But I think she was often loth to do her duty as she saw it.

She was a character, and a most important member of the family, being wholly devoted to their interests, and honest, faithful, and true in every respect.

She had like Mrs. Gilpin "a frugal mind," and never threw away or wasted anything. She was in her position also the recipient of many more or less valuable gifts, and this combination resulted in the course of years in a vast accumulation of plunder. Her cottage was quite large and all the way round it, from the foot of the bed there was a row of bureaus, trunks, baskets, boxes, in some parts

---

[*]Cynthia Peters, a negro slave, given by Felix Gilbert to his daughter, Sarah, when a child.

three deep, one in front of another. She had three bureaus that had been given her from time to time, and everything was full to bursting. She hated to see scissors go into good material, and used to afflict me very much, bringing me bonnets to trim, but begging me please to put the ribbon on some way that it would'nt have to be cut, which was a difficult thing to do. She once bought the black silk for a dress, but kept it three years before she had it made, because she "did hate to think of its being cut," and yet cut it had to be.

When Porter was a cadet at West Point, she came out one morning in a most extraordinary dress, and I said "Mercy! Mammy where did you unearth that dress?" She smoothed the front of it tenderly down, and said, "*This* dress, Miss Clifford, *this* dress? Why this is the dress I nussed Marse Porter in."

When she died she left 135 dresses, 37 shawls, over 40 bonnets of various vintages, numerous breast-pins, and hoards of all sorts of things, old and new. She left a will and bequeathed "her jewelry to her white children," as she called all of us, and any of us were to keep any of the things we especially wanted, and Alice was to have one of the bureaus which she designated. Then everything else was left to a niece, of whom she was especially fond.

Mammy never married, but always lived a moral life. Indeed, for the last half of it she was an humble and devoted Christian—a great reader of her Testament and hymn book. She never left her old home after freedom, and was tenderly cared for there until the end.

M. C. H.

Harriet Alexander to Her Sister Clifford.

Home, Monday p. m. Jan. 3rd '53.

Blessed Sister—In judging me as a correspondent, judge me according to the time I have, and not according to what I have not. I have but little of the article at my command, of late—and not energy and spirit enough to use even that little, to advantage. If I write to you at all, I dont know what I will write—for there is nothing happening round me that strikes my attention—and I have no thoughts and no feelings to tell. I believe I am turning to stone. If anybody wants a receipt for "great wretchedness," I would give them one that I tried this morning—There: they interrupt me, call me off, and for an hour I am busy marking, arranging &c "fine old Wines" and "fine old Brandies" &c. Aunt Lou has taken to brandy for her daily potion, and as she is to be here on Wednesday, it set Father to search into the hidden mysteries of the liquor closet. Great treasures has he drawn forth from thence—treasures buried and hidden there for twenty and thirty years.

Now I'm going back to the morning's melancholy occupation. I sorted over *my* old treasures—relics of my happy, childish days—and as I consigned one after another to the flames, I shut my eyes that I might not see the piteous sight. Oh! it was most sad—and the fire burnt in spots into my heart. When I went to the glass to smooth my hair for dinner the sight of my gloomy brow startled me. I have seldom seen it so utterly clouded. The wind blows furiously, howling like an angry fiend, round the house—and it seems a fit accompaniment to the dirge-like strains of my own spirit. In short, I am about as far from the tender, smiling, blissful mood in which young women in my condition are supposed to exist,* as the east is from the west. I feel hard and stoney—and as if I cared for nothing in the world but Dot and Mammy. But oh! my kind, thrice blessed Aunt Loulie now on her way to aid me and cheer me—do not I love her? With my whole soul—and the tho't of her breaks the icy fetters in which I have been bound. Cliff, in spite of me, they *will* have "a table" and my wretched Mammy is making Fruit cakes today! Oh! I do not wonder that the wind howls and the skies weep, beholding it—I know it is that cake and the clothes on the line, that have raised the commotion—it is to typify to me the storm that is to rage in my soul, in the dread hour when that cake is cut and those floundering, flying, flapping petticoats are tied round me. And that reminds me to tell you that my trunk has come—and that I thank you on bended knees and with melting heart, for the precious treasure that came to me therein. The likeness is perfect—and the setting, worthy of the jewel. Everybody pronounces it a "ne plus ultra," and oh! its value to me! Writing of it, made me hone after it—and I have stopped to get it and look at it— Oh Cliff! how I thank you for it. The other things suit me well. The blue dress suits my taste perfectly, and it fits like wax. The combs, the shoes, the fur-cuffs and the sleeves. As for the collars, I own that they look to me a good deal like the pattern of old Mrs. Wylie's—those that they sent me—and I shall stick to my old ones, for the occasion. The trunk, carpet-bag and satchel, are all that I desired them to be. Those, I think, were the only things they sent up. The rest await me in Sav. and I will give you my impression of them when I see them— Ah! but not in a letter, it occurs to me as I write—I will see you with my own eyes, so soon after I am there. I leave home on the 13th, and from what Aunt Lou says, I suppose you will sail from N. Y. about the 15th. Then,

*Written a few days before her marriage.

two weeks from tomorrow, we may meet! Oh joy! I will meet you at Aunt Loulie's—and you must forget that anything is changed since we were there last. If you reach there on that day, it will be, I think, exactly two years since you and I left there together, with Wallace and Joe for our companions.

Cliff, Mary Semmes is dead—the wild Mary we knew as children—with whom it seems impossible to associate the idea of sickness and decay. How all earthly things change! Has any one written you since Mr. Robert Randolph's death? He was ill only a short time. Cousin Lizzie and Lizzie Colley are both better. I suppose there is hope now for both of them.

My engagement is still so little known, that none of my friends at all suspect it. I meant to have gone to tell Lizzie Barnett about it, today—but the weather has prevented. Cliff, I will write you but once more, my Sister— Oh! the tho't, the tho't! I do not at all realize the change that is before me. It seems to me that something trying hangs over me, but I never realize what it is—A sort of shadow gathers over the family circle—they are sorry to have me go—and I feel guilty when I see it, and wretched when I think of the parting. But I am ungrateful. God has blessed me abundantly—and I ought to be thankful and happy. I have written you a poor letter—but I write no other, in these days. I have no thoughts, no feelings that are definite enough to express—and I do not notice outward events enough to write of them. Dot is with me constantly—but I no longer laugh at her odd ways and I only sigh to think how soon I am to leave her. I am ashamed to send you such a letter but I dont know how to write better now. Goodby—I will write you again in a few days. This letter came for you from Ella and I took off the envelope to get it in mine—"only that and nothing more." All send love.

Tuesday. A letter from Wallace this morning causes a change to be made from Thursday to Wednesday the

12th, as our day for leaving. We are to go by Macon and Atlanta. He leaves Savannah on Saturday, and will be here Monday night. Aunt Lou will come tomorrow. Oh Cliff.

H.

Harriet Alexander to Her Sister Clifford

Tis Sabbath at home, darling, and I must give you a portion of the sacred, precious time. I come to say my last words to you. Oh Cliff! what can I say to you to tell you all the love for you that fills my heart—all the sorrow that makes it throb and ache when I know that we are to spend no more happy months and years together in this dear home of our childhood. I have been thinking much, today, of the last Sabbath that we spent here together. Do you remember it, and can you recall the sweet sunset hour when we sat together in my window—and when we talked so sadly together? And that last morning—when we parted—oh! it is so well, my darling, that we will not have to suffer that again. I am glad that you are not here. It would distress me far more, to go—if I had to leave you. In looking back, it is sweet to feel that we have nothing but loving and kindly memories of each other. We have been much to each other, dear Sister. God grant that we may still be. We must not think of this, nor speak of it, as a separation between us— for we must not let it separate us. It need not, it shall not. I thank you for the loving words you wrote me— they reached me yesterday—they are the last I shall have from you here. They cost me agonies of tears, but they were precious words still. The thought of you awakens much feeling in my heart, dearest—and I often sorrow over the thought of your being here without me. I wish I could prevent it—could keep you with me—but if duty calls you here, I must not shrink from it for you. Aunt Loulie, my priceless, precious Aunt Loulie, is everything to me in these last sorrowful days. When I am gone, she will write and tell you all about it. The church-bell summons me away. Oh Cliff! dearest, precious Sister—Goodbye—goodbye. "The fondness of long years, I pour into the word."

Goodbye—God bless you, now and forever more.

Lovingly,

H.

A Visit to Sunbury.

Sarah Alexander to Her Daughter Clifford.

Hopewell, Feb. 20, 1853.

My dear Cliff:—

So much of this holy day has been spent in reading, that I find myself unable to continue it any longer, and I lay aside the book for the pen, that I may hold communion with those dear one who are *scarcely* ever out of my mind, though so far distant.

I had a headache and felt much fatigued from the various exciting scenes and changes of the last three days, so I did not go to Midway with your father to-day, especially as it is very cold and windy. Indeed I am not fond of going such a distance to church—then, after one sermon an hour is spent necessarily in a crowd in conversation, etc., with no place for rest or retirement, even for a moment. Then follows a second sermon and it is nearly 4 o'clock when one arrives at home; often too much fatigued to enjoy and improve the remainder of the day in a suitable manner. These two Sabbaths I have spent alone at home have been very sweet and precious time to me. I have enjoyed the privilege of quiet communion with my own heart—and I trust with my Savior—and have tried as well as I could, to afford some of these poor negroes the means of grace in reading the Bible to them as much as I was able. They seem most thankful and willing to hear, but I fear there is very little religious feeling among them, and there are but few who even make a profession of religion. Those of them who are able to go have abundant access to preaching addressed to negroes, but there are

176

several on the place too old and infirm to go any distance. The poor creatures seem so fond of us and so rejoiced to see us, that I feel condemned whenever I remember how long we have left them, and resolve fully, as far as is in my power, they shall never again be so deserted and neglected. The little favors distributed daily in turn, from the table, among them are received with such thankfulness and so prized, as our up country servants know nothing of, and every one seems to think it a privilege to wait upon us.

We returned last eve from our excursion to "The Salts," and the visit was a time of great interest and feeling to myself as well as your father. I know not that I have ever been more deeply impressed with the sense of the fading and transitory nature of all connected with earth, and of the grand and solemn realities of the eternal future, than from this return to the scenes and places, where I passed one of the most interesting periods of my life, where I appeared as a bride, and was presented by my husband to the friends and companions of his boyhood. Very many of these have passed from time to eternity, and of the scenes where we met and walked and rode and were merry together, not a vestige remains. Of our old dwelling, where he was born and his father died, only a few broken brick can be seen, to point to where once we gathered around the fireside. Even the old trees, the old houses, the streets are gone, and cornfields occupy the place of the streets, the gardens, the houses,—God's handiwork alone remains unchanged, and the noble river opening to the wide ocean, and rippling on with its ceaseless murmur to the winds and the tides, looks like old Sunbury. I longed for privacy to indulge the feelings which stirred up my heart to its very depths. All the way we rode home the words "passing away" seemed written before my eyes and ringing in my ears, and thro' the night, which was a wakeful one, still were these affecting words the burden of my thoughts. I thought how youth had passed away, and friends and relatives and companions had also gone, and I felt that I too am passing away, and must soon be numbered among those whose places shall know them no more on earth. But blessed be God, His word and promise is not thus frail and mutable; the hopes and consolations of the Christian are not thus uncertain. Our trust is built upon the Rock of Ages, and amid all the changes of this changing world, we may rest secure on that unfailing anchor. My soul wait thou only on the Lord; all my expectation is from Him.

I have anticipated the account I intended to give you of our excursion in narrating first the feelings to which it gave rise, but I will still return to the particulars which may interest you somewhat. We waited for the mail on Thursday, and received Will's letter and a very pleasant one from Lou Toombs* and then set out to pay a visit at the settlement called Dorchester, and then go on to John Stevens. We reached there at sundown, after a ride of eleven miles, and passed the night in the house which was once old Dr. McWhirr's, which looked as ancient as himself, and seemed to me to be haunted with his presence. Next morning we rambled about among the venerable oaks and cedars on the banks of a beautiful salt-water creek, and then took a circuitous route to Col.'s Island, stopping to see a pretty place which is the summer residence of Dr. C. C. Jones.

We were most cordially received at Social Bluff, the place belonging now to Laura Maxwell, by her uncle and aunt, Col. and Mrs. Maxwell. They are two charming old people, and remind me, in their warm hospitality and friendly manners, very much of Mr. and Mrs. Gilmer, and seem to be regarded by all the county very much as they are (Mr. and Mrs. G.) among their own people. I was perfectly delighted with the place and the people. The house is on a bluff overgrown with magnificent oaks and cedars, and surrounded on three sides by a fine wide river

*Then engaged to Will.

(Newport) which opens off at two points to St. Catherine's Sound, and where you can see the Florida boats pass and repass, and from whence they have the sea-breeze in perfection. I could scarcely sit still in my chair from the constant desire to look out upon the fine water prospect, to which I am so partial. Your father was full of reminiscences of boyish sports enjoyed there with Laura's father, and enjoyed it all highly. We were saddened, too, with the memory of poor Charles Maxwell, to whom this fair inheritance had descended and who had formed many plans for beautifying it; and I sat and looked with painful interest at the very spot where his mother received the news of his death, at the very hour when she expected to welcome his return, and where she fell to the floor as if struck by a shot. Mrs. M. delighted to talk of him and dwell on his many fine qualities and the high promise of his opening manhood. I saw there, too, the trunks and boxes marked with his name and containing his clothing, books, etc. as sent out from the North, and they struck a chill to my heart as I thought of my own promising sons, each one as dear, it seems to me, as if he were the only one. We left this charming place and kind people with regret, and with promises to return and make them another visit, and your father and I were agreed in the desire to have a summer residence out there, if we remove to Savannah. It would be very convenient to this plantation, as we could have constant communication by a boat with it. How would you like such a home? It would be very retired and perhaps lonely, unless the beauties of nature could supply to you the want of society.

We took a snack along and called by for John Stevens who piloted us through the cornfields to Sunbury, where we remained till the afternoon, and rode home, thoroughly jaded and worn with fatigue and excitement. Indeed, I felt as if we had travelled one hundred miles, and it was really thirty and forty in the three days, though on these fine roads that distance seems trifling.

179

Monday—I am quite busy to-day, preparing for a visit to Savannah. Sister wrote to beg that we would go in to attend the party she is to give Hattie on Wednesday, and as I have several reasons for wishing to go for a few days, I am quite willing, and she promises to return with me. Your father will not hear of going, so I must leave him alone, unless Sarah comes out to stay with him, which she spoke of doing. I shall take my letter down and finish it there, as it will reach you just as soon.

S.

MARY CLIFFORD HULL (*b.* June 14, 1830)

From a daguerreotype taken in Savannah, Georgia, when she was about twenty-one years old, by Carey, who was widely and favorably known for the unusual excellence of his work.

Clifford Alexander to Her Mother.

Home Feb. 23rd 1853.

My dearest Mother

I tho't that a real boisterous day would secure me against interruptions, and enable me to devote the freshness and dew of the morning to my letter, but a visit from Fred Andrews, before I had so much as read my Bible, has made my expectation vain and belated me considerably. Alice however came for a sheet of paper just now "for to write to Pa on," so I shall trust to her contribution, to supply the shortcomings observable in my hurried letter. She was vastly delighted yesterday at the receipt of father's to her, as her speedy reply may prove. Of all the things in the letter nothing seemed to afford her such unmitigated satisfaction as to hear that you had *cried* because you were away from her and wanted to see her so much. Like those who are older and wiser than herself she likes to feel of some importance, and necessary to the happiness of others.

Father's letter was a general benefit and pleasure, and I for one was more edified to hear of your double chin than I was to hear of your tears, tho' I'm afraid if you indulge much in the latter you will do away with the former and wont be able to present such a full front when you come home. I think too you must be getting very gay and dissipated in your tastes to ride forty miles to a *party*—you go quite ahead of the girls there, tho' I don't wonder you want to show your double chin.

I hope Aunt Lou has better weather for her party than we are enjoying here. It rained all day yesterday, and a good part of the night as tho' it had never rained before, and did not expect to have another opportunity to do so in years to come. Today it is blowing great guns—almost a hurricane—while the clouds and the sun are struggling for the mastery, the latter doing its best to shine and the former to prevent it. I shall wish and expect to hear very particular accounts of the party, and that the Bride* looked lovely of course. Yesterday's mail brought me such a delightful letter from Sister Sallie. I don't know when I have enjoyed one so much. It was profitable for everything, and I found in it, doctrine, encouragement, comfort, affection, amusement and instruction. Letters are great pleasures to me always, but greater now, it seems than ever.

The Spirit of Reform has possessed me for a week past, and I have spent one or two very busy days making alterations and improvements in my room. Somehow, I had a desire to have it look different from the old way when it was Hattie's and mine together, for it seemed to me then I would miss her less. So I have just helped myself to one or two pieces of furniture, in exchange for one or two others, and moved out and moved in, and altered and arranged and rearranged until Sallie and I were both exhausted, by which time I had succeeded in getting fixed quite to my own satisfaction. I only hope when you return you wont find it necessary to put your veto on my bill of appropriations.

I am busy, busy from morning until night, and haven't as yet found any time for reading or sewing. Everything goes on famously still, and we continue to be a most thriving family. Mercer† is about again—that is, he is up, and will be able to go out to his work as soon as the weather permits—and there are no new cases of the measles. Fannie Turner and Edwin Anthony have both been desperately ill, but are out of danger now. The cases of Pneumonia this winter are very violent. Alice is

*Harriet Alexander Cumming.
† Body servant of "Uncle David" Hillhouse.

the picture of health, and enjoys a continual flow of the highest spirits. I hear her read every day, and tho' she always seems willing enough to say her lesson, I don't think she is *remarkably* fond of her book. I read to her every day, and there is no lack of appreciation then. Her last new play is "Sister now play you was a lady what didn't understand things, and I was going to explain 'em to you. Now play you asked me what did '*explain*' mean by." Some of her definitions you may be sure are well worth hearing, and tend to throw great light upon the subject under consideration.

Miss Lizzie Whitney, or Mrs. Putnam rather, has sailed for California, and in a vessel with 960 passengers, amongst whom she had *one acquaintance*, and that one a lady! Fred Andrews is coming here to tea with Felix tonight, and as a balance I have sent for Lou to come to tea with *me*. Friday Lou and I are going to spend the day with Mrs. Alick Pope, tho' I have to keep it very dark, as Alice weeps whenever it is alluded to. She cries bitterly sometimes when I go out to walk in the afternoon and her only comfort consists in having a party, and plenty of tea-kettle tea at it, in which she drowns her regrets at my absence.

C.

Marriage of W. F. Alexander to Lou Toombs.

Louisa Gilmer to Her Husband.

April 30, 1853.

If I perish for it, my dearest, I am determined to get off some kind of a letter to you this morning, and if it is a very mean kind, you must take my many infirmities as extenuation.

The grand affair is happily over, and I know you will all want to hear from it, and as Cliff, who will be expected to give the most interesting account of it, is too busy today to think of writing, you will have to content yourselves with this until a more convenient season. I write to you, my darling, because I know you value my poor letters, not for their manner and matter, but because they always carry my best love to my dearest and best husband.

Well, the grand affair, as I said, *is* over, and over in the grandest and most satisfactory manner. Thursday evening about five o'clock this establishment began to be in a flutter, and petticoats and dresses, and vests and pants, and ribbons and flowers were flying hither and thither all over the premises. Marion and Alice could not wait until dark to put on their wedding clothes, so they came out bright and early, like pink rosebuds, and were ready then to be in everybody's way for the rest of the evening. I began to dress very early, thinking to be ready to help Cliff, but I was not half touched up before the boys came to have their cravats tied, and before that was done, who should come in but the *groom* in dishabille, with a handful of collars and cravats and I had to go out to his room with him before he could be suited to his mind. While I was there Mr. Wright came, blushing red to his finger ends and shaking like a willow, to ask if I could *tie his cravat, too!* I said yes, of course, but he was in such a perspiration by the time I began that the cravat all stuck to his neck and the pins would'nt go in, and altogether it was quite a job. It took me so long that Cliff was calling out of the window for me before I was done, to come and fix her wreath, and so by that time the carriage was at the door and I was not half fixed. I had been very busy all day, making blanc mange and jelly for the dinner, so that I was tired by night and not much in the mood for anything but bed, but finally we were all fixed and got off just before the groom and his attendants, who had another carriage.

The house* was crowded when we got there, and the servants said some people had been there an hour. The family, ours and theirs, were asked into the right hand parlor, and the doors of that were kept closed and nobody else was to be admitted there until the tableau was formed. Lou sent for me when we arrived, and I found her sitting quite disconsolate waiting to have her veil fixed and nobody could do it. I got it all right for her and the attendants by that time were all ready, and the company more than ready. Lou looked perfectly lovely and her dress was the handsomest I ever saw. She wore a white silk, something like mine, but the figures were smaller and closer and between the figures it was watered. She had a deep Honiton lace around the neck and sleeves, which could not have cost less than fifty dollars, and her veil and wreath and handkerchief were all handsome enough to correspond. She had a beautiful pearl necklace and bracelet, and she looked almost as fair and delicate as the pearls themselves. I think she was the prettiest bride I ever saw, and she reminded me of some of the romantic descriptions in novels of "fair and fragile" brides—too fair and frail I am afraid for much of the wear and tear of life.† Will looked remark-

---

*Mr. Robert Toombs' house.
† She died two years later.

ably well too, and they behaved in quite a dignified manner considering they were'nt used to it. Tell Aunt Lou he had on the diamond pin, and it was pronounced like the monkey's tail in pea green "neat but not gaudy." I am giving you this minute description of the bride's dress for her benefit, for I know you will not understand the details of silk and Honiton lace, unless she explains it to you. The bridesmaids all looked very blooming and pretty.—Sally T., Cliff, Mary Pope, and Emma Dawson, but the groomsmen did not have much beauty among them.

Mrs. Toombs had a splendid supper table and provisions enough on it for three hundred people. I went down before supper and saw it, but I was so tired when the folks went down that I went upstairs and lay on a sofa in Lou's room until it was time to go home. The carriage was late coming and I don't believe I ever was so tired in my life as by the time I got to bed. Yesterday morning we had to be up bright and early to get ready for the dinner here, but alas, alas, when it was all done and the ladies began to dress, I began to undress and had to go to bed with a dreadful sick headache, so I did'nt see any of the fun of the day. Mother had a very nice dinner, or rather Cliff and I did, for we took all the responsibility and only let Mother help some. They had the meat table in the dining room and then we fixed a beautiful dessert table in the sitting room, and the company adjourned there when they had finished the first and second courses. It was an idea of Mrs. Toombs' to have them separate. She said she had seen it done in W. City, and it answered remarkably well here, for the servants are not accustomed to such entertainments, and would never have gotten the dessert on right, I am sure. I heard it went on very well and that the girls looked very pretty, but I did not see any of them except Lou who came in my room for a little while dressed very handsomely and looking very sweetly.

Mother has stood it all remarkably well and I never

saw her look as well and as pretty as she did yesterday when she was dressed for dinner. Cliff is flying around this morning getting ready to help Lou receive company at home. Will was over for a little while this morning and seems to bear his honors with great composure. We all miss him very much from the house, and I think Father and Mother felt really badly at having him go away.

I have written more than I thought I could when I sat down, and have helped Cliff dress in the meantime, but it is nearly mail time now and my letter must go. Excuse the scratching and scrawling. I received yours this morning and felt very like crying when I heard you were to be in T. so long. I have been calculating all along to go down with Ed. and shall try and meet you there by the 25th at least, if that suits him. I would not ask you to take this long and tedious journey twice when he is going, and shall make myself quite contented with him for an escort; but there will be time enough to arrange the particulars.

Give my best love to Aunt Lou and Uncle and Sallie, and believe me, my dear, dear husband, ever your longing, loving,

Wife.

Read to Aunt Lou and Uncle all about the wedding for I can not write any more.

Sarah Alexander to Her Son Porter.

Savannah, May 26, 1854.

My dear son:—

This is your birthday and I feel as if I could not let it pass without a few lines of love to show you that I remember the day. My heart is full of tender thoughts and memories of your infancy and early years, and is melted into praise and thanksgiving when I think of the grace and mercy of God which has given you a name and a place, I trust, among his own children. You have been a precious son to me and the remembrance of your duty and affection is very sweet to me in our long separation. I think sometimes I may not live to see another of your birthdays,* and if I do not you may comfort your heart, dear son, with your mother's assurance that you have been to her all she could expect or desire at your age, and no pang for neglected duty towards her need ever wound your heart.

I am longing to hear from you. Capt. Anderson told your father of the painful accident which happened to Smead of Geo. and it seemed to revive and renew my anxieties about you, exposed to so many dangers.

Your father, Cliff, and Charlie left us last night for home. I have been very sick ever since I returned from Florida, and the Doctor said I would have to give up the plan of going home at all and must go North by sea, so we decided that your father should go and stay a week at home and then return here and sail for Philadelphia on the 7th of June. From there we will come down the Chesapeake to a little place called Hampton, within a mile

*She died during the ensuing winter.

of Old Point Comfort, where I can have sea air, and sea bathing. There and in Virginia we expect to remain till September. I am not able to travel about and must be stationary where I can be very quiet. If I get better so your father can leave me, perhaps he may go on for a few days to see you, but I shall not be able to enjoy that pleasure.

We miss Cliff here a great deal, but I am glad she has gone home to collect the family together again at home. Mr. Wright has been quite sick but is better again. Hattie has just been in here and sends you a birthday greeting.

I am not able to write more and must conclude with warmest love to my dear son from his

Affectionate mother,

S. H. A.

Adam Alexander to His Daughters.

Philadelphia, July 11, 1854

To Marion and Alice,

My dear little girls:—

I have been five days on a visit to your brother Edward at West Point and returned to your mother last night. It was while there I received a letter from your sister Hattie, informing me of the death of her dear little boy.* The letter was written the day before his death and he was not even sick then, for she ended it by saying he was a picture of health. A postscript in pencil added the next morning told me that she was sitting beside his little dead body. I was struck dumb with astonishment and grief, and for a moment thought it was only a horrid dream—but it is such an one from which alas! there is no awakening. It is too true. I do not grieve for Charlie, but for his poor afflicted mother. How lonely the house will seem to her, all this long summer through. We are writing to her today to beg her and Wallace to meet us in New York, and go thence with us to West Point, hoping it may help to divert her mind from her great sorrow. This will be better than going home to Washington, for there she would be perpetually reminded of her loss, where she had anticipated so much pleasure and pride in showing her little boy to so many friends. May this sad lesson in our own family teach you, dear children, how uncertain is life, and lead you to an instant preparation for Heaven, where already three of our dear little infants have gone to await our coming. You loved him very tenderly and if you want to see him again, you must fit yourselves for

*Charlie Cumming.

190

the Home and the company where he now is. We can't tell whose turn will come next, for you know he was the youngest of the family, so all should be ready.

Your mother was quite unwell again with fevers while I was gone, but I suppose it was owing to her distress of mind for poor sister Hattie. She is better again today and has been out walking and riding for several hours. We hope to leave here next week for New York, where we will stay only a very few days, hoping that sister Hattie and Wallace will join us. Dr. Willis has kindly offered to take Wallace's place in the bank, that he may go as long as he pleases, so we hope he will be induced to come to us, when we will together visit brother Ed.

Mother longs to see Ed and so does Mammy. He is a fine looking fellow now, though he is as brown as a nut. We had many pleasant walks together, and never one without speaking of you both, and wishing that you were with us to help us admire the great mountains, that have pitched their camp around West Point, and the glorious river that flows between them. I hope you may live to see them one day, for there is no place like it on this side of Heaven. Indeed, Heaven seems to be nearer there than anywhere else,—But I must end my letter with this sheet which is not half big enough for the messages which Mother and Mammy would send you.

Remember me, too, to all the dear family and think as often as you can of your

Affectionate father,

A. L. A.

Adam Alexander to His Son Edward Porter.

Home, Jan. 12, 1856.

My dear son—

In looking over my list of letters I see that I have written to my other children since I last wrote you. Your letter of the 25 ult. is safe in hand, and as you have safely received my last remittance I now send you $5.00 more. I shall send no more till I hear again that you are in want. My remittances at any one time will be small, since you have no safe place to keep your funds, and West Point (unlike Heaven) is a place where thieves do break in and steal. My letter will probably reach you, about the close of your examination, thro' which I hope, and have no doubt you will have creditably passed, so I venture to congratulate you upon its result. They are always trying ordeals, and it is a pleasant thought when one is over, that the number remaining is one less. Let me know the result of this one as soon as you can.

You must be having terrible weather, if I may conjecture from what ours is and has been for a month past. Constant rains and sleets with less than four days of sunshine has been our lot in all that time, and at this time our ground is covered with snow seven inches on a level, and the trees breaking down with ice. "It blew, and it snew, and it friz" is the short history of a month. What must it have been where you are and what the edge of the winds that come down upon your plain through those mountain gorges!

I had very pleasant letters from all your sisters* in Savannah, telling me of their Christmas reunion at their

*All married and in Savannah for Christmas.

Aunt's table on that day. Felix joined the party, very unexpectedly to all of them, only an hour before they sat down to dinner, and he carried to each of them $1,000 which I had sent by him as their Christmas present. They all write and say that my contribution was not the *least* pleasant incident of the day. I am sure, however, that it gave me more pleasure to give it, than they felt in receiving it. Indeed, it was my only pleasure this Christmas to contribute to that of my children and servants. When I think of myself, it is only to compare my present loneliness with the sweet society of her, whose presence never left me anything more to wish. I spend much of my time in the shadowy society of the sweet faces that look down from the parlor walls. My wife, Sarah Brackett, and Cousin Felixina are all now in the sitting-room, where, too, I have Lou Toombs, Uncle, and my grandmother—a blessed company. They make the best company I know and I gaze at them so earnestly, that the pictures seem as if they were the realities and their blest and sweet originals were only the shadows.

Do you ever see my dear Mrs. Walker? Her kindness has taken a strong hold upon my affections and I love her as I do my sister. Do remember me to her when you see her and also to my dear friend, the Colonel.

Our school begins next Monday and we have the promise of a large number in both. Our Seminary is in excellent condition now; never indeed better.

No news to send you. The little girls send you love and so do I. God bless you my dear son.

Your father,

A. L. A.

Harriet Cumming to Her Sister Clifford.*

Savannah Dec. 6th 1856.
Saturday night.

It was a cold, bleak night in December. In a small but brilliantly illuminated apartment a young Matron sat bending over her work. There were no marks of great wealth or luxury around her, but upon her beautiful features there sat a smile of such content as told of a mind satisfied and at rest. A lovely tidy was upon the back of her chair, and the charming castors upon the sideboard betokened that she sometimes ate catsup with her beef— Now if Sallie Gilbert had'nt cried just here and broken the thread of my discourse and put my elegant ideas to flight and wasted my time, there's no telling what a lovely letter I might have written you. But she did do all that, and the next work the young Matron found herself employed on, was oiling the baby's nose, and as she did'nt know how to make that poetical, she concluded to dismount from her elevated steed and write henceforth in a more sensible strain. The truth is, Kitty Clover, I've been wanting to write to you ever so much and ever so long, and I just resolved I would not write till I could do it at my leisure and say all that I wanted to say. I'm tired of writing little business letters with not a bit of chat in them and I just mean to take solid comfort in this one and chat as much as I please. Wallace has gone out to look after some business, and as I am alone, what better can I do than to invoke your gentle shade to sweeten my solitude.

I am resting on my oars after one busy week and preparatory to beginning another of the same sort. The Com-

*Recently married to George G. Hull.

194

mercial Convention opens on Monday, and as there are many more delegates expected than our Hotels can accommodate, we have all got to open our doors. So I have been getting my house in order for whatever "angel" comes unawares upon me. I shall not be reluctant to do my part, if Cora continues as well as she is now; but if she should go back to bed, I'd feel like going there too, with company in the house and Mary Ann in the kitchen. Mary Ann can cook very well, but she needs somebody at her elbow to keep her up to her work, all the time.

There has been a dear, delightful old Dr. Humbug here, that has nearly cured Cora's rheumatism. Jerry came home from Market one day, and told great tales of a man (a stranger) whom he saw there curing rheumatic pains of all degrees and sorts. So, immediately, Cora sent for him. For a month, her arm had been as stiff and immovable as if it were iron, and she had not slept a night without Morphine or Opium. Much of the time she was unable even to feed herself. The old man said that hers was a bad case, and that he could'nt cure her in one rubbing, as he did most people. However, he rubbed something on her arm, and left her, promising to come again. The next morning when I went to see her, I found her with both hands over the top of her head, and she in high glee because she had slept all night without the Opium. The old man came once more and rubbed her, and since then she is about, and sews all day. She still has some pain in her arm, but she can use it and does not suffer acutely with it.

We had some funny scenes with her while she was at her worst. Sometimes she would seem in paroxysms of such unbearable pain, that I gave her chloroform to help her thro' them. The instant she began to breathe it, it was wonderful to see the change in her. Before taking it, every breath was a groan of agony, and instantly she would break in some exulting tone, laugh, say she was so happy &c, and load me with every blessing and praise. One Sunday afternoon, I laughed at her till the tears rolled down my face. She was suffering greatly and sent for me to give her the Chloroform. So I gave it, and finding she seemed perfectly quiet and sound asleep, turned to go upstairs. But as I got to the door, she burst into such an obstreperous flood of song as quickly brought me back to her. "I would not live alway" she shouted, and then she knotted her face up and wept profusely for a minute. "I ask not to stay," she continued in a yet louder key, sobbing and weeping. Louder and louder swelled the song as she rose "dark o'er the way." At this juncture her miserable husband ran breathless into the room, crying "What's the matter with Cora!" I was trying to hush her mouth, but Sam's frightened face set me to laughing and seemed to add fresh fuel to the flame of Cora's desire to depart. Recall the tune and perhaps you can imagine how she got thro "the few lurid moments that dawn on us here." She fairly yelled by that time, and when she came to the high note, she held on to it and quavered it and slid up to it and down from it in a style that would have done credit to Lucy S. Cliff, I laughed until I did'nt know what to do with myself, and yet the poor creature's sobs and tears made it positively affecting too. I wondered what the neighbors and the passers-by would think was going on. She finished the first verse and was most anxious to favor us with the second—but Sam and I finally prevailed on her to put it off for another time.

Monday— I am so religiously resolved on being in bed in good season (for the preservation of my health, beauty and freshness) that I was obliged to say goodnight to you on Saturday night, while in the full swing and enjoyment of writing. I say *enjoyment*, because tho' I hate to begin a letter, I do enjoy it after I get a-going, and furthermore I am so benevolent as to enjoy anything that will give pleasure to another, and so vainglorious as to be sure that my letters do please and interest you, poor sick exile that you are. You speak of envying us, Mavourneen, because we are together. Yes, it is sweet, very sweet—and yet we are less together this winter than ever before since I have been living here. I find it my duty to spend more time at home, looking after the ways of my household, than I have formerly done— So I cannot visit the other houses as frequently and at my leisure as I used to— You know how much the others come to see me— And in the afternoon I very often have charity visits to make, where they do not care to go. And so it happens that we are not as much together as when you were here. Have you heard of the sewing-machine that has been introduced at Aunt Lou's. She bought it and Sister is to work it. It keeps Sister pretty close at work, but so far, it has not seemed to me to accomplish much. Perhaps when she gets more used to it, it will do better.

I've just had a dance—a dance that has made me feel good. Some strolling musicians came by, harping with their harps, and I stopped them to play for Sallie Gilbert. There was quite a crowd collected round them in the piazza, and while they listened, upstairs in my solitary chamber, I danced to my heart's content. The music got into my heels, and I could'nt help it. I had no intention of dancing, being a sober and serious woman in the main; but it was irresistible. So now I feel thawed and amiable. It has been a very cold day and I have felt rather crabbed until now, being unable to keep up a sufficient amount of caloric in my system.

H.

Louisa Gilmer to Her Sister Clifford.

Savannah Sat.
Jan. 17th 1857.

My dearest Cliffy

For two weeks it has been my settled determination every day to answer your last letter wh. I *did* receive, but have not been able to accomplish it. All last week, I did not try very hard, because I thought I might go up with Charlie to pay you a visit. I thought about it seriously and was very anxious to do so—but Mr. G. could not make up his mind to let me go. I did not think of taking the children, because I was afraid to have them travel in such very cold weather as we have been having—but I thought I might go myself and stay a while with you, leaving them to Aunt Lou—but Mr. G. felt very much about me as I did about them. I believe Father thought me very foolish and very precious of my delicate self—but I have suffered so much with neuralgia in my face within the last few months that Mr. G. was not willing to run the risk of having me exposed to the cold air late at night or early in the morning, and of course I would not have enjoyed going without his full and free consent. I *intend to pay* you a visit tho', dear Cliffy and the pleasure is only *deferred*, not lost. I could not take Henry travelling in the winter, for he is a delicate child, and has a constant cough, which sometimes makes me very uneasy, and I have to be very careful with him. Loulie is none too delicate but as I have only the one nurse I could not take her, unless I played waiting maid to her myself, wh. I am not ambitious of doing. Speaking of her Ladyship, she heard your last letter to Hattie, with George's "Vindication" read out aloud, and it made such an impression on her, that she reads it to herself now, in every book she takes up, with sundry remarkable variations in the narrative, wh. would be quite new to you—this morning I heard her, to herself on the couch. "And Cliffy went in the garden and picked *them turnips*, and she *cussed* me, and said I done it" which is supposed to be an imaginary extract from George. Her gift of language in her readings is quite remarkable you will perceive, and she has a wonderful store of facts laid up on wh. to draw whenever one is missing in her experience. She reads Bible stories to Henry who listens with the greatest gravity to the adventures of "the prophet Aberam" in a series of encounters with bears and tigers after he had "shotted" a ram, instead of Isaac—interspersed with moral reflections not always very pertinent to the subject. Henry listens in decorous silence to all the reflections, but when the crisis comes in the affairs with the wild beasts, his enthusiasm kindles intensely, and when the prophet, Daniel, *Aberam* or Moses as the case may be, finally slays the monster, as he invariably does, he breaks forth like Deborah in a glorification and clasps his hands and says *"Aha"* most vociferously. All Loulie's heroes, whether sacred or profane, have adventures with bears, and none would pass the gate of heaven, if she kept the keys, who had not proved their prowess as hunters. I hope her taste may become less bloodthirsty as she grows older.

L.

Louisa Gilmer to Clifford Hull.

My dearest Cliffy.

All the morning have I been trying hard to get to my desk to write you, but here it is past two o'clock and I am but just commencing. I had an opportunity to send my daguerreotype on to Ed by Col Hardee, who left at 12 o'clock, and I went out directly after breakfast to try and have one copied—staid there an hour and a half and did not succeed at all, so all that time was thrown away. Then I had a little shopping I was obliged to do and when I came home found Hattie come with her work to have a talk, so I had to get mine too, and have a talk instead of a *write;* she is just gone, and now I must scratch away as fast as I can to get my letter mailed by four o'clock.

I got home all safe on Sat. at half past one—and found nobody expecting me and nobody at home, except poor little Henry, who was shut up in his room, with most dreadful sore eyes. He was delighted to see me and clung fast to me for half an hour, but would not speak a word. When he did open his lips I was quite astonished to hear how he had improved in conversational power, *quantity* I refer to, I must say, however, and not quality—for almost the first thing I heard was when the Dr. came to see his eyes and he exclaimed in very intelligible English, "I tick oo out housh"—which sounded all the funnier for his eyes being very red and weak and his whole appearance being anything but that of a Sampson. He is delighted with his book and most particularly with the picture of the soda-water shop — in which he delights to imagine himself and drinks imaginary draughts from the fountain with the greatest possible relish.

As for Loulie, you guessed rightly that she and Æsop's Fables are a nuisance to the whole house. She goes around with it under her arm and assails anybody and everybody with her pressing request to read to her. Yesterday I tried to taboo it, on the plea that it was Sunday—but in vain—and I am quite surprised to see how much she understands the point of them. She was in quite a pious frame of mind yesterday, part of the day, and indulged as she always does at such times, in various anticipations of Heaven, for which it would be hard to find her authorities. She said "she would *try* not to worry the Angels when she got there, but she did wonder what they'd say if she did," but as I had never heard of their being subjected to any such trial or temptation, I was unable to enlighten her. I believe I told you how she tickled Custis Lee one warm evening not long ago, when she had been running on the pavement and came up the steps where he was seated with me. "Oh, my," she said, wiping the perspiration off her face with her apron, "I *shall* be glad when I can quit this nasty, hot, sweatty world, to go to heaven." He says he never heard such a descriptive expression and he thinks of it every time the sun is hot.

I had a very nice journey down, and was highly successful with all my goods, boxes, dirt and all. I have come to the conclusion conductors are much nicer than husbands to travel with, because whatever their thoughts may be on the quantity and quality of your travelling equipage they keep their remarks to themselves. George's conductor was very civil and had all my plunder transferred to the Waynesboro Road without any trouble at all to Will. I thought I should have died laughing as I sat in the omnibus to see a man come tugging along with the bag of dirt, and when he got to the omnibus he calls out breathless "Here, Dick, do for gracious sake help me wid dis bag of sugar." Mr. Gilmer was not here to see my arrival and favor me with his comments, and since he came home I have been so strenuous on the subject of the politeness of conductors that he has felt a delicacy in saying anything that might by any possibility suggest a contrast.

He did not get here until Sunday morning—the boat being a whole day behind its time. The plants all came very safely, with the exception of both the camellia buds being knocked off, by the weight of the dirt. Sat. aft. I spent planting out my things, and as a fine rain came on at night, they are looking first rate. I had another sick headache in consequence of my ride and my gardening exertions, but felt quite well again next morning.

Henry has just come in and when I asked what I should say to Uncle George he says without any prompt-ings—"Tah tah I shen five tish," evidently remembering the book. I asked Loulie the same and she said she had already written a letter to her Aunt Clifford and sent it—and she told her all she had to say—so I hope you may get it—but she added "you can tell her I have got a head dress on of silver curls." I wish you could see it—made of paper and a manufacture of her own. Give my best love to George. All send love to you both.

Ever my dearest Cliffy yr.

Aff. Sister   L.

E. P. Alexander to George G. Hull.

West Point, May 2, 1857

Dear Brother George:—

Your most acceptable letter came to my hands in the usual time (although you may not have thought so) and was made most welcome on its arrival as it deserved to be. Allow me to present my most sincere congratulations to you and Dearest Mae, and the same accompanied with my warmest love to the juvenile stranger* who is the cause of so much joy and happiness. As a token to her of my esteem and affection, please kiss her for me now and ask sister to remember to let her off the first castigation her depraved nature may merit for her in future.

I would have written long before now on this interesting subject, but I am absolutely hard at work every minute, except a half hour after supper every night, from five o'clock Monday morning to twelve o'clock Saturday night of every week. The twenty-two years of my life that were fated to be devoted to scrambling up the hill of science, pursued by forty or fifty school-teachers, and tortured by "blamed long equations, infernal combinations, tormenting permutations, eternal slight reductions and double and twisted fractions, and the Lord knows what" (as a cadet song eloquently expresses it) have now dwindled down to five weeks, and then the long agony will wind up with a grand observation to determine to what height I have ascended.

My altitude having been determined I hope to take a final leave of this place where Uncle Sam "teaches the young idea how to shoot" about the 12th of June, and as

*Lucy Harvie Hull.

I expect to return South by the road from Virginia to Tennessee, I will probably call on you on the way home sometime in June. It is yet so uncertain exactly when I will be relieved here that I can not tell exactly when it will be, but if I get time I will write again and let you know more definitely.

I entertain strong hopes of being entitled to wear the Engineer Uniform which I have had made, and to do this I daily ascend early and descend late, and fly around during the day with the utmost agility, continually hoping that my friends will not require many letters from me now; and then, some of these days, when I am Lieut. General they will be proud to recollect these little things and will often amuse their grandchildren with relations of them. I hope your old age may be enlivened with such recollections.

I am very sorry to hear that all of the fruit is killed in Georgia, as I had anticipated spending many pleasant hours with it. But is probably much better for my health that it is so. Spring, which is so late everywhere, has got what the cadets call a "frigid absent" here. There is not yet a single green leaf visible anywhere, and but very few small buds, and not even a maple has put out. The weather, however, is splendid for the "Shanghai" drill which has been adopted by the authorities at Washington, and after them, though much against our inclination, by ourselves, and we run every where.

I am sorry for your sake that I have no news to write, but as such is the fact I had probably much better stop at once. So with much love to dearest Mae and yourself, believe me ever

Your most affectionate brother,

E. P. A.

Adam Alexander to His Daughter Marion.

Savannah, May 7, 1857.

My darling:—

You little thought on yesterday how near I was to you. For the greater part of the day I was in sight of the beach of Daufuskie, and often strained my eyes if I might see you and your young companions in the distance, thinking that my heart at least, if not my vision, would recognize you even that far.

The morning promised fair for the day, but proved faithless in the performance. But I was tempted to trust it and with a strong desire to renew again the pleasures of my boyhood by a sail in a little boat, I went with Mr. Dunning to Tybee and Cockspur Islands. We rowed down and attempted to sail back in a little two oared skiff and were overtaken by the storm eight miles below the city. We were repeatedly nearly capsized and for more than an hour exposed to the fury of the gale, finding the utmost difficulty in keeping the boat alive, while attempting to make shore. We finally about dark reached Mackay's rice fields, where we landed and walked to the Overseer's house, when I hired a horse and rode through wind and rain, reaching the City a little after 8 o'clock. I found them all in the greatest anxiety about my absence and infinitely relieved, of course, to see me again. But I must not occupy my paper wholly about myself.

Your Aunt, Uncle, and Alice, with Sister Sallie's family went to the picnic in Liberty County, and had from their accounts a pleasant time of it. Alice will attempt a letter to you, and I leave to her an account of the pleasures and marvels of the day.

On my return last night I found a letter from Hilly awaiting me. He is doing well as usual and occupies much of his letter detailing the troubles which occurred at Charlottesville between the students and some of the storekeepers in the village, in which, however, he was not a participant. He asks my permission to visit Niagara in company with a classmate and two of his sisters, but as I don't know either classmate or sisters, I don't think I shall consent. I remember my own impressibility at his age amid such scenes, and though to me the result was most auspicious, I feel that it was not by my own prudence and foresight such a result was secured, but that I was led by a kind and overruling Providence and by a path that I knew not. A day never passes over me now without my remembering with feelings of the profoundest gratitude the series of kind providences which first brought me acquainted with your Sainted Mother, and afterward united us in ties of love which Death is unable to dissolve, or even for a moment impair.

Today is your brother Felix' birthday, and sure I am you will remember him. But while you think most of him, I think most of her who bore him, and while I love him as he deserves to be loved, I love her better than all the world beside. I can recall every incident connected with his birth, as tho' it happened yesterday.

I have written this note in anticipation of Miss Lizzie's going down to you tomorrow, and with the hope, too, that I shall hear from you tomorrow on arrival of Mrs. M's boat.

I hope not only that you and your young friends will enjoy yourselves, but that you will also be pleasant company tó your kind friend who has provided such an entertainment for you. It is a great privilege to be able to spend a few days at such a place, and to a cultivated and refined mind the memory of it even will be a perpetual joy. If the places in which we live, or which we may visit, help to develop our minds and to deepen the foundations of our character, as assuredly they do, you will appreciate Mrs. M's kindness in affording you your present pleasures, more than if she had manifested it by the gift of some costly jewel which money could have purchased. The one could have ministered to your vanity only; the other to the advancement and improvement of your higher nature. If your Mother's spirit dwells in you, my darling, (as I think it does in the love you show to me), you will show it also in the refinement and exaltation of your heart by the scenes amid which your favored lot is now cast.

My paper and time admonish me to close. Your Aunt is going with me to look at a set of silver which I wish to buy for you, on sale at Wilmot's. I think it beautiful but shall defer to her better judgment and tastè. It is one of Bailey's handsomest workmanship; six pieces and costs $470.00 and matches well with the waiters I bought for you.

Sandy is still very ill, and his case extremely doubtful; Lucy is also laid up with a sore and swollen foot; Beverly being our chief waiting man and doing well.

Present my most respectful regards to Mrs. Mongin; remember me to Miss Carrie and remind her of my promise made her long ago, and for yourself, darling, receive the greatest love I have left for anything living.

Your affectionate father,

A. L. A.

E. P. Alexander to His Sister Clifford,

West Point, Nov. 11, 1857.

Dearest Mae:—

I received your letter yesterday and find myself arraigned in it on following charge and specification viz. charge, general worthlessness and neglect of duty; specification, in this that I have willfully and shamefully neglected to write to you for the period of seven weeks. All this at West Point, N. Y. where I am no longer a cadet, and to which charge and specification I will plead as follows: To the specification guilty, except the words, "willfully and shamefully," and to the charge guilty, except the words "general worthlessness and"—for really ma chère soeur I have been intensely busy, and I can modestly say unintentionally and unwillingly so. Part of the time I have had three or four drills a day to attend; part of the time I have had to stay with the Company, superintending its work from 7 to 11:30 A. M. and from 1 to 4 P. M. and lately I have been on a courtmartial which has given me forty pages of large size letter paper to write, of which twenty-seven had to be without an interlineation or erasure; and to fill up the spare intervals of my time I have had over thirty visits to pay, the most of them after tea; very many letters to write and my room to fix up in a comfortable style.

But most of these jobs are completed now and I gladly seize my pen with my right hand, back up, between my thumb and first and second fingers, the nib of the pen down —but steady—I've been explaining how to seize hand-spikes and rammer-staves at artillery drill till my head runs on it. It is quite immaterial how I seize my pen so I induce your judgment and good nature to give as a verdict that, though I am "guilty of the charges and specifications mentioned, they attach no criminality thereto." But before I lay aside these legal forms let me reply briefly to the series of cross-questions you put in your letter, and then proceed to the news. The answers will suggest the questions to you.

I go into company as Phoenix says "slightually," having much inclination, no time that I can conscientiously spare, but fortunately a convenient and pliable conscience. I have formed some very pleasant friendships and could form more, and more intimate ones, if I had time and I've no doubt that they could be cultivated so as to assume both length, breadth, and "thickness," about which physical proportions you inquire so particularly.

Baylor has been quite ill with typhoid fever and only went to Watervliet a short while since, but I have heard from him and he is very much pleased with his post. He does not know Cousin John yet, or did not when he wrote, but he likes him very much in anticipation on general principles. He paid me a short visit on his way to Troy and gave me a most pleasant surprise, for I did not know that he had left New York until he was in my own room.

But last night about half past ten I had a surprise. I was about going to bed (in unmilitary costume), when up came Lieut. Donelson with a telegraphic despatch to say that I must hold myself in readiness to start for New York immediately on the receipt of another despatch, in company with the Company of Sappers and Miners, to protect the Subtreasury there from being plundered by a mob of the "unemployed," "plug uglies," "deadrabbits," etc. As my monthly pay comes out of the Subtreasury and the government would feel very badly about it, if it could not pay me promptly when it was due, I patriotically obeyed the order. It required but little preparation. I only curled my moustache up at the corners, and then—

if the Subtreasury could have seen me it would have felt easy.

We have been waiting all day for further orders, but as yet none have come. Whether they will come or not, I can't say, but I am afraid that such a little trip as that is too good luck to fall to our fate here, and I can hardly suppose that the danger will justify it.

This is all the news I have to tell and moreover the end of my sheet, so with the greatest love to yourself and household, and many kisses to Miss Lucy, I am as ever,

Your affectionate brother,

E. P. A.

E. P. Alexander to His Sister Clifford.

Dearest Sister :—

Some people might think I have commenced this letter too soon, but I have'nt. I intended to commence it a heap sooner, but I did'nt. I would apologize for my negligence (apparent) but an apology suited to the occasion would take up all the letter and so I won't. But now I think of it I have not got anything else to write about, and so I believe I will. But on the whole an apology is always so abominably stupid that I had rather freely forgive anybody at once than read one, and so in mercy to you and at the same time in justice to myself I will split the difference and tell you as *news* what I have to do and let you draw your own inferences. In the first place I have to get up every morning regularly, and being once up, I generally decide to dress myself, during which process visions of buckwheat cakes float thro' my head to such an extent that I am induced to go to breakfast almost invariably. After breakfast I rush madly over to the section-room, when I lean back in my chair and give the young idea lessons in shooting for three hours, after which I devote an hour to preparation for mortal combat with the worthy Conner and the big brothers of the Judson Society, by boxing and fencing lessons and broadsword exercise, after which I pronounce myself tired and go to my room for a rest and read the morning paper, and feed my prairie dog, etc. until 1 o'clock. At this time I go to a place I know of where there is some cheese and crackers and occasionally a little cider, with which I while away a half hour, and then for the afternoon I usually have some Company duty to attend to (for I am on duty with it as well as with the cadets now), or I read or pay a call, or take a walk with some fair creature, or semi-occasionally as at present, I write. Dinner comes at half past four, and I usually digest it with a game of chess, and then read over my lessons for the next day, and look thro' other books for new ideas on it, after which beginning to feel sleepy I go out visiting until about half past ten or eleven, when I come back home to read a little more, and then, as I remarked to the Judson, I go to bed, having as a precedent therefor the example of some of the most illustrious sages of antiquity.

Last week I got a leave of absence for a few days (four) and occupied it in a trip to Washington City, which was, you may be sure, very pleasant, and is the only holiday I have had except one day when I went down to New York to hear Piccolomini at the Opera.

There is little society on the post here, except married ladies, but I prefer that kind very much to all others, and intend to marry somebody myself some of these days on purpose to enjoy it.

I am afraid there is little chance of my seeing any of you this winter, as being on duty in two departments I can not get a leave of absence for even a few days without a great deal of trouble. Perhaps about the first of May I may have an excuse which will touch Col. D's heart enough to get me two weeks' leave, in which case you will get a glimpse of me, but what the excuse is or will be is too far off to mention yet. As brother G. advised me I did not apply to be relieved from this place, but will wait for something to turn up. I am very pleasantly situated and enjoying myself as much as I could almost anywhere. There are two or three or four or five families of the young officers here where I am very intimate and call just as if I were at home.

Write to me whenever you can, dear sister. I have so many correspondents everywhere that it takes me very long to get around at the speed I go, but then I am the best appreciator of a letter you ever saw.

Give my best love to little Miss Lucy and kiss Brother George for me.

Ever you most affectionate brother,

E. P. A.

P. S. I have got the funniest books in the world and am dying to show them to George. They are A. Becket's "Comic History of Rome and England," illustrated by Leech.

E. P. Alexander to His Sister Clifford.

Long Island, Nov. 10, 1859

My affectionate Sister:—

I know your family owes me a letter and if I had any correspondents to whom I was indebted I would write this to them; but I have had two leisure days at this gay and festive location, owing to the prevalence of rain, and no books, and I have just set myself straight correspondentially with everybody, and will now give you this, the first free letter I write, as you are my best correspondent usually and deserve the medal. I have, however, one crow for plucking even with you, or rather George. I wrote a long letter to him about the 3rd ult., explaining the duty I was ordered on and giving my address and asked to have it all communicated to Father, etc., which he never did, thereby involving me in the trouble and expense of another letter to Father, and cheating me out of various letters which would have been written to me had my address been known. George, therefore, stands legally indebted to me, at least three letters, one as a reply to mine, another as a reply to the one he made me write Father, and at least one which *somebody* would have written had my address been known. Please tell him I am expecting these letters daily. For yourself I will simply say that my address is "Care of Lt. R. K. Meade, Box 1373, N. Y. City," and you are authorized to make as free use of my name on the backs of your letters as you please.

We are going on to Washington City next week to experiment before the Secretary of War and and the War Department, and will probably be there a week or ten days. Please write me about this directed there, as soon as you can, to "Willard's Hotel." When we finish there I am going to Virginia to see her* for a short while. After that I expect we will be in New York most of the Winter. At present I am picking up a precarious subsistence between this place, New York City, and Sandy Hook, keeping my trunk in Dick Meade's room, and traveling on my carpet-bag, eating at restaurants, and lunching at the bazaars of itinerant apple and peanut venders. There are no regular means of communication between most of my business localities, and so I walk with my valise and satchel in my hand when I ain't lucky enough to meet a lagerbeer or sodawater cart, or a fellow with a boat who is good-naturedly tight. One of these last took me two weeks ago seven miles out in the Outer Bay to a wreck and landed me aboard a tugboat which purported to be coming up to the city, and would probably have done so had not the Captain been intoxicated and ordered the pilot to run out to sea first. (The pilot was $\frac{drunk}{2}$ and said he would run to Ireland, if he said so, but the engineer who was about $\frac{drunk}{3}$ said he would not shut off steam.) Then there was swearing for fifteen minutes faster than I could keep up with it, and then the boat started like an arrow out to sea, and all was still except the engineer who was muttering gently, but emphatically, about the amount of fuel it should cost the Captain, and the pilot praying for the "Great Eastern" to come and run over us because the Captain had had all the boat's lights taken in. I sought an offered berth and laid down, and would doubtless have gone to sleep had I not caught several specimens of an unknown but very suspicious looking variety of small bug running an exciting race from my left temple to my chin. I was in a great hurry to reach the city and we were then forty miles from it and steaming towards Gibraltar as fast as a railroad car, and I was just sea-sick enough to feel precarious,—no place to lie down and the night cold. I think I would have given five dollars a letter

*Miss Retty Mason, to whom he was engaged.

for an allowable synonym of the verb "to check the flow of water by obstacles." Being aboard, however, as a guest and not a passenger, I could do nothing more than hold a convention of feeling in my own chest, and pass resolutions condemnatory of everybody and everything from the smoke-stack to the algebraic bugs. I call them algebraic from their suggesting to my mind, at the moment when I first discovered this race going on, (and with great dexterity caught the hindmost one and held him out to the light), the algebraic expression or formula d minus n. We ran out to sea till one o'clock at night and then to my surprise turned back, but it was long after sunrise when we got back to the city.

The Doctor and I are succeeding admirably with our signals and using nothing but light and portable pole and flag for day, and the same pole and two copper torches for night, can converse readily in any weather except fog or falling rain over fifteen miles. No military signals have ever been sent over eight miles before and they required machines. We can communicate, too, in a million ways besides with flags. For instance, today there is a heavy fog and the Doctor is at the Highlands, fifteen miles off, and we have made no arrangements or concerted no signals for this emergency, but I fired, a little while ago, from Ft. Hamilton, thirteen 32 pounders, and if he heard them at all, I feel perfectly confident that he read the message, "Do you understand?"

I don't expect to go back to West Point when this duty is finished, but will most probably go to California. I have had a falling out with Col. Delafield on leaving there and rather have the upper hand of him in it about some Ordnance Property I left there.

Did I ever tell you of my having met Maj. and Mrs. Laidley last summer and of their inquiries after, and love to you? I saw, too, Mrs. Ella Clinch in New York a month ago (I had to ask her husband's name!), also Miss Annie Camak.

My love to the Unjust George and a kiss to Miss Lucy, and one also with my respect and congratulations to Miss Mary Cooper, if that is her name. I have received but one letter since her advent and was written on the supposition that I had heard all particulars, and so omitted all but a mere reference.

Ever affectionately your brother,

E. P. A.

E. P. Alexander to His Sister Clifford.

Fort Steilacoom
Washington Territory, Nov. 11, 1860.

Dearest Mae:—

My last letter to you, I believe, was from West Point and was devoted to my combinations and arrangements at that locality, for the peaceful enjoyment of my quiet conscience and all other blessings; but the magician Floyd has said presto, and now the little joker undergoes quite a permutation, and addresses you from the fir (off) forests of Washington Territory. His quiet conscience, however, has not deserted him, and Peace and Innocence still cheer his fireside. In fact I am just as well satisfied here, as I ever was at West Point, and though I miss the morning papers at breakfast, I still contrive to get up an appetite proportioned to any amount of salmon, trout, or slapjack that Bessie can provide.

I have written little accounts of our surroundings, etc. to so many that I suppose you all have a sufficient idea of how we are situated and I have become tired of the story myself, so I will judge your feelings by my own and not formally recur to them again. There is not much in them that I think would excite your envy, except the scenery and the walks and rides. The novelty alone is the charm of everything else, and I apprehend that over twelve months would reduce the charm to a very poor apology; but of the ever-changing aspects of old Mt. Rainier, the dense forests and little lakes, and the magnificent gravel roads, I don't think I would ever tire, and I enjoy them now as pleasures I will always look back upon with delight. I have not much to do and amuse myself with reading,

218

EDWARD PORTER ALEXANDER (*b.* May 26, 1835)
Reproduced from a daguerreotype taken soon after his graduation
from West Point and before the Civil War.

chess, hunting, and fishing; and Bessie devotes herself to making a talma, sugar biscuits, pies, and a variety of other useful articles too numerous to mention. She is very much amused and interested, too, by the specimens of the aborigines who come here very often with game, fish, berries, etc. to sell, or to beg for old clothes and crusts. Our servant (the affecshunate An) has some in daily pay, who come for the crusts and scraps, and in return will squat tailor fashion and clean fish, or pick birds until they are nearly smothered in feathers.

But speaking of this filial female, reminds me to thank you for your kind epistolary remembrance of Sept. 17th (the day we arrived here) which we got on the 8th inst., with one from Uncle in New York. Letters are our greatest excitement here, and we tell each other all over the Post how many we expect, and whether they all come, and if we have heard any news.

Don't tell George of it, but your likeness which I have has attracted much attention and praise from two officers here, and I have told them a good deal about you, and now if I can only say that you write to me very, very often, and oh! such funny letters, there's no telling what chances may be in store for you, if you ever need them. Minnie, too, is quite a belle here in spite of her seclusion at home.

Preparations are being made in this Department for a strong campaign against the Snake or Shoshonee Indians, next Spring, and I expect, unless some order takes me away from here before the time, to go out in it, either with the Company of Sappers, or to introduce and use Myers' signals. They are a large tribe and have long been troublesome. They very recently murdered a large emigrant party, only one or two, half starved, escaping to tell of it, and Bob Anderson with Capt. Dent and 100 men are now out to try and find survivors and bury the dead. Their country lies to the Southeast, across the Mountains, and is very rough and but little known.

Of course, we are all much exercised now to know

the result of the election which is all over, but which we can not hear of for three weeks yet. We suppose from the latest news we have that Lincoln is elected, and if so I *hope* and *expect* to be called in to help secede. If he is once inaugurated, it will be too late to oppose him, as the purse and the sword will be in his hands and the Army and Navy are sworn to obey his commands. If he is elected I believe the interests of humanity, civilization, and self-preservation call on the South to secede, and I'll go my arm, leg, or death on it.

The rainy season has set in here and you had better believe we are having a juicy time and no variety but dried apples. A dry joke would be a perfect luxury, but they can't be dessicated in this country.

I don't know that I've ever explained that the father of his "afecshunate An" did not get the letter to Minnie which was from Bessie, and eventually mailed to her in San Francisco. It was intended to be mailed at Acapulco, but in the hurry I mailed the wrong letter, not knowing of its existence, and the bona fide turned up afterwards. We had amused ourselves very much imagining Minnie's receipt and perusal of it, although we did not before know of An's orthographic attainments. I suppose she thinks about spelling like the Irishman about playing the fiddle—she supposes she can do it as it looks easy enough.

Please say to George in remembrance of me that my "pen is bad, my ink is pale, my love for him shall never fail." Our double, double breasted, laminated, long-range affection to both of you and your chicks, and the usual osculatory accompaniments to boot. Always think of me as a male, and let the thought suggest long letters and lots of em.

Ever affectionately your brother,

E. P. A.

Extract from "The Sable Cloud; a Southern Tale with Northern Comments."

"A Southern gentlemen, who was visiting in New York, sent me, with his reply to my inquiries for the welfare of his family at home, the following letter which he had just received from one of his married daughters in the South.

"The reader will be so kind as to take the assurance which the writer hereby gives him, that the letter was received under the circumstances now stated, and that it is not a fiction. Certain names and the date only are, for obvious reasons, omitted.

The Letter.*

" 'My Dear Father,—

" 'You have so recently heard from and about those of us left here, and that in a so much more satisfactory way than through letters, that it scarcely seems worth while to write just yet. But Mary left Kate's poor little baby in such a pitiable state, that I think it will be a relief to all to hear that its sufferings are ended. It died about ten o'clock the night that she left us, very quietly and without a struggle, and at sunset on Friday we laid it in its last resting-place. My husband and I went out in the morning to select the spot for its burial, and finding the state of affairs in the cemetery, we chose a portion of ground and will have it inclosed with a railing. They

---

*The above letter being shown to the Rev. Mr. Adams, a Northern friend of the family, was used by him as a text for "The Sable Cloud," a book in defense of the South published by him in 1861. The names here given are fictitious. The child referred to was named Cynthia for Mammy. Her mother was the Cora so often referred to in these letters who had been maid to H. V. C. since childhood and who will be remembered by many of the family in Savannah.

have been very careless in the management of the ground, and have allowed persons to inclose and bury in any shape or way they chose, so that the whole is cut up in a way that makes it difficult to find a place where two or three graves could be put near each other. We did find one at last, however, about the size of the Hazel Wood lots; and we will inclose it at once, so that when another, either from our own family or those of the other branches, wants a resting-place, there shall not be the same trouble. Poor old Timmy lies there but it is in a part of the grounds where, the sexton tells us, the water rises within three feet of the surface; so, of course, we did not go there for this little grave. His own family selected his burial-place, and probably did not think of this.

" 'Kate takes her loss very patiently, though she says that she had no idea how much she would grieve after the child. It had been sick so long that she said she wanted to have it go; but I knew when she said it that she did not know what the parting would be. It is not the parting alone, but it is the horror of the grave,—the tender child alone in the far off gloomy burial-ground, the heavy earth piled on the tender little breast, the helplessness that looked to you for protection which you could not give, and the emptiness of the home to which you return when the child is gone. He who made a mother's heart, and they who have borne it, alone can tell the unutterable pain of all this. The little child is so carefully and tenderly watched over and cherished while it is with you,—and then to leave it alone in the dread grave where the winds and the rain beat upon it! I know they do not feel it, but since mine has been there, I have never felt sheltered from the storms when they come. The rain seems to fall on my bare heart. I have said more than I meant to have said on this subject, and have left myself little heart to write of anything else. Tell Mammy that it is a great disappointment to me that her name is not to have a place in my household. I was always so pleased with the idea that my Susan and little

Cygnet should grow up together as the others had done; but it seems best that it should not be so, or it would not have been denied. Tell Mary that Chloe staid that night with Kate, and has been kind to her. All are well at her house.' "

H. V. C.

"Of the persons named in this letter, Kate is a slave-mother, belonging to the Lady who writes the letter. Cygnet was Kate's babe. Mammy is a common appellation for a slave-nurse. The Mammy to whom the message in the letter is sent was nursery-maid when the writer of the letter and several brothers and sisters were young; and, more than this, she was maid to their mother in early years. She is still in this gentleman's family. Her name is Cynthia; Kate's babe was named for her, and called Cygnet. Mary is the lady's married sister. Chloe is Mary's servant. The incidental character of this letter and the way in which it came to me, gave it a special charm. Some recent traveller, describing his sensations at Heidelberg Castle, speaks of a German song which he heard, at the moment, from a female at some distance and out of sight. This letter, like that song, derives much of its effect from the unconsciousness of the author that it would reach a stranger."

Adam Alexander to His Daughter Marion.

Savannah, April 22, 1861.

Dear Minnie:—

You have been out there* long enough and must come in, if you expect to see me at all. I have fixed upon no time for going, but feel that I may be called home at any hour.

War has commenced and will be formally declared before you can come, I think. Hilly may be ordered away at any hour, and in that event I must return home. You have been away long enough any how and as long as Charlie begs you will not have resolution to fix upon a day, so I do it for you and shall expext you in on Wednesday.

Companies come here and depart on every train; now chiefly to Norfolk. The Navy yard there has been burned and abandoned by the Devils, and is now in possession of Virginia troops. Washington City will probably be attacked this week, if not sooner abandoned by the miscreants, in which event they will blow up everything before leaving, but which *we* don't care about. Maryland will certainly follow Virginia, and they have already cut off all passage by land for any more Northern troops. You will see telegrams in this morning's papers.

Your Aunt has a headache this A. M. but joins with me in saying you had better come on Wednesday. The carriage shall be at the depot. Tell Charlie, if he comes with you, not to forget the musket, etc.

Love to the people and much for you and Charlie, dear child.

Yours,

FATHER.

*At Hopewell.

Felix Alexander to His Father.

Dear Father:—

I am just now in receipt of your letter of the 29th and hasten to reply.

When I wrote Porter to resign I told him not to wait to hear from Washington City, but, if possible, to come on at once with his resignation. This I hope he will do, as other officers have done. I met last night a Lieut. Walker of Virginia, who left California on the 4th of April, coming with the mail that brought his resignaticn. He resigned on the news of Lincoln's inauguration. I do hope Porter will be home now soon, as other officers from that section have already reported. Walker spent the evening with Sister Lou on the 3rd, and says that Gilmer does not intend to resign until North Carolina secedes. He then did not believe that the Border States would come out. Walker says that Porter was expected in San Francisco on the 7th, and I fervently hope he will have taken the steamer on the 11th.

Two days ago President Davis sent for me and told me that he was sending a special messenger to meet Gen. Johnston at Havana or at Panama, wherever he could find him, with instructions to him and all other Southern officers to come over to New Orleans, and he advised me to send a letter to Porter by the same messenger. I therefore did so, and if he did not take the steamer of the 11th of April, the messenger will intercept him. If he did take the steamer, he will be in New York probably tomorrow, and if he will be prudent can come home by the Western route. Don't say anything publicly about the messenger to Gen. Johnston. I think it will stagger

Gilmer mightily when he finds Gen. Johnston has resigned and entered our service. I am told by a gentleman from North Carolina that John A. Gilmer is a fiery secessionist.

You can have no idea of how the war spirit rages throughout the country. Tis manifested here in importunate applications and angry complaints that they are not mustered into service. I believe that we can put 150,000 volunteers in the field without resort to drafting.

I sent you yesterday a copy of the President's message which is a most admirable State paper; also a pamplet copy of the laws passed by Congress. There seems to be a general disposition to accept the invitation given by Virginia, and to move the Government to Richmond, in the event that the popular vote of Virginia ratifies the ordinance of secession.

I have very little doubt that we will be in Richmond a month hence. We will probably make no move upon Washington, until or unless Maryland secedes. In that event Lincoln will receive notice to quit. We are sending mortars and shell down to Pensacola and ere very long will be ready to pitch into Pickens.

I hope that the State Bank has removed her Northern balances, for I have reason to believe that they will not be safe a few days hence.

I shall be very sorry if you go home without paying me a visit here. I know you will enjoy it. Mr. Toombs has gone to housekeeping and I am living with them. This is much more agreeable to me. Please give much love to all for me, and let me hear as often as is convenient. What has become of Minnie?

Ever your affectionate son,

W. F.

A Trip from San Francisco to New York in 1861.*

In January, 1859, Capt. J. F. Gilmer was sent to
San Francisco as engineer in charge of the harbor fortifications there and the whole Pacific Coast.

He was a Southerner, sent to West Point by North
Carolina, but married and living in Savannah, Georgia,
up to the time of this appointment.

There were other Southern officers of the U. S. Army
then in California, many of whom became prominent in
the war which followed so soon: Gen. Albert Sidney
Johnston was in command; Maj. Mackall, his Chief of
Staff; Custis Lee, Robert Anderson, E. ˜P. Alexander, etc.

From the time of Mr. Lincoln's election in 1860 rumors
were rife as to the secession of the Southern States, but
excited no interest in San Francisco. It was considered
a kind of a joke rather. Even the actual secession of
South Carolina was looked on as a piece of braggadocio,
tho' we did feel individually some excitement at so unfore-
seen a thing. (Your aunt, Mrs. Mackall, and I heard
it down on the street first). Your father being a North
Carolina cadet, determined to wait for his State, hoping
and believing its secession would not come, and that
the affair would blow over, but in May or June, 1861,
North Carolina did go, and when we got the news your
father determined to send his resignation to Washington.
He had to do this as no officer out there was able to receive
them, he being ranking engineer and taking orders only
from the Department. So soon as we knew of North
Carolina's secession the resignation went, but in those

*As narrated by Louisa Gilmer to her daughter.

days the mail took a long, long time, and we determined to keep it secret till the answer was received.

Meanwhile, however, Gen. Sumner had been sent by the Government to supersede Gen. A. S. Johnston, and he issued an order commanding all officers to renew their oaths of allegiance to the United States. Capt. Gilmer took no notice of this, not being amenable to an officer of the line, and then Gen. Sumner issued a special and most arbitrary order to him by name, superseding him and ordering him to turn over the office, and immense property of the United States to Capt. McPherson (he was in his office.) This was a most unprecedented piece of interference, but Gen. Sumner considered himself justified by the exigencies of the time. Your father had gone off on business when the order was handed in and Capt. Elliott brought it up to me. Wildly excited and angry we decided to send your father a note to the boat by which he would arrive, telling him to come straight home, and not to go to the office by any means. This was so I could tell him and he not know it otherwise.

He came home and I told him, but now a most extraordinary thing and one which changed the whole face of affairs,—the acceptance of Capt. Gilmer's resignation arrived that very night by the pony express, with a most complimentary letter from the War Department as to his service and especially as to his settlement of a lawsuit concerning the land for the Lime Point fortification. While we were rejoicing at this stroke of luck, there arrived an old officer—renowned as a gossip—who plainly came to talk over the suspension and who walked into his subject almost without preliminaries. "Capt. Gilmer," he said, "I can't tell you how much Gen. Sumner is blamed for the order he has issued to you, and how sincerely we all regret the treatment to which you have been subjected. What shall you do about it?" Your father replied, "I have nothing to do, being in no way amenable to Gen. Sumner. The War Department has accepted my resignation and directed me to turn over the office to Capt. Elliott." This produced a tremendous effect, and the good man could scarcely wait to say goodnight. We heard that he jumped into his buggy and rode from place to place for the pleasure of telling the news. It was just the way we would have chosen to have it spread,—socially. No notice was taken of Gen. Sumner's order at all! He was greatly mortified, especially as his own aids had warned him he was going out of his province, and they all knew the snub he got in return.

Well your father had resigned; we were no longer "Army people." We would have started home immediately now, if we had been independent as regards money matters, but we were not and we had to remain till our house could be rented and our furniture sold. Gen. Halleck invited us to spend our last days at his house, and we worked as fast as we could to get ready. But, while we were packing our last things,—a few cases with books, etc. which through the kindness of Mr. Alverd were to be sent by the Horn and stored with friends of his in New York, and which, by the way, lay there five whole years unclaimed,—on the day we were to leave the house and sleep at the H's your father began to complain of his wrist, his eyes. By next morning rheumatic fever was declared. Our passage in the steamer (which left then only every two weeks) was transferred from steamer to steamer and still your father lay there, unable to let the sheet touch him even. The weeks went on.

One night we heard something in the city roaring like a fire, or a distant wind storm, and upon the hill on which we lived, we could see lights moving about hurriedly, and the tramping of crowds. It was late, however, and we did not learn till morning what had so strangely excited the city. The news of Manassas had come by pony express the night before. When I came down to the breakfast table Mr. and Mrs. Halleck looked curiously glum and uneasy, and he began with, "I suppose you have heard the news?" "No, no, what?" "A battle has been fought and the Southerners have whipped the Government Army." "Let me go tell Mr. Gilmer," was my first reply, but I am afraid I showed more joy in my manner than was strictly polite. Gen. H. held me by the arm and said, "No, sit down and take your breakfast. I'll tell him myself." When he went, however, I followed and heard him say: "Well, Gilmer, they let Beauregard and Johnston get together and they whipped old McDowell!" Your father was very ill, but, of course, it excited him. He had more self-control than I, and the two men discussed it calmly—so calmly that it seemed like a dream to both in after years, when they were several times face to face in the two armies in Tennessee and Kentucky.

Well it was not till the 21st of August, 1861, that we dragged your father, his arm in a sling, his eyes under a shade, to the steamer and set out for the long voyage. There were crowded steamers in those days before the Railroad, and we had between six hundred and seven hundred passengers on the ship. A large party of U. S. officers with their wives and families were on board. They were all as kind and considerate of us as possible, and when Capt. Hudson attempted to put a slight on us by putting us at the Mate's table, they resented it to a man. I declined to be moved back to the Captain's table where they all sat throughout the voyage; nor did I find myself at all to disadvantage, for the so-called Mate, Capt. Dahl, was of great authority and gave me many privileges and showed me many kind little attentions.

When the pilot came out to meet us at Panama, we were all greatly excited to hear the news. We had been out two weeks and all were interested. A young officer named Hawkins got the paper first, and appeared in our group on the deck, exclaiming, "Come, come in the cabin and I'll read you all the news. Jeff. Davis is captured; the Sumter is captured and destroyed; there's been a big fight in Missouri and Gen. Lyon has been killed!" I did not care to go but Mrs. Hancock took me by the hand and said, "Come, come, you had better hear it all. Nobody knows if it's true anyway." (She had brothers in the Confederate Army and Gen. Hancock—Captain he was then—told me he would be hung yet for her tongue). She dragged me part of the way but I slipped into my cabin and then back on deck. When she saw me again she came up saying "Was'nt so bad for Dixie after all, and they got old Lyon."

We did not know what was true but when we got to Aspinwall, the Sumter was evidently not considered destroyed. The whole town quaked and a terrible old tub escorted the steamer a tiny way out into the Gulf, putting back long before she could possibly have expected to see the dreaded *Pirate*. The Captain of the steamer was awfully afraid of her. He would not allow any lights on the ship or in the cabins. The only one was under the saloon table and we had to make out as well as we could. All the men passengers were drilled, so as to resist a boarding party if we were attacked, and great was the horror and excitement when a sail was seen on the horizon. Gen. Benj. Butler's mother was on board, I remember, and once during the periodical stampede caused by "a sail," she accosted me by remarking that I did not seem alarmed. "No," I said, "they are friends of mine on the Sumter. I only wish they may come on and take us." "What do you think they would do?" she queried. "Well they would take all the gold on board, make prisoners of the officers, and (just here a wicked thought struck me) of you." "Me!" she screamed, "why? why?" "Because of your distinguished son, madame." "But they would not know who I was." "But I should consider it my duty to point you out." Terrible was her state of mind and it really pleased me. I who had so much more to fear!

One day a Capt. Mason who was from Ohio asked me what we were going to do when we got to New York.

"Try to get South," I said. "But your husband will be arrested, will he not?" "We must try to go by the West." "I will give you a piece of advice, Mrs. Gilmer," he said, seriously. "Do not go to the ———— House in St. Louis. All the Army officers stay there and Capt. Gilmer would be recognized instantly. I will give you the address of a quiet little hotel on the river near the boat you will wish to take. It will be much safer." My story will show how greatly this counsel aided us, and I think also that it proves how little these officers realized we were bona fide enemies. The esprit de corps, so great then in the army, was stronger than any political opinion.

When we passed up the Southern Coast I longed ardently for the Sumter to take us. How convenient to be carried in to Savannah or Charleston, then unblockaded. What a cutting of all our knotty problems! No Pirate appeared conveniently, and in September we approached New York.

A brother officer, Mr. Merchant, came in the pilot boat and warned Capt. Gilmer that the papers for his arrest were at the Metropolitan Hotel (then quite an Army headquarters) and that he must drive from the pier and go—anywhere to get out of New York, even if he abandoned his baggage. There were some breathless escapes on the steamer wharf, but they all got off for Cincinnati before it was known in New York that the passengers were landed.

L. G.

Alas! I can not remember now all the details of this journey. How they went to the little hotel by the river in St. Louis; how they came down the river and then separated, Capt. Gilmer cutting across the country on horseback, Mrs. Gilmer and her little boy traveling as they could by boat, train, or wagon. To Cincinnati, Maj. Porter, her uncle, had sent money to the care of a former Savannahian, Mr. Law, who risked much in coming to see them even, and who warned them to move right on. In the end they both got to Atlanta and met, I believe, at the house of her sister, Mrs. George Hull.

L. P. M.

Charles Alexander to His Father.

Dear Father:—

Your kind letter was received three days ago, and as I have not had a chance to write home in some time I will try and improve the present one, poor as it is. The wind is blowing so that I have to keep one hand before my short piece of candle all the time to keep it from blowing out, and it is turning cold very fast. My hands are perfectly numb now. We had quite a cold snap here the same time you did in Washington; ice was plentiful one morning. Since then it has been quite warm again until tonight, when it rained a little and now is blowing off very cold.

I wish I had my hogs fat. I would like to kill some this morning.

Since I last wrote you Capt. Winn's family have moved to our place and are now living there. They wanted to move to their plantation to be near the Captain and Willie, and as my house was much more comfortable than theirs, I offered it to them, being glad to have an opportunity to return some of the many kindnesses I have received from them. They gladly accepted the offer and are now comfortably quartered there. I find it a great advantage to have them there for several reasons. Mrs. Winn is very kind in attending all cases of sickness on the plantation and in doing many little things, which relieves me very much of the anxiety in leaving the place; and she does many things for me in camp, which add very much to my comfort and convenience.

Camp life agrees with me finely. At first the exposure

and rough and dirty work went rather hard, but now I am used to it and never got along better in my life.

I wish you would let Ben make me a strong heavy pair of boots. There are none to be had in Savannah to fit me and the ones I have now are about to give out. I believe he has my measure, but if he has not, tell him to make them just a little large for Hillie and be sure to make them high enough in the instep. I want them strong and water tight.

How has the wine and vinegar I made in the summer turned out? None of you have ever mentioned this in any of your letters.

My fingers are so cold I can hardly hold my pen so I will put up for tonight.

With much love to all,
Yours affectionately,
CHARLIE.

E. P. Alexander to His Sister Clifford.

Headquarters Army of the Potomac,
Centreville, Va., Dec. 3, 1861

Dearest Mae:—

The *two* most delightful and *too* rare letters from Hattie and yourself, which reached me last night, have imposed such a burden of gratitude upon me, that to enjoy my rest to-night I must make immediate reply direct to you and thro' you to her. I came up to my room early to-night intending to give you the best part of the evening, but my next door neighbor, Prince Polignac, came in with a letter to read over to me to criticise the English, and we have talked and smoked, and the stove has smoked, and it is now after ten, and my eyes are almost watering, and a little cough is getting to be a big one so fast that I'm afraid it is not doing you justice not to defer your letter, but "Procrastination is the thief of Time," of which I have little to spare, so I think it better for both you and my conscience, the interested parties, that I should just apologize and proceed.

In the first place, Bessie and the Prodigy* are both well. Not having yet seen the latter, I fear I can give you but an inadequate idea of her wonderful pulchritude, which is admitted by all from whom I've heard on the subject—even by her mama. The descriptions sent to me have been a little irreconcilable in details from some cause, though on the whole satisfactory to one possessed of vanity. As a sample, Bessie writes "She is the sweetest - - - - baby - - full suit of long black hair - - avoirdupois 9 lbs. - - - the very blackest of eyes - - -

*Bessie Mason Alexander.

236

very red face - - - - no teeth yet - - - - exact image of her papa - - - affectionate wife, etc." You will notice the discrepancy which exists between some of these statements, but on this occasion I have concluded not to say anything about it to her. In her last letter she says the Doctor considers the dental destitution nothing to be alarmed at, and hopes he can cure it soon. To meet the requirements of this event, I have issued the following set of Infantry Regulations, which are to be more unalterable than the Koran: Ist, No daguerreotype, photograph, or any other unlikeness shall ever be taken of Prodige (her present name) before she is au fait in closing the oral aperture, and has overcome all wandering tendency in the visual organs. 2nd, The practice by her of gratuitous osculation shall be always discouraged, and the art kept a secret from her, especially before attaining the first acquirement mentioned above. 3rd, She is not to be killed by low-necked and short-sleeved dresses, and I bind myself to burn and destroy all with which any one may attack her.

Beyond, or rather within these points, I think her mama may be trusted, and she is to have absolute control. As for the swap you propose, although it would prevent any recurrence of any assertion of resemblance, my tastes in the matter of sex, as well as the wide-spread reputation of Prodige, while I never before even heard of the young Hull, render the thing impossible.

To say when I can go to see Bessie involves the answering of more questions than I can write, and to none of which can I give even a probable answer, but I fear it will not be before Christmas. I have'nt yet felt justified in even asking to go. We are still in daily expectation of an attack, that is the Generals are, and the Army is in position for it, though the men don't believe it. Our friends in Washington warn us earnestly to look out this week for a desperate attack by overwhelming numbers and there are facts which corroborate their views. We are very strong here, and if we can manage to fight here will have no objection. This is to be *the battle* here, and we feel very confident that Providence has not yet forsaken our banners. Our men never meet the enemy in scouts without routing them easily, and have acquired great morale from it, and McClellan seeing how his are losing by it, keeps always very near his lines. Our pickets go over two-thirds of the distance between us.

I suppose you have heard of our beautiful new Battle Flag and I wish you could have seen its presentation a few days since to Gen. Longstreet's Division. It was done with much formality and religious ceremony, and accompanied with the greatest enthusiasm among the Regiments and a striking *omen*. It was a very cloudy day but just as the order was read, committing the flag to the men, the sun broke out brightly on the stands of flags, and the arms and uniforms, making the most beautiful display and attracting everybody's attention by its suddenness.

Hilly is still with me, and Will in Richmond. No news of H's commission. I am going to build a log house for winter quarters as soon as I find out where they will be. I am trying to get board for Bessie in some railroad town near here, if possible, for the winter.

My cough has now changed into a sneeze, the smoke in my eyes is now a case of cold toes, and ten o'clock has given place to bed-time, so you must excuse, dearest Mae, the termination of this epistle, to which I now beg to lead you with the most delicate remembrances to Brother George, the usual compliments to enquiring friends, and the same heartfull of affection for yourself, which has been yours ever since I have been your

Brother

E. P. A.

James Hillhouse Alexander (*b.* June 6, 1840)
From a photograph by Dana taken about 1882.

Hillhouse Alexander to His Father.

Richmond, Va., June 30, 1862.

My dear Father:—

I telegraphed to you last night of the safety of all our family, and of the casualties of the Irvin Artillery,—the latter because I hoped to relieve the heart breaking anxiety of the community at home. I tried to telegraph you the night before but could not get in the office, so I wrote a few lines. I have not seen Porter since the battle began but have heard of him often. He is chiefly engaged ballooning and has not been in the fight. Brother was in on Friday, I believe, and came out safe. I hope he has written, or will write soon his personal experiences. I can only speak of my own. I joined Gen. Lawton as soon as he came near the scene of action and was with him all day Friday, the fight coming on, on one side, about an hour by sun that evening. His brigade was in the hottest part of the field, and it did excellent work, turning the tide in our favor, as I believe in the nick of time. His six regiments went cheering into the fight and it was not long before we had the advantage. It seemed as though it was certain doom to any man to go where we went, and how we ever did go there, and how we ever came out are wonders to me now. I never realized before what a close face to face battle with 50,000 men was, and when I got in I never expected that I could by any possibility get out again. We were hotly engaged for about an hour and a half, tho' it did not seem like more than 5 minutes. There was a perfect hail of lead and iron, and men fell like leaves in Autumn, and to my inexperienced view it seemed impossible for anybody to come out safe. I was about with the Staff all the time, each one doing his best to encourage the men and keep them up to the mark. I had my horse crippled by a spent ball, and my martingales torn off by a shell, and later a button cut from my coat tail by a ball. That was in the closest quarters we had and a soldier who was wounded and lying on the ground told me when it was done. He saw it he said, but I never felt it. Capt. Chivis of the Staff was shot through the heart, and Capt. Lawton was hit on the leg by a spent ball, which bruised him a little, and these were the only casualties on the Staff. Capt. Colley it seems was hit not only in the hip *slightly*, but also in the shoulder, the ball passing through and breaking two ribs, making a severe but not very dangerous wound. This is what I hear from his men. I could not find him myself.

The enemy broke before us about dark and we pursued some distance. I being on foot fell in with a regiment which I thought was one of our brigade but which was not, and when I found it out I was lost from Gen. Lawton and could not find him again till next morning. I slept on the ground with a Yankee blanket I picked up in the pursuit. On Saturday I left my wounded horse at a country house where I think she will soon recover, as the wound was but slight, the ball cutting the fore knee joint a little and making only a bad bruise. The horse belongs to Major Moses M. Toombs' Commissary, who lent him to me for the occasion. I pressed in service a horse from the farm house—a trifling little creature, which however, served to bring me back to Mr. Toombs where I found brother and the Irvin Artillery, and heard the sad results of the engagement they had.

This fighting which I saw myself was hotter than ever I imagined it could be, and now that I have taken so much trouble to look up a fight and have at last found one, I am satisfied. Next time I go into such a place it shall be in discharge of my duty, and if duty will suffer me to stay out, I will stay. It it all exciting enough while it is going on, and when I got once used to it I was not much concerned, but now that it is all over and I think of it and see the field and the blood and carnage I stepped over so lightly at the time, I am fully convinced that I was foolish to want to go into such business, for I don't want to be killed yet unless it is necessary. So the next time I won't look up a fight as I did this time, for it would be just throwing my life away for fun. I came in town last night thoroughly exhausted and worn out. The intense excitement so long continued and all the dreadful sights I witnessed, which were finally all brought home to me by seeing my own friends from the camp lying so mangled and bloody, have unstrung my nerves completely. I was quite sick last night and this morning, but after sleeping quietly for several hours I feel quite recovered now. Tomorrow I will go out to Gen. Toombs to find brother or else look up Porter and see how they are getting on. I don't know what is going on while I am here. The City is so excited I can't find out any reliable news. I hope to get through my indoor duties for the Signal Corps as soon as I can find a quiet hour to report finally to Mr. Randolph that my work is done. He could not think of anything but the great fight progressing now if I were to go to him. When I can report to him I hope I will be relieved and ordered to the field. I am applying to be sent with Gen. Lawton and he will apply for me he says.

I received today your letter of June 25. It came in strangely—a letter so full of quiet things and home pleasures on the busy matters here. How I would like to be at home *even a day* to see all the dear ones there! I can almost wish I had a nice little wound of honor to go home on a while. I thought of you all at home so often while surrounded recently by the dreadful scenes of battle. God has favored us greatly up to this time and we have promise of a complete and glorious victory now in 24 hours, but verily the price has been dearly paid for our dead and wounded cover the earth for miles around. I feel tho' that nothing is too dear to give for our country.

Love—very much love to all at home. My brothers would join if they knew I was writing.

Goodbye—

Affectionately,

J. H. A.

P. S.

My address is box 998, Richmond, Va. I send a trophy captured in the Yankee camps on Friday night.

The Battle of Fredericksburg.

E. P. Alexander to His Father.

Dear Father:—

I've just finished such an eventful week that I almost despair of being able to give you any adequate idea in a letter of all its occurrences, but will, nevertheless, try what can be done in my brief leisure for a letter.

You know already the general position of the armies preceding the commencement of active hostilities. I had posted most of the Artillery and had reserved for my own Battery the open ground between Fredericksburg and Falmouth, (one mile above Fredericksburg) where I thought the enemy would make his most earnest efforts, and had made little works for a few of my guns on its most exposed and commanding positions. On the night of the 10th Gen. Longstreet gave us intimation that the ball would open the next day, and about two hours before dawn the signal guns indicating an attack by the enemy were fired. Our tents were immediately struck and wagons loaded and moved out on the road out of range, while the Batteries moved into a hollow immediately in rear of their positions, except two which occupied the pits we had dug at once. By this time a scattering musketry fire on the banks of the river and in town, with a gradually increasing Artillery fire of the enemy, told of his efforts to construct bridges. Our men held the town, however, so well that it was night before the enemy could complete his bridges and cross over. In the meanwhile we had shelled the town with 145 guns nearly all day. The firing was the heaviest I ever heard and the poor Burg is riddled and considerably burnt. The spectacle was a grand one as you may imagine. That night we all slept at our posts, expecting the grand attack at dawn, but, tho' he had built five bridges, the enemy was all day in crossing his immense force. I opened one battery down the streets occasionally thro' the day and elicited warm responses from the other side, but without suffering any, and we spent Friday night as we had the night before. On Saturday morning a heavy attack was made on the right of our line near the R. R., and very soon afterward a similar one on a little bluff and range of hills on the outskirts of the town where we had a good many guns in pits and some infantry behind stonewalls and in gullies, etc. The position is called in the papers "impregnable," but it is in reality of scarcely ordinary strength, and was but as an outpost to our real "line" which ran along a secondary range of hills, half a mile back of it. The Washington Artillery in these pits and our infantry repulsed this attack and several others, in which I assisted with two Batteries coming behind them on the second range of hills and firing over their heads. I also searched for their pontoon bridges with some "Napoleon" 12 Pr. Guns and found, as I have since seen, the most important one. What damage I did I don't know, but I drew on me the fire of three batteries as hot as they could kindle it, and they kept it up on the position I had taken all day long,—hours after I had gone elsewhere.

About 3:30 P. M. the Washington Artillery ran short of ammunition and sent for me to relieve them, which I did under the heaviest fire I ever saw. Innumerable guns in every quarter fired over the slope outside of the pits, and the houses and streets of the town were filled with infantry who kept the air so full of minie balls that their sound was as constant as the flow of water. I lost fourteen horses and one man killed and a few wounded in running in, but once in we were comparatively safe. The enemy saw the Washington Artillery leaving and thought we had given it up and gave a loud hurrah and dashed at us again in immense columns, but my chests were full of canister and everything else, and the fire I kindled soon showed them their mistake. They pressed it, however, very hard and by dark, when they ceased their firing, my guns had averaged 100 rounds a piece at them. The infantry under us said that we killed more than the Washington Artillery had during the whole day.

About an hour after dark the enemy marched what we hear was Sykes Division of Regulars and there was great cheering in their lines, shortly after which they made another dash at us. We could see nothing but the flashes of their guns, and could scarcely aim at them, but we poured out one second case shot and canister loose in the dark, and their prisoners call that repulse the bloodiest of the whole action. They certainly gave it up very soon and their flashes died out, after which I gave them a few farewell shots, and then we had a quiet night of it. One of my best men in the same pit with myself was killed in this action while sighting a load of canister. The next morning we expected a renewal of the engagement, but the entire day passed off with only an annoying fire of sharpshooters from the town and a continuous shelling of their heavy batteries across the river, to which we did not reply at all, saving our ammunition for their infantry. That night I got two Napoleon guns in a ravine on our left, from which I could see their reserves of the front line of skirmishers and sharpshooters lying behind some banks, and on Monday morning I had my own fun opening on their flank to their entire surprise. They stood a few rounds and then broke and ran for the City. This brought them in sight of our infantry and the Artillery directly in front of them, and the mercy that they showed them was no great thing, you may be sure. Before this, however, I had taken a special shot with a 24 Pr. Howitzer at some extremely annoying sharpshooters who had loop-holed a brick tannery very close to our lines and hurt many men. I tore a hole two feet square in the wall beside the most important loop-hole and killed the sharpshooter at it and scattered about a hod of bricks and fragments of shell over the room, so that not another shot was fired from the building.

We had replenished our ammunition the night before and I went along the line firing the different guns at various squads and regiments of them all day. The next day we were *sure* they would come at us again, but to our surprise and great disappointment the morning showed them all on the far side of the river, and their bridges taken up, except one which is cast off and floats against the other shore. Their repulse on the right has been as complete as the one in front of the town, and the ground everywhere is so strong that Burnside is afraid to face the music. His enormous force is now encamped where it was before, and for ten square miles, at least, the smoke hangs over his crowded camps like over a city on fire.

The fruits of our victory are entirely *moral* but most important. If his men fought as well as *any* of ours, he would have carried the position at Marye's house at the *first* assault, and I don't think they will ever fight as well again. Of the condition of the City you will doubtless read in the papers, so I will only say that it is the saddest sight of the war. The house of a cousin of Bessie's living there was pierced with about forty shell, many of them exploding, and was then completely gutted of even the doors by the Yankees. What is going to be done next, it is useless to conjecture in a letter, and so I will leave that to be told in my next.

The weather is now bitter cold and a severe snow-storm preceded the fighting. I, however, manage to keep very comfortable for camp-life in the Winter. Since my last I have received one letter from you, which having been sent to Bessie, I can not *answer* now, if any answer is needed. I remember, however, in it your kind invitation to come South and pay you a visit. Ah, would not I do it if I could!—but if I get seven days to run down to Richmond and see Bessie, it will be the height of my boldest hopes at present, and just seven times as much as I have ever gotten since the war commenced.

Ask Will what ever became of the bottle of whiskey sent for me with the brandy, for if he drank it, I will expect him to bring me on a gallon to make it up. Please send by him my big blue overcoat to Bessie. I left it in my big chest. My dinner is waiting for me and I must come to a close or my pork will get cold.

Much love to all the family in communication with you, not forgetting Mammy, and a Merry Christmas and a Happy New Year all around.

Ever, Dear Father, your affectionate son,

E. P A.

P. S.

I forgot to narrate that my "horse de combat" Dixie, was somewhat lacerated with a piece of shell near her caudal appendage, but is none of the worse for it. Another whole one lit between her feet and I thought for a moment that we were about to have another balloon ascension, but it fortunately failed to explode.

Camp near Fredericksburg,
Thursday, Dec. 18, 1862.

Battle of Gettysburg.

E. P. Alexander to His Father.

Dear Father:—

The last letter of mine which you have probably seen was written to Cliff on the 1st inst. from near Greenwood, Pa., on the pike from Chambersburg to Gettysburg, and fifteen miles from the latter place. While I was writing that letter the battle had already commenced at Gettysburg between A. P. Hill who came down from Carlisle, and three corps of the enemy who came up from Frederick City. At dark on the 1st we received orders to march at 2:30 A. M. on the 2nd for Gettysburg, and at 9 A. M. that morning we were on the field. Gen. Longstreet's corps was ordered to attack the enemy's left, and I was directed to assume command of all of his artillery on the field, three battalions including my own. Much time was occupied in getting position, but about 4 P. M. all was ready and the ball opened in earnest. I occupied myself personally with my own and Cabell's battalion, which I got into position within six hundred yards of the enemy's line of battle, sending the third battalion (Henry's) to our right flank with Hood's Division.

Our fight was the severest and bloodiest artillery fight I ever saw, four companies of my battalion losing in forty minutes as much as the whole battalion lost at Sharpsburg, which was the bloodiest of all previous battles. My mare Dixie was severely cut in the thigh by a fragment of shell, and I got a ball thro' pants and drawers, grazing my right knee, but the skin was not broken. We silenced the enemy's batteries, however, and killed many of their infantry supports in this time, and then our infantry charged and we limbered up what guns we were able to move and advanced with them, and occupied the enemy's line, opening on their flying troops and artillery and causing them to abandon several guns. They retreated about three-fourths of a mile, to a high ridge and very strong position, where they were reinforced and stood, repulsing our infantry line which had followed them vigorously under our artillery fire, tho' but a single weak line. Our guns now occupied their original positions and we fought a duel with them until dark with much effect on them, but our infantry did not attempt another charge.

It was in this charge that Barksdale was killed, leading his men most gallantly. He had just before lent me four men to help work my guns which were getting short-handed, and two of them were killed at the guns.

I slept that night among the guns in position on the field, and at day received orders to take command of all the guns in the vicinity and prepare for a grand assault on the enemy's position. I accordingly put seventy-five pieces in position bearing on the enemy's batteries and the point of attack, and nine others in reserve.

The attack was ordered by Gen. Lee, though Gen. Longstreet was opposed to it as the enemy's position was so powerful, entirely sweeping the 1200 yards over which we had to advance, that it was of doubtful success. Pickett's Division was to make the charge—unsupported it afterwards appeared in rear—and Pettigrew's Division of A. P. Hill's Corps was to go on his left. I was ordered to take a position to observe the effect of our artillery fire, and at the proper moment to give* Pickett and Pettigrew the order to charge, when my nine reserve guns and all that could of the seventy-five in line were to advance also. Accordingly when all was ready I took my position and gave the signal and immediately my batteries all opened, aided, too, by about fifty or sixty

*See "Military Memoirs of A Confederate," by Gen. E. P. Alexander. Chapter XVIII.

guns of A. P. Hills' corps on our left. The enemy replied
with a line of batteries a mile long and the fight which
followed was, as you may suppose, something to be
remembered. Smoke soon hid almost everything. The
firing was as rapid as musketry, and shot and shell flew
in flocks. I stood behind a tree with my glass and watched
the Yankee line of fire carefully for forty minutes, when
there being no material diminution of it, and our ammunition, I knew, burning low, I sent word to Pickett, and
Pettigrew also, that they must advance then if at all,
before our ammunition burnt out. Five minutes afterwards
the most formidable Yankee batteries limbered up and
traveled. I waited five minutes more to see if others
were going to replace them, but none came and there
was a gap of four hundred yards at least in their line. I
then sent two other messengers to Pickett to hurry up
as our fire was already slackening materially, but it was
still, at least, five and I believe ten minutes before his
lines went thro' my guns and then our ammunition was
reduced from five to fifteen rounds per gun. I had sent
for my reserved nine guns, but some General, I have
never found out who, had sent them to some other position
and they could not be found. I collected a few of the
most serviceable guns near me and rushed them on after
the infantry for a short distance, when Pettigrew's Division
on Pickett's left broke and fell back under the fire, the
enemy having brought up new batteries, and a strong
force advancing against both his flanks as he went into
their lines in front and took their guns. Those on the
right were nearest me and I turned my guns on them
and drove them back, but those on the left, assisted by
their reserves in his front, broke Pickett's lines and his
Division fell back in disorder, losing many prisoners and
colors. Had he been properly supported the result would
have been very different, for the charge was as gallant
as was ever made.

That ended the fighting except some desultory artillery

fighting. We slept on the same ground that night. The next morning we fell back to our original lines and on the night of the 4th the whole army marched in retreat, almost entirely out of artillery ammunition, and leaving many wounded, across by Fairfield, Monterey Springs, and Waterloo to Hagerstown, where we encamped on the night of the 6th, just after terrible night and day marches thro' constant rain and mud, with jaded and insufficient teams.

On the 9th the enemy appeared in our front and we took line of battle and offered fight for four days, which, however, they declined.

On the night of the 13th, having finished a ponton-bridge (the river was too high to ford), we recrossed the Potomac and are now encamped about 12 miles in front of Winchester.

Our campaign has cost us in killed, wounded, prisoners and sick about 20,000 men, but we are receiving reinforcements, ammunition, and supplies, and are again in fine fighting trim. Loss in my battalion was 131 men and 101 horses. I do not think we can ever successfully invade, the ammunition question alone being enough to prevent it. Moreover, our army is not large enough to stand the casualties even of a victory in the enemy's country.

There are many interesting incidents which I would like to write you, but time and space are wanting. We have had awful marches and very hard fare and are reduced to such a small allowance of transportation that we are living anything but comfortably. I am now commanding my own battalion and the Washington Artillery as the reserve of Longstreet's Corps. Frank Huger, my Major, is a fine fellow, first rate officer, and very pleasant companion. We mess together with an ex-English Captain Winthrop who has espoused our cause, and is assigned to me to be made useful generally. He is as agreeable a companion as any Englishman can be.

Our next move I can't conjecture, tho' I think Gen. Lee means fight, and we are all anxious for it, thinking that we had not a fair showing at Gettysburg. The enemy must have suffered very heavily to have been afraid to harass our retreat and to recoil from our line at Hagerstown from the 9th to the 13th. We are listening with much interest to hear from the West and Charleston. The loss of small arms at Vicksburg and Port Hudson is a calamity, tho' the loss of the positions, I think, is of no importance at all, and on the exchange list we are so far ahead that we can get the services of the men again as soon as we can arm them. The river has been worthless to us for a year and the Yankees will find it worthless to them, as the market on its shores no longer exists, and its sole remaining use is as a highway to Europe, and our guerrillas will soon put a stop to any travel except ironclad. They are now attacking Charleston in the only feasible way and I watch the result there with interest. With the "opening of the Mississippi River," I even hope that the West will lose interest in the further prosecution of the war.

I received a few days ago Hilly's "cards," and extend herewith my warmest congratulations and best wishes. Their constancy deserves reward.

My last news from Bessie was the 7th inst, when she was well and as comfortable and happy, as far as surroundings are concerned, as could be, tho' quite the reverse mentally as she had heard nothing of me since the Battle. Capt. Woolfolk, at whose house she is staying, was badly wounded in the shoulder with a shell, and has gone home much to my envy.

For my new Adjutant I hope to get Lieut. Haskell of South Carolina, one of my particular friends.

Reports just in say that the enemy is advancing from Harper's Ferry, and part of our army is moving towards Charleston, and I must close and get ready to receive orders myself.

Much love to each and all at home. You don't know how I long to see you all again and how brightly I anticipate peace and its re-union. God grant that it may not be long and that there may be none missing from our circle, which His mercy has so signally spared thus far.

Ever, dear Father, your affectionate son,

E. P. A.

Pickett's Charge at the Battle of Gettysburg.*

GEN. LONGSTREET TO COL. ALEXANDER.

About 12 M.

Hd Qrs. July 3d—'63.

Colonel. If the Artillery fire does not have the effect to drive off the enemy or greatly demoralize him, so as to make our effort pretty certain, I would prefer that you should not advise Gen Pickett to make the charge. I shall rely a great deal upon your good judgment to determine the matter, & shall expect you to let Gen Pickett know when the moment offers. Most respectf'y

J. LONGSTREET
Lt. Genl. Comdg.

Col E P Alexander
Arty.

COL. ALEXANDER'S REPLY.

Near Gettsburg July 3 1863.

Lt Genl. Longstreet, Comdg.

General. I will only be able to judge of the effect of our fire on the enemy by his return fire as his infantry is but little exposed to view, and the smoke will obscure the field. If, as I infer from your note, there is any alternative to this attack, it should be carefully considered before opening our fire, for it will take all the Arty ammunition we have left to test this one thoroughly & if result is unfavorable we will have none left for another effort

*Copied from General Longstreet's original letters in General Alexander's scrap-book and from General Alexander's copies of his own letters.

& even if this is entirely successful it can only be so at a very bloody cost.

Very respectfy yours
E. P. ALEXANDER
Col. Arty

GEN. LONGSTREET'S LETTER.

About 12:30 P. M.
Hd Qrs July 3 1863

Colonel.

The intention is to advance the Inf: if the Arty has the desired effect of driving the enemy off, or, having other effect such as to warrant us in making the attack. When that moment arrives advise Gen. P. and of course advance such artillery as you can use in aiding the attack.

Most Respectfy
J. LONGSTREET
Lt. Genl Comdg.

Col. Alexander.

COL. ALEXANDER'S LETTER.

About 12:40 P. M.
Near Gettsburg, July 3, 1863.

Lt. Genl Longstreet Comdg.

General   When our Arty fire is at its best, I will advise Gen Pickett to advance.

Very respfy yours
E. P. ALEXANDER
Col Arty.

COL. ALEXANDER TO GEN. PICKETT.

1:25 P. M. July 3, 1863.

General.

If you are to advance at all, you must come at once, or we will not be able to support you as we ought.   But

255

the enemy's fire has not slackened materially, & there are still 18 guns firing from the cemetery

Respfy yours

E. P. ALEXANDER,

Col Arty.

COL. ALEXANDER TO GEN. PICKETT.

July 3, 1863, 1:40 P. M.

To Genl Pickett. The 18 guns have been driven off For God's sake come on quick, or we cannot support you. Ammunition nearly out.

E. P. ALEXANDER,

Col Arty.

CHARLES ATWOOD ALEXANDER (*b*. November 4, 1838)
From a photograph by C. W. Motes of Atlanta.

Harriet Cumming to Her Sister Clifford.

Savannah, Dec. 23rd 63.
Tuesday night.

I'm most too sleepy to write to you tonight, old Sweet, but I have been in your debt already too long. I dont have time to write except at night, and oft times I am too sleepy to attend to it then.

Thursday night. It's a melancholy truth, My dear, that I went to sleep with my pen in my hand on Tuesday night, thereby proving the truth of the proposition with which I set out—I just could'nt keep awake. Last night we had to go to Uncle's for Ida and Charley to say goodbye; and tonight I am writing against tide—having had to fortify myself with two cups of green tea, to allow even a hope of being able to get thro with a letter. My little Junior has a vicious propensity for waking before day and keeping me in attendance on his humors till it is too late to go to sleep again. It is that that makes me so sleepy-headed at night. Tonight however I have a double-barrelled excuse—for my breakfast bell rung this morning before six o'clock to enable Charley and Ida to make a timely start for Liberty. They have gone to those delectable regions to spend Christmas and kill hogs. Charley has applied for a thirty days furlough, to enable him to look after that important work on both his plantations—and from Liberty he hopes to go to Mitchell. He selected Christmas, thinking it well to have some white person on the place at that season. Wallace went to Augusta on Tuesday to look after some of "Mother Bank's" business, and is to return tomorrow morning. So tonight I am all alone. I took my solitary cup of tea

257

and eat my cracker in haste that I might seek your sweet society before I get too sleepy. When I have done this, I shall go upstairs and perform the duties of Santa Claus to the best of my ability—tho there's not the pleasure in it that there usually is when Wallace helps me, and when I have "full and plenty" to share out. I could'nt let the darkies hang up their stockings as usual this year—for with candy at six dollars a pound and apples 75 cts. a piece, I could'nt even furnish them those luxuries. Sallie and Mary have hung up theirs, and I have some few little trifles for them; but my preparations for making gifts dont go much beyond that. I had a little loaf of cake baked for Henry and Loulie—and I have some stockings for Cora and Maria—That's all—To make it up to the darkies, I give them a certain amount of provision towards a quilting party that they want to have on Monday night. The colored singing-class, that have had the use of our kitchen for two nights in the week for a year past, have sent a present here for Wallace—a plain white and gilt cup and saucer, (for which they paid $15!) and a fine gobbler for Christmas dinner— Then this afternoon he had a most valuable Christmas present of a hamper basket, containing a sack of salt (two bushels) and a half dozen fine large spare-ribs to rejoice the soul of his cracker wife.— Wont that be a sweet morsel under my tongue! I dont know who sent it—but suppose it must be either Joe Clay or Gaston Allen—the latter having promised him a sack of salt of his own making, some time ago— That will be the beginning and the end of Christmas presents with us, I imagine—tho two or three outside friends have sent little presents here for Sallie and Mary.

We have the promise now of a clear and very cold day. Wallace and I are to dine with Auntie as usual. The poor fellow will have a cold ride of it tonight. As I sit here alone tonight, writing to you, old times come back to me— Christmas eves of long, long ago— I can no more realize that I am the same person that used to write to you in those years long past, and that used to enjoy everything belonging to this season so much, when we shared its duties and its pleasures. Cliffie my darling love, very pleasant hast thou been unto me, My Sister, my Friend. Thank God, in all Time's changes there's never been any *there* —and as I sit here tonight, a happy contented Matron with my children's stockings hanging in my room upstairs, I write to you just as freely and out of as loving a heart as in those dear girlish days. When I look at my two daughters and wish good things for their future, I hope for them that they may be to each other thro' life, what you and I have been. I'm sure that for more than twenty years, there has never been an unkind tho't or feeling to mar the pleasure of our intercourse—not even when seven-pence mashers had caused a strange and unaccountable silence on my part!

H.

Sarah Lawton to Her Sister Clifford.

Richmond—May 9. Monday. Mr. Lawton came up-stairs after dinner and said to me "I have made arrange-ments for all of you to leave, day-after-tomorrow." It came like a thunder-clap upon me. Our arms had seemed so successful that we were beginning to breathe freely and to think the enemy were foiled. At least *I* cannot go away.

May 10. Tired and sick tonight—after a sad and busy day—preparing the children to go—they are all ready now. Corinne was bitterly opposed to going—but her father talked to her a long time and she now seems cheerful and reconciled.

May 11. They are gone. I feel sad and desolate enough—but have not time to indulge it. I must pack my trunks, so as to be ready for anything. Paul is very useful. Under my direction, he can do all the packing.

Thursday, 12th. Rain—but I went visiting. I had been at home for several days and knew little of the state of feeling in town. We heard last night that the children had safely reached the end of their railroad journey, so I felt relieved about them. Mr. Lawton was kept up late last night and waked up early this morning by business connected with getting a train of corn thro' to Gen. Lee's Army. Well, I went visiting. I went first to Mrs. S's—found her tete a tete with Mr. T.—made the acquaintance of that silver tongued Frenchman and learned from his magnetic eyes the secret of his power over the bewitching and bewitched lady.

I learned that on Tuesday night there was great alarm in the city. Many ladies sat up all night, dressed in all their best clothes with their jewelry on. Congressmen besieged the war department all night—so that Gen. Bragg was called out of bed to go down to them after midnight. We knew nothing of all the excitement—absorbed in the grief of our expected family parting. We slept as we best could each in our quiet chamber.

I went to see Mrs. Field—found her looking very sad and anxious. Came home by the Gibson's and Grattan's —learned that old Mr. Grattan had just returned from his long detention at Wilmington—had walked part of the way —but as soon as he reached home, began to prepare to go out with the militia.

Friday—13th. Early this morning we were waked by the tidings that the Danville road was cut. We next learned that Gen. Stuart was dead—sad news. After break-fast I had a trunk or two to pack—while thus engaged, Mrs. Stanard sent for me to sit the morning with her. About one o'c I set out to go to her home—went by the Grattan's to leave a bottle of wine for Mr. G., this led me to Col. Preston's. I found three of the young ladies sitting on the steps, sewing and darning stockings—they stayed there all day, *to hear the news*. I had a very pleasant morning with Mrs. Stanard and returned home just before Mr. Lawton and the Doctor came to dinner. Mr. L. hurried off soon to be pall-bearer at Gen. Stuart's funeral. Not long after, the Doctor returned to his office —rain set in—I had a dreary afternoon—we are all alone this evening—a rare occurrence. The gentlemen are talking about how terrified the Congressmen are—how anxious to get horses. We are now hemmed in on all sides.

Sunday 15th. I could not write yesterday evening, for we went to spend it at Judge Perkins. I had heard that Mrs. Perkins was very uneasy—or rather that some-body was laughing and saying that Mrs. Bragg was telling how uneasy Mrs. P. was and Mrs. P. was telling how uneasy Mrs. Bragg was. So I wanted to see her. While we were out, Will and Lucy came here with a telegram from Porter announcing all safe after three days hard fighting.

The excitements yesterday were the cannonnading at Drury's Bluff—and the impressment of negroes to work on the fortifications. Jake was caught. Paul and Lysander took flight and hid—and all day Paul did not dare go out.

There is much feeling against Gen. Bragg and about Pemberton's being put in command of the artillery around the city. Members of Congress are much excited and there is indignation against the President on his account.

Today we had some cannonading at Drury's again. Beauregard is preparing to give the enemy battle. We expect a heavy fight in a day or two. A train went off on the Central Road today. Several families left on it, en route for the South—with them Fannie Gay went and I hope is at home this evening. Mr. Carmichael, Will and Lucy have been in to spend the evening. The Doctor is gone to sit up all the night at the office. He and I took a little walk this afternoon, while Gen. Lawton was out, hunting up the Georgia M. C. All nature looked her loveliest. This beautiful city is dressed in her fairest robe of leaves and flowers—and amid all the commotion of men, we drew a lesson of peace from gazing awhile on these works of creation. The God of creation is the God of Providence too—and all will be well, however it may end.

Wednesday 25. For a week we have been more quiet. Business begins to receive attention. Letters are once more delivered. We are expecting, however, daily to hear of a terrible battle between Lee and Grant. We have all been much excited by the tidings that Gen. Johnston has retreated below Marietta and abandoned upper Georgia.

Friday, 27. 10½ P. M. Yesterday evening we had a succession of visitors. Mr. John Gilmer came early, about six or seven o'c. then Drs. Moore and Leyburn, then Mr. Robt. Barnwell of S. C., then Maj. Basinger, and last Mrs. Gen. Huger, son and daughter. I like Mr. Gilmer, he is a straightforward, earnest man and commands respect and friendly feeling at once.

Today I have been sewing all morning—and to prayer-meeting this afternoon. Col Urquhart dropped in to tea—saying he had to sit up all night in Gen. Bragg's office and he wanted a cup of my nice tea. My tea is very popular and it gives me so much pleasure to have it enjoyed by my friends. The Col was advising me to leave Richmond in view of the approach of the contending armies towards the city. His advice made me feel as if it would scarcely be wise in us to bring the children home —of wh' I am so sorry. I am becoming so anxious to see them.

Richmond

May 30—Sunday.

9½ P. M. Gen. Lawton has just returned from a long ride. He has been out to Gen. Lee's headquarters at Atlee Station, 10 miles from town. He reports the Gen. very unwell and looking worn down. No wonder—the wonder is that he has kept up so long, with so intense a strain upon his mental powers. Gen. Lee seems to expect that the enemy will attack him tomorrow. He telegraphed for Beauregard who went up to him this afternoon. Butler is said to have been heavily reinforced— and I suppose Beauregard will not venture to stay long away from his command. We are all discussing the probability that Grant will not attack, but will cross the Chickahominy, thus forcing Gen. Lee to the city. A siege is far more to be dreaded by us than a battle.

I was greatly shocked this evening, as I was standing under the front door, by a gentleman coming up and (introducing himself as a Member of the Y. M. C.) saying he came to inform Gen. Lawton that Col. Millen of Sav'h, was killed yesterday and his body had come in with a cavalry escort for immediate interment. Gen. Lawton had left, so could not join in the last rites to his old friend.

Mr. Lawton was saying how alone Gen. Lee seems to be in his responsibilities. Ewell is out of the field—

broken down, Jackson gone, Longstreet wounded—So few on whom he can rely for counsel. Porter is on the Mechanicsville road—ten miles off. I feel quite excited at the idea of their all being so near us.

June 12. Sunday night. We are just from church. Gen. L., Lulu, the Doctor and I. Since I wrote last, two weeks have passed. We have had the sorrow of poor Ed Willis' death. He was mortally wounded May 30 and died next day. His body was brought here and sojourned one night with us on its way South. We have had Col. Berry with us, sick and wounded—also Charlie Lawton—they left us yesterday, transferred to hospitals nearer home.

The children all came home on the 3d. How glad I was to get them home again! they came looking so well and so delighted to return. We have had a lull in military excitement for several days. Grant seems to be preparing for a siege. Our news from the Valley is discouraging—raiders in possession of Staunton and Lexington and threatening Lynchburg. I am anxious to hear from our friends, the Gays. I wonder whether they fled from home before the approach of the Yankees or whether they stayed to brave the devastation. My housekeeping is seriously interfered with by being cut off from Staunton—whence came my supplies of eggs, butter, &c.

June 19. Sunday. My record seems of late to be confined to Sunday nights. It seems very difficult to write these warm evenings. Nearly always there are visitors and when there are none—we are sitting out on the porch. Richmond has been full of excitement and rumors all day. The enemy have been beleaguering Petersburg and shelling it. Refugees from there have been coming here and there are uncertain tidings of great battles—but nothing authentic is known. We here, feel still very calm and cheerful and never think on the ifs of Grant's success. Household matters still fill up my daily life, as in peace times, and the struggle to live comfortably requires considerable effort and forethought. We continue to have all our wants supplied. I send to market every morning and get fresh vegetables. We have fresh meat in small quantities, some two or three times a week—the rest of the time, ham. I will append my market bills for a week. Wednesday, 5½ lbs. of veal, $33.00. 1 peck green peas $12. Thursday. Lettuce $1.50. Cherries, 2 qts. for $3.00. Friday, Squash, 1 doz. for $6. Asparagus, $3.00. Saturday, Snap beans, $4. gooseberries $2.00. Butter, 4 lbs. for $48.00. Sunday and Monday— nothing. Tuesday, Lettuce $1.50. Beans $4, Raspberries $20.

We have been to church this morning and tonight. I think all the sermons we hear now, show want of thought. Our ministers have no time for study—they are so engaged with visits to the afflicted, to hospitals, to the wounded and with funerals.

Tuesday 21. Yesterday I heard that poor Major Alston died out at Jackson Hospital. Several friends would have taken him to their houses but he was too ill to be moved— so after the poor tabernacle of clay had suffered its last pang and the spirit had departed, it was removed to Mr. Miles' house, and lay there to receive the last sorrowful tributes of friends. A courier came here yesterday from poor Joe McAllister's command, confirming the tidings that he was killed in the battle of the 12th. Last week we walked, about sundown one afternoon, to the Armory to see Mrs. Gorgas. She has just heard that her brother-in-law was severely wounded in the same fight. Mrs. Bayne, her sister, was there and was telling of all the care and trouble she had with a wounded officer who was staying with her. The air is full of sorrowful tales. At Mrs. Gorgas' I found Mrs. James Alfred Jones, who is my special admiration of all the ladies I have met in Richmond. She resembles Mrs. Ward in style, manner and appearance, which is perhaps one secret of her attractions in my eyes. We generally sit with her at Dr. Moores' church. She was spending the evening with Mrs. Gorgas, and being invited, we also stayed to tea and spent the evening.

Friday—June 24. Very hot and dry weather. All our railroads cut. Enemy fortifying on the Weldon road. I am busy with a woman who sews for me by the day, getting the girls' work done and some dresses made for myself. The Gen'l. getting very anxious about the supplies of corn for the Army. The Doctor working hard with the sick and wounded at Jackson Hospital. 2300 patients there—thermometer at 92. Daily prayer meetings. I could not go this week; they were held too far off.

June 25th. Lucy* and baby went in the country yesterday very sick—but we hope much from change.

I understand that reports are current in the Army that Gen. Johnston has been hampered in his movements by orders from Richmond &c &c—a sort of effort to throw the responsibility of his retrograde movement on Gen. Bragg. It is all false—he has had all possible resources put at his command—and Bragg has shown every disposition to have him furnished with all he desired—and the Gov't here was *very anxious* for him to *move forward* into Tennessee—and *did all but order* him to do it. That they could not do.

S.

---

*Second wife of William Felix Alexander.

Sarah Lawton to Her Sister Louisa.

Richmond, Va., May 16, 1864.

Mr. Carmichael of Augusta was here last night, my dear sister, and said he would try to go South to-morrow, so I avail myself of the opportunity to write, as I know you will all be anxious to hear from us. I can not write much, as I must write to father, to Cliff, to grandfather, and to William* also. We have no mails now at all, and nearly all places of business are closed. I have gone once more thro' a general packing up, and my things are all in trunks ready for, we know not what. People in general have not done so and few seem to think of moving, but in certain contingencies Mr. Lawton says I must go, so I am prepared. I am, however, very unwilling to leave my "things" to the mercy of the negroes and the fortunes of a disorganized city. "What would man be," says Carlyle, "without his blankets," and what would I be without mine; not to speak of those supplies for the inner man, which I now husband so carefully and distribute in the house and out of the house where they are needed.

We directed Corinne to write to you from Halifax C. H. where they all four went (with Mary and Milton) to stay at Maj. Carrington's, till we can decide whether they can safely return, or must go on South. The roar of artillery is shaking the air today, and we hear that Beauregard is giving them battle on the South Side. Custis Lee has at last a chance and is there with his city troops, some 1500. Gen Ransom commands one wing. Many people augur ill to the city, from the fact that Bragg

---

*Brother of A. R. Lawton.

and Pemberton are commanding here — Bragg as Chief, and Pemberton Chief of Artillery. But on the whole, there is great confidence and calmness, and people smile on danger and death, as only repeated acquaintance with both could enable them to do. Stuart's death was received with a mingled sadness and sense of glory, truly touching. He was personally much beloved.

We have just had a cheerful, brave letter from Ed. He says Eddie Willis is *slightly* wounded in the shoulder. All our officers, whom we know, seem to be covering themselves with honor. Oh! who would wish a nobler life or death! Men who have been thro' such things will be fit to inaugurate a millennium! In such thoughts I realize the glory, but yesterday I felt the horrors of these dreadful days, when at the street corner, coming from church, I encountered a procession of hundreds of the wounded just come down on the Fredericksburg road and marching (if marching that could be called) to the hospital So haggard, so emaciated, so suffering, so ragged, so uncared for, they looked, that I said to myself, "Can these be the materials of that heroic army, the world's wonder!"

I have written too much. I am never at all excited till I begin to write. I have felt for many days that I *could not* do it, and indeed have been too busy preparing the children to go and then packing myself. Love to all at Wallace's. I received Hattie's note some two weeks ago. Love to dear uncle and auntie and all at your house. We hope brother Gilmer is now resting and recruiting. Felix and Lucy are well. He talks of sending Lucy South with Mrs. Gilmer, but is hesitating. They had the baby christened yesterday after church at their own home. He is a lovely child.

Goodbye, dear Sister, and much love from

S. A. L.

Sarah Lawton to Her Sister Clifford.

Richmond Sept. 7 1864.
Wednesday.

My dearest Cliffie,

I have no record of having written to you since the 29th of June. In that time great changes have occurred— but we are so accustomed to stirring events that they no longer excite us. For my one part, I look tranquilly on all the occurrences of these momentous days, sure that a Hand directs them which will bring all things right at last—and therefore neither my hopes or fears are ever great, nor my desire fixed on any special course of events —as in reading a novel by some master-writer, the apparent untowardness of circumstances which surround the hero and heroine never deprives me of the assurance that all will yet end well, and these very ill pranks of fortune be made to contribute to a prosperous and happy denouement. In our daily prayer-meetings here, it is the custom for some of our most earnest and devout leaders to lay out military programmes for Him who rules in the armies of earth and heaven, and to implore him earnestly that Sherman's communications with his rear may be interrupted —that Grant's sharpshooters may not prove so very accurate in their aim—that Atlanta and Petersburg might not fall, nor the Weldon road get into the enemy's possession. But for my own part I never feel like joining in such prayers—not because I think we may not freely spread our wants and desires before the Mercy-seat—but because *I do not know what we want*—it may not be what we *wish*—and so I prefer to say "Our Father, thy kingdom come—thy will be done—remember us with the favor that thou bearest unto thy people—oh! visit us with thy salvation." I am learning more and more to prize the general terms in which Scripture is written. The same promises, the same prayers, the same precepts that suited our days of peace and prosperity, now answer for these darker times—only breathing a new significance, with each change of circumstances, which proves them to have been spoken by One who could foresee all events when He dictated them. I am afraid, however, you will think all these moral reflections very dull for a letter. I was writing unconsciously—as I often do in writing to you—and if you will pardon them, I will promise to say none the less of other things for the space they have taken up. I generally limit myself to a certain length for each letter because I have so many to write that I find it necessary—but I will give myself both longitude and latitude in this. I am just prepared to go to the State Library, where I have long promised myself the luxury of spending a morning—and stole this much of time for you before going. The Examiner of this morning has a piece on the attractions of Atlanta, prepared probably to cut Yankee combs—but it is so good, I mean to cut it out—and if you dont see it otherwise, I will send it to you.

We all feel very anxious about things in Georgia—not because Atlanta is taken—which has always been expected here, sooner or later. Gen. Johnston was thought by military men to have pretty well settled that question when he abandoned the line of the Chattahoochee. But the condition of Hood's army is not satisfactory—there seems to be a want of harmony and confidence among the leading officers, which forebodes no good. There was a great desire, among many here, that Beauregard should have succeeded Johnston. But the Presid't does not seem to have a high opinion of Beaureg'd as a fighting man. Whether he will yet yield to the pressure of public opinion and send him there, we do not know—he yielded to such a pressure when he placed Johnston in command—for he did it in opposition to his own judgment. Hood certainly, whatever his merits, does not seem able to harmonize those elements of strife which have long fomented in that army. Hardee has asked to be relieved, it is said. He is such a favorite with the President that we all wondered at Hood being placed over him, and the Pres't did write him a private letter explanatory of the reasons—which were that Hardee was understood fully to endorse Johnston's policy, to wh. the Administration was opposed—but the nostrum did not soothe. Perhaps you knew all this—but at any rate—it is told now. We talk so much of these things that I cant help writing them. Well, after all we are greatly indebted to Hood for holding Atlanta till the corn crop of Virginia was in a condition to be used, at least for horses. We fear the whole of Georgia now lies open to destructive raids—but Washington is off from the probable track. Should the Yankees go there, we all earnestly hope that father will not think of staying at home. It could do no possible good and would certainly do harm. Here in this raid-visited section, the men are wiser—they all leave home, as a matter of course, on the approach of the enemy—for long experience has taught them that women are the best defenders of themselves and their property under such circumstances. I would much rather have you and Lucy and Hattie to defend me against a party of Yankee freebooters than any three men. I trust in the mercy of Heaven, that they will not be allowed to strip us of everything—for we have yet before us, I fear, a long time of need. I cannot yet discern the bow of promise in the clouds of war. And I often think that the fall of Atlanta, coming just at this time, was designed for one great benefit to us, which is to dissipate those strong hopes of Peace which we feared would have an injurious effect on our country—ungirding the loins of our minds and relaxing our vigilance and courage.

Well, the first sheet is full of public affairs—(I read the Examiner too much) and I must now dedicate this to matters which some might call less, and others more interesting. I believe I will not go back so far as to tell you about my visit to Staunton, other than that it was very pleasant—devoted entirely to Idleness and Ease—and I think it has done me good. I dont dilate on my trip to Rockingham, where grandfather Gilmer and mother used to visit—and to Weir's Cave, the region of our ancestral home.

Our weather here is cool and delightful. I am beginning to think about autumn clothing and to be busy renovating. Dont you want a word on the fashions? Mrs. Stanard has a box from Paris, wh. contains two black silks, *made* up—so I presume that is about as recent authority as we are likely to have. They are made just according to the modes wh. prevailed here last winter and spring. One has two points in front and swallow-tail in the back— skirt trimmed with wide bugle gimp put on in festoon or scallop style. The other has one point in front and one behind—skirt trimmed with velvet ribbon put on thus VVV with a row of chenille fringe below—skirt trimmings in both not coming within ⅛ yd of the bottom. Sleeves of both, coat sleeves, rather smaller at the hand than at the elbow not wide at either—but requiring undersleeves. Mrs. Gibson says she has seen recent fashion prints from Baltimore, and Garibaldi waists are still worn. So I mean to proceed on the styles prevalent hitherto. I think I shall certainly cut off my velvet cloak this winter into a sack—or do something with it—I hate to wear it—so few persons have any such now. It will make me a sack and a waist—dont you advise me to do it? I suppose Corinne wrote to thank you for the silk you sent her. It will indeed make her a handsome dress. I mean her to go into company this winter. She will be improved by it—and should I go to the plantation I will not carry her there—but will arrange to leave her here if I can. I enclose you her last from Staunton to show you how she spends her time there. It is carelessly written and is only for yourself to see.

Thursday, 7th. My plans for yesterday were interrupted by a message from Mrs. Caskie asking me to drive with her at 1 o'clock, which invitation I accepted. In the evening, we all took tea with Lucy, who is now a housekeeper—her mother and sisters having been away since July. And a real Virginia housekeeper she is—with a bountiful eye—and much we all enjoyed her Sally Lunn, tea and coffee, rolls, nice butter and ginger-cake—with peach ice cream and cake at ten o'clock. Lucy looked so pretty too, that was the greatest treat of all. Sally Irvin and Hilly were there and the Gilmers.

We all feel so much for your losses, dear Cliffie. They are indeed serious, as they now appear to you, but I hope in the end you will find more saved than you think for. China and crockery seem to me the most serious—for father has supplied to you the ruined garden and the fowls—but what friend loves another enough to give her glass or china now! Sister received your long letter, which was much enjoyed. I have also to thank my dear father for his of the 23d which reached me on the 5th. I will write to him before long. Kiss the little ones all round for me and tell Mammy many howdyes. Much love to Marion. Ask her if she cant come on next month and stay till I go South—the fall here is delightful and I wish you would persuade father to let her come. If any of you wish to send abroad for anything Mr. Lawton can send for you—if you will take the risks and pay the exchange. He has sent for several things for me. Dr. Richardson has heard from his family—they are at Long Branch New Jersey—but he heard nothing satisfactory, as it was by flag of truce. He says they have friends there and he seems to prefer their being there to either Canada or Kentucky. Does father like Dr. Richardson as well as ever? He never mentions him now and he used to write often about him. Goodbye—you see it is hard to say it, even now. My love to George.

Your most devoted

S. A. L.

Adventures of the Assets of the State Bank of Georgia

The Story of how the assets of The Bank of the State of Georgia were hidden from the Yankees during "Sherman's March thro Georgia"—my Husband being the Cashier of the Bank.*

Late on the evening of Monday, Nov. 28th, 1864, my Husband came home from a meeting of the Directors of the State Bank, and told me that he was ordered to leave Savannah on the next Wednesday morning at 8 o'clock to take the assets of the bank out of danger.

Sherman's army was then on its march toward Savannah, and all the Banks, warned by what had happened in other places, were hurrying to get their possessions out of reach.

We were to have a special train—to go toward Thomasville—and to hurry to cross the Altamaha before the bridge was cut by our own troops to stop the Yankee progress in that direction. I was to take my three children and my servants with me, and we were to shape our course according to circumstances, when once we had crossed the river. It was pouring rain on that Monday— the week's wash was all wet in the tubs, and the servants could be no help, as they were to pack up to go with me. I was to carry plenty of cooked provision with me, as we would be probably some days on the way—to take blankets, mattresses, chairs, cooking-utensils, &c, that we might sleep in the baggage car, and be prepared to camp out if necessary. To prepare, we had only one day. It is

*Written by Harriet V. Cumming for her grandchildren.

useless to try to describe that day. But on Wednesday morning we were all ready at eight o'clock, leaving the empty house with all our earthly possessions in it, just as when we lived in it. There had been no time to arrange for what we were to leave behind.

Saturday night found us landed in Thomasville and as the sun went down, I sat on a pile of lumber in the street with my children and servants, while my husband rummaged the town to find shelter for us. It was dark before it was found. Then a lady whose husband was in the Army, offered to let us have the second story of her house, if we could furnish our own bedding, and if my husband would undertake to forage for table supplies for the crowd.

We spread our mattresses on the floor, had our own chairs, made the best of everything—and lived there six weeks. An empty store was hired, and there all the gold, bank books &c were stored. The gold was in kegs, such as are used for the transportation of heavy nails, &c, and we were supposed to be carrying spikes for the use of one of the R. R. companies. Our servant Jerry slept there at night, and Mr. Cumming and Mr. Ross (the Teller of the Bank) took turns in staying with him at night—all armed.

In January, Gov. Brown sent down a large number of State troops from the upper part of Georgia, to check the advance of the Yankees in that direction, and Mr. C. decided that our safest plan would be to hire some of the returning wagons to take us across the country to Albany, where we could strike the R. Road and could go to Macon. There the State Bank had always had a Branch Office and there was a building, vault &c where the money could be stored. The Yankee Army had then passed Macon and was in Savannah. So we hired seven wagons and loaded them, each driven by a long-legged cracker from the Mountains. We sent Cora's family back to Savannah, as the darkies there were faring well, and they remained in their own quarters in our house till our return a year and a half later—and worked for the Yankees who took possession of it. Wallace Jr. was about 18 months old when we took this Journey. We were three days and nights on the road. At night the men drew together great trees of dead and fallen pine, and made a roaring fire, round which we camped, and where we cooked supper and provisions for the next day. We reached Macon late in Jan. and made our home with Mrs. Thos. Nisbet, Mr. C's Sister. There we remained for six months. Early in April, news began to come that a second detachment of the Yankee army was on its way thro the State—and what to do with the money, became an anxious question. Wherever the Yanks had found Bank money, they had seized it as spoils of War. We had with us between $150,000 and $200,000 in specie, besides many chests of family silver belonging to friends and Directors of the Banks. The specie was in the vault of the Bank—the silver stored in a rented room. After much thought it was decided to bury and to wear what gold we could, and to sink the rest in a deep well. Each member of the household wore a wide belt, made of heavy linen, and stitched full of $20. gold pieces. The front yard of the house was a mass of large, beautiful rose-bushes, in full bloom. Mr. Nesbit had a large iron Foundry and Mill— and there he cast a long, round iron bar, like a lightning rod, the size of a $20. gold piece, and sharpened it at one end. Freshly-dug ground would have betrayed our secret to the enemy, but the lighting-rod could be driven in close up to the root of a Rose-bush, where it would never be seen. Every day Mr. Cumming made several trips between the house and the Bank, and came home loaded each time, till many thousands of dollars were safely landed in our room. When night came, we waited till everybody was in bed and the town was dark and quiet. Then Mr. Nesbit and Mr. C. went to work. The rod was run down close up to the root of a Rose-bush, and as deep as their

united strength could sink it (they were both large men)—
the hole was filled up with gold eagles, dropped in one
by one and loose earth was thrown over the top. They
worked till near daylight, while Mrs. N. and I kept watch
and gave notice if any one was passing, so that they could
get out of sight. The roses were in full bloom. My
recollection is that between thirty and forty thousand
dollars were buried in that way. Mrs. N. knew the name
of every rose, and a record was kept of what was buried
under each. In the mean time we kept up a vigorous search
for boxes that might serve our purpose for the rest of
the money and they were quietly stored at the Foundry.
When all was ready and the near approach of the Yankee
army warned us that we must act, Mrs. N. and I went in
her carriage to the Bank, where Mr. Cumming awaited us.
The day was cold, and we had on heavy cloaks. Each of
us passed several times in and out, between the carriage
and the Bank, and each time we came out loaded with as
many little canvas bags full of gold as we could carry, till
the seat was full of them. Then I stayed and sat on them,
till all had been brought out, and covered them with
my cloak and skirts, while I rode to the Foundry. The
others walked, as the weight was great. Mr. N's foreman
had been in the habit of staying alone at the Foundry
while the Workmen went to dinner—but that day Mr. N.
said to him that he could go with the others, as he
(Mr. N.) had business that would keep him there for
an hour or two. So the Mill was empty and Mr. N.
awaited us. In the centre of the building was a very
large, deep well, ten feet in diameter, which supplied all
the water for the machinery. We got all the little bags
safely inside and having had an hour to work, filled the
boxes as rapidly as possible, corded them tightly, and one
by one the two men consigned them to their watery grave.
I never saw my Husband look as he did then—for he was
taking an enormous responsibility on himself, and his
good name hung on his being able some day to bring

up again from that deep, what he then consigned to it. The date was April 19th, 1865. Two days after this the Yankee army took possession of Macon. There were two or three other Savannah Banks whose assets were in the City in charge of their Cashiers and they had decided to try to escape and hide in the surrounding country. But they were captured and the money seized.

Mr. C. was arrested when the Army came in—but all they could find in the vault of the Bank was some barrels of Confederate money to which they were welcome, and a few hundred in silver which we had not been able to hide—and which they confiscated. The money remained in the well more than two years. We returned to Savannah in May 1866, leaving it there—and it was not till the troops were withdrawn from the State and the reign of Martial Law was over, that Mr. C. went back to Macon and took up his task of recovering what had been so long buried. It was a dreadful time for him—full of risk and the keenest anxiety—but I can tell little about it, as I was not with him. I only know that Mr. Nesbit gave out that he would have to stop work for a week or ten days, to clean out his well and repair his machinery. The work of recovery had to be done at night—all the sand taken from the well and sifted, the boxes that had not broken taken out and carried to Mr. N's house—and the work done by Trustys that could hold their tongues. Mr. N's colored driver of course knew all that had been done, but he was staunch and faithful, and most useful in all this trying work. All the money was recovered and returned in safety to the Bank of Sav. with the exception of one small package of gold one-dollar pieces, which being so very small and light were lost in the water, mud and sand taken from the well.

But when it was all done, my husband came back to me ten years older, for the few weeks of anxiety and care thro' which he had passed.

The chests of silver were all returned in safety to their

owners—and the watch which Wallace wears was given to his Father by the Telfair Ladies, as their expression of gratitude on the return of theirs. It was made in Paris and was the first stem-winder we had seen in this country.

H. V. C.

Clifford Hull to Louisa Gilmer.

My dearest Sister Lou:—

The surprising object of this letter is to beg for one of Brother Gilmer's old coats, and I will proceed to explain why and for whom I want it. Do you remember an Episcopal minister who used to live here named Hunt? Well for years past they have been living in Marietta where they owned a little home, and managed to eke out a small living, and having nothing but their home in the whole world, old Mrs. H. tried to stay and take care of it. But they were driven away, and went to Savannah, where he was taken very ill, and has been there for some months on the poor Drysdales. As soon as he was able they came up here, and are living in Mr. Plumbs' house and they are just as poor as they can be. The old lady (over 60) does all their work, for they have no servant, and tho' Lizzie R. offered to let them have one for nothing, Mrs. H. said they were obliged to decline, for they were not able to feed one. He looks wretchedly and is so dilapidated you would be sorry for him. His coat is just a bundle of *patches*—it is almost literally in tatters, and all mended and darned, so that it looks more fit for a very *seedy* darkie than a white man. Father looked to see if he could spare a coat to give him, but is short of clothes himself, and then is so much stouter than Mr. H. his clothes would not fit him at all. We were talking about them the other night and it occurred to me Mr. Gilmer might have some civil (not military) coat laid away among your things here that you would give him, and I would write and ask you. He is just about the size and make of Bro. G., only a little shorter, and he and his wife both look like the most pinching poverty. They have four children: one son in the Army, one at home disabled by a severe wound in the hip, one daughter at school, and another teaching and her salary is what they all have to depend on. Father sent them a ham and a middling, and afterwards when Mr. H. saw him he thanked him, and then added he hoped he might never see the day when even a small present of meat would be so acceptable to him.

I know you have tho't of us all in the exciting times we have had. We feel so thankful for the dangers averted, so much for those poor people who have suffered what we so dreaded. At one time father had his wagons and mules and all the negro men up from the plantation, his and George's trunk packed, and all ready to load the wagons with meat and valuables to go off at short notice, but they took another course. Many persons here did send off everything they had the means of sending, and long trains of wagons from the country, between here and Greensboro, were passing out on the Petersburg road all day. It was the first time I have been really afraid they would come. In the country thro' which they have passed the people have suffered terribly. They spent Sunday in Eatonton—entered the town with all the bands playing and their banners flying, and their horses and themselves dressed in their very best,—Gen. Slocum's horse magnificently tricked out. They went to every house and did more or less mischief. *In every instance* where persons had buried or hid their valuables, they were compelled to show where. None saved them but those who could say solemnly they had been sent off, and they did not know where they were. They killed all the hogs, poultry and cattle, and what they could not carry off they left dead, and carefully destroyed all the salt they could find anywhere that the people might not save the meat. In every instance they poured out all the syrup—thousands of gallons—and they burned all the corn and grain they could not carry off. They found out the names of the young ladies, and called them all by their first names, and wherever there was a piano they forced them to play, and they would all sing their national songs. In one house there the ladies determined not to notice them, and when they entered just went on with their work as tho' they did not see them. The officers roamed all over the house, and then went out and told their men to come in and pillage, and there everything was very badly treated. We heard this account of their doings in Eatonton thro' Mrs. Dr. Dunwody who lives not very far from there, and whose daughter had been there since on a visit. They carried off a great many negroes, but almost all had made their escape and come back to their owners. Two negro women were confined at their camp on that Sunday, and after they left, and our men went there, both these women and their infants were there dead. They say in Milledgeville they violated several respectable females, but I don't know how true that is and am disposed to doubt it. Such things they have done here, but generally at country places and not in the towns. If they take Savannah and Augusta I fear our turn will yet come. Every one seems to fear they will get Savannah and Augusta yet, and then no part of the State will be safe. We have felt so troubled about Aunty and all her family. Father wrote to beg her to come here, but fears it was too late. If they take Savannah, they will hold and occupy it, and it is no use to try and stay where they are, unless you can make up your mind to submit to every insult, indignity, and oppression from them, and from your servants,—like Cousin Carry for instance. I had rather die than submit to what she has had to submit to. And then perhaps be driven out as the Atlanta people were. I suppose you have heard from Aunty about Hattie's going to Thomasville, and if Aunty can't get here I hope she will go in that direction. If they shell the City I believe the constant state of anxiety and excitement would be too much for Uncle. Aunty seems to feel so uneasy about him. Georgia is now being punished for her sins, and I feel as tho' it must come home to us all.

We feel very uneasy about Sister Sallie. The last we heard of her was thro' Dr. R. who said he had had a dispatch from her at Weldon. We were amazed that she would try to come at all in the present state of things, especially to go to Savannah, but suppose she is there. I fear she will get into great difficulties. We hoped when she heard the state of things she would come here first and were quite disappointed. I do long to see her and hope nothing will prevent her coming here.

We heard from our house in Atlanta. It is standing, but horribly abused. All the blinds and sashes gone, all the locks and door-knobs, and everything on the lot carried off that could be carried. Every building between that old Methodist church near me and the corner of Whitehall, beyond McNaught and Ormond, is destroyed,— just one vast heap of ruins. All the hotels and depots and R. R. buildings are burned.

Indeed, nearly the whole town is destroyed. Persons are going back fast, but while the war lasts I don't see how it will be possible to rebuild. I can't myself bear the idea of ever going back there to live. I have wanted to quit there for three years past, and do wish Providence might now open the way for us to live some where else. I do want to live where I won't have to keep an hotel for wayfarers That is only one of many reasons, but I tho't of that first because all that country being swept of provisions, stocks, poultry and negroes for 30 miles round, hotel keeping will be particularly hard there for a few years to come.

When George is well enough he will go to Augusta and thence to Atlanta. He is improving now very fast. We have had 16 cases of measles on the lot and plantation, and it has been pretty severe measles too. My children were almost the first, and for several days were very sick.

They are pretty nearly over it and its effects now, tho'
I have not turned them loose to run in and out at liberty
yet.

The weather has been so mild and delightful all Fall
and Winter, except one cold (bitter cold) snap, that I'm
afraid the vile Yankees will fall in love with our climate,
and after peace be for coming back here to live.

I had no idea of writing you so long a letter and
feel quite exhausted.

Yours very affectionately,

M. C. H.

Washington, Ga., Dec. 7, 1864.

Harriet Cumming to Her Sister Clifford.

Kiokee*—Jan. 10th 1865.
Wednesday.

My dearest Puss: Late yesterday afternoon I reached these peaceful shades and while Sallie is busy with her household affairs I will begin my story and ease my pent-up heart by writing "to you all." I received Marion's letter and your note yesterday, when I met Sallie in Albany, and right glad was I to hear from you. Since the last of November, I had known nothing of any of you. I wrote you a long, full letter from Thomasville, and enclosed it to Savannah, asking to have it sent to you via Charleston—but I suppose you never received it and all its valuable information is lost to you—as I am sure I cannot go as much into details again. Then I commenced another letter to you in the wagons between Thomasville and Albany, but when I separated my baggage to come here, that and my knitting were both forgotten. So that is lost to you too. Now I mean to do what I can towards telling you of our past, present and future, hoping that Sallie can devise some certain means of getting this to you. I seem to be in some troubled dream "from which 'twere joy to wake and weep." I cannot realize my own identity. I cannot realize that I am a homeless wanderer—that all these discomforts at the bare thought of which I shuddered when it was first proposed to me to begin this pilgrimage, have been already habitual, and that I must look forward to nothing else. I was so *rooted* in my pleasant home—one comfort after another had been added till I was wedded to them, dependent on them, and

*General Lawton's place near Albany, Ga.

could not bear any interference with them. The thought
of living with all my little family in one room was dreadful
—now, I shall be thankful to find at my journey's end
that I can have even that. I can see that I needed this
discipline—that I had learned to love my ease too well
and was in danger of forgetting that I am a stranger and
pilgrim here. I only pray now that I may learn my lesson
with patience and cheerfulness, and be helped heavenward
by the sundering of so many bonds that made earth
pleasant. We were five weeks in Thomasville. During
four of them we were every day trying to get away, and
four separate times we had three days rations for a large
party cooked ready for starting, and then were disappointed.
I was comparatively comfortable there, and had much
kindness showed me by my hostess. She was a Mrs. Stark,
a niece of old Mr. Guest of Liberty; so she knew a good
many people in whom I was interested and knew my
belongings. Our room was a very large, nice one—but
entirely bare of what we call conveniences. I soon learned
to live in trunks and baskets tho' and then I did'nt mind
it. She kept a nice table, and took a deal of pains to
please us in everything; so that when I turned my back
on Thomasville, I felt that I had only good to remember
of my sojourn there.

Of our journey, I can give you no idea. We started
in a train of nine wagons, five loaded with the Bank's
and our effects, the other four with government stores.
We were up before day on Friday morning to make an
early start, but with the delays of loading &c, and then
waiting two or three hours for the forage-master to eat
his dinner and take his smoke, we camped only three miles
out of Thomasville that night. Baby and I got permission to spread a mattress in an empty room where
the wind whistled and played thro' the wide cracks—the
rest slept in the wagons and around the fire of the camp.
The roads were indescribable—the mud, the mire, the
mud-holes, the corduroy—but by dint of hard work we

got thro' *thirteen* miles the second day and slept in a house again. We had good weather for three days, and tho' it rained some after that, we managed to keep dry. The third night we slept in the wagons and were more comfortable than we had been either of the other nights. Hard rain and heavy wind overtook us on the fourth day, but we were near Mr. Merrill Calloway's, and there we took shelter—and there we found such a bountiful welcome and such a profusion of turkey and hog-meat and eggs and butter and syllabub and jelly and cake as made my ideas turn a complete somerset. I had'nt seen good things in such a time that I scarcely knew the names of them. We stayed overnight with them and on Tuesday morning Cora Butler sent us into Albany in her carriage. There we found Sallie and George Lawton waiting for us, and heard from you and from the children in Macon. We lingered about his car, and then we—i. e.—Sallie and I, with Baby and nurse,—were all aboard for Kiokee. Dr. Richardson was keeping house in Sallie's absence, and had a good meal waiting for us. So we washed our faces, refreshed ourselves with a good cup of coffee, and then sat down before the bright blaze for our talk. You can easily imagine of what we talked—Savannah, our friends and homes there—and all that the loss of it involved. I feel so restless to hear what is going on there, how they are faring, what becomes of my home— tho'ts flitting from one household to another and imagining the circumstances of so many whom I love.

You know I brought out nothing with me in the way of furniture, except three or four chairs in which we rode on the cars. I have some blankets, sheets, pillow cases, towels, and table-linen with me, but left some of all behind me, because the house was still occupied. I brought out all our clothing and new cloth—a few plates and dishes that I tho't would be necessary to us if we located on Charley's place, and a few pieces of that handsome set of glass which used to belong to W's father.

I left everything else—my china, most of the glass, all the furniture, carpets, bedding, curtains, quilts, nets, books —and many, many little things that I valued from old association, and which money cannot replace. I believe I grieve most for some of them—tho' I count the carpets the greatest loss as far as comfort goes. If I had them and my mosquito nets, I could manage for most other things. I dont like to sit down to think over my home and what was in it. It makes it harder to be content. I think I own but three books in the world now—my Bible, Bogatsky, and Trench on the Miracles. As for Cora and her family, I can give no guess. I *expect* them to be faithful. I believe that Cora will save for me what she can, and that if they are allowed, they will remain where they are. But many others have trusted in such cases, and been deceived. I think Sam will be less likely to be led astray by the tho't of freedom than Cora will—for he has better sense about many things, and is a more humble servant, if less attached. He has so little reason to think that he could better his condition by any change, that I dont think he will care to try it. I dare say our things will be better cared for than if they were not on the lot, and I dont know how we could take care of them if we had them here.

We cannot hear the truth definitely as to whether Sherman is requiring the oath or not. Accounts vary. We have heard that provisions were plenty and cheap, private property respected, and everything going on as usual—and three firms gone North for goods. But others say it is only to last for 20 days and then comes the test. I dont see how those who come out can bring much, with all the roads cut. Aunty has all her silver there—could'nt send it out with us. I am sure she will stay if it is possible for her to do so, rather than lose all she would in coming out. Poor Leila! I think constantly of her and hers. As for Hopewell, it has been swept. All Liberty is devastated. I heard thro one of the scouts of

Charlie's horses being taken, and that James had remained at his post up to that time—but I could not hear how many of the negroes had stayed with him, or any particulars of the place. I only know that in all the cases of families of whom we especially heard, they had not left them a *morsel* —that the ladies lived on rations served out to them and on what the negroes gave them— They took clothing, money, furniture, everything. I heard a letter read from one of Laura Jones' sisters, saying that they had not a change of clothing left in the house, and that she had had to walk eight miles for as much salt as she could bring in the palm of her hand— They had not molested the ladies otherwise than to steal from them.

Sallie's messenger is getting ready to go into Albany and she advises me to let you off with this much for this time and send the rest by some other opportunity. I am so glad to be writing to you again, that I think I could go another sheet, if I were let alone. This is for my dear Father and Minnie and all— I know you all think of us and feel for the trouble that has come upon us. I hope to be in regular communication with you again after this— Direct to Macon— Let Emma and Mary hear from me thro this. I am truly grieved to hear of poor Mary's illness. What a pleasure it would be to go over with you to see them and tell my story instead of writing it. My love to Mammy and tell her to think about me. My baby stood the journey across pretty well. I need'nt tell you how comfortable and happy I am at old Kiokee and what nice talks Sallie and I have. I told you that she expects to leave here next Tuesday, if she is not detained—but will write again before she leaves. She says she will have to carry Dr. Richardson to Father's house with her; but that as a cot in the parlor is all he gets when he goes visiting with her here, she is sure you can find some place for him. Goodbye dearest—I have'nt said all I wanted to. Tell me if you think of going back to your old home. Where is George and what is he doing.

Faithfully,

HATTIE.

Felix Alexander to His Father.

Richmond, Va. Jany 16, 1865.

Dear Father :—

Yours of the 6th reached me this morning and was a great pleasure to me. We had heard nothing from the South for some time and were very anxious about you all. I am daily hoping to hear that uncle and family will come out from Savannah. They must feel their isolation from all the rest of the family, and as uncle can not discharge his duties as President of the bank, I can but think that he will come out. God only knows what we have to look forward to. We hear this morning that Fort Fisher has been taken. This puts a stop to blockade running. We have enough in, with what we make, to keep the army furnished with quartermaster supplies for some months; but the loss of Wilmington will cripple us most seriously. Meanwhile the spirit seems to have gone out of the people, and herein is our most serious danger. If there were *heart* to continue the war, I believe we have the power for another campaign; but there seems to be a restless feverish disposition that does not give promise of that cordial support that will be necessary.

I hardly know whether to let my box of crockery come on, for I would hate very much to lose it. Yet the probabilities seem that Richmond will be evacuated, unless negotiations for peace are entered upon. I think I will ask you to have the box kept in Augusta to await further orders, if it has not left before this comes to hand.

One good may come to us from the fall of Wilmington. As we lose our seaports, we concentrate and form in the interior an army able to preserve our communications.

Ed will give you all the news. I am glad that you will have him to talk to. God bless him! A more noble and gallant soldier never breathed. The President says "he is one of the very few men whom Gen. Lee can not do without."

Give warmest love for Lucy and myself to each and all at home, and may God grant us to meet again. I see no possibility of my getting away just now.

Ever your affectionate son,
WILLIAM FELIX.

Harriet Cumming to Her Father.

Macon, Ga., April 30, 1865.

My dearest father:—

I hear contradictory accounts as to the possibility of getting a letter to you, but as I am sure that you have suffered a good deal of anxiety about us in the last ten days, I shall risk at least a note to tell you how we have fared since we have been in Yankee lines. To have endured exile to escape them, and then to have fallen into their clutches after all! We had been in some fear of them since hearing of the fall of Selma and then Columbus, but on the 19th the news came of the armistice and orders from Beauregard to send out to meet any force that might be advancing against this place and advise them of it. The flag of truce went out on the 20th and we had dismissed all fear of Yankees, when as Wallace got half way to town after dinner, he was met by a negro with the news that the enemy were already entering the town. Knowing that we were alone and the children in the street, he hurried back to warn us and in ten minutes time the advance was straggling thro' the street. They had met the flag but refused to respect it as the town was evidently in their power, and as our batteries had been warned of the armistice and told not to fire, they came in without opposition. Generals Johnston and Sherman are to determine whether this is a captured city. The first night and day was an anxious, exciting time. A good many of them rode into the yard, some to ask for food, some to water their horses, etc., but we kept the house closed. Mr. Nisbet or Wallace answered all calls at the door, and those who asked food were fed in the kitchen, so we were not molested in the house. A good many persons had their houses entered and their watches, etc. taken from them, but we escaped with the loss of a horse and mule. The mill was sacked and all the corn and flour carried off, but at the house we fared better than most of our neighbors. The Army seems to be under good discipline and there has been an evident effort to prevent plundering. W——'s precincts have not been entered at all, tho' due precautions had been taken beforehand. If circumstances here do not forbid his leaving, he may go to see you for a few days to talk things over with you. Writing is not safe.

Little Wallace and Mary were both sick most of the week. And in the midst of all this gloom and anxiety came the news of Gen. Lee's surrender—our death blow. Oh! I have grown old in the two weeks that are past. What faith it requires to bear this blow patiently! The cause which we still believe was a righteous cause, for which so much has been endured patiently, baptized with so much precious blood, for which prayers and tears have been continually offered up—all lost; and those godless wretches triumphant. Did ever faith have a harder trial! "When I thought to know this, it was too painful for me." What have our dear and honored leaders been called to endure of humiliation and trial?

This is but a line at a venture, dear Father, to let you know that we have not suffered bodily harm, and also to beg earnestly for any information you may have of Porter, the Gilmers and Lawtons. We hear nothing— are cut off from the outer world almost entirely. What can Army men like Gen. Gilmer and Porter look forward to? What future lies before them?

Do beg somebody to write and tell me about my sisters and brothers. W. received the money for the salt. I wrote home the day before the Yankees came. Tell Charley the key and letter have come. I will send the things when I can do so safely. His provisions have not reached here yet, and now we will probably countermand the order as he won't want Confederate money.

Affectionately your child,

H.

Monday, May 1st.—I find that no mails are going from here as yet, so I shall get Mr. Tyler to send this to George and beg George to forward it to you. If you write to me, you would better try the same route.

Our servants have not seemed at all shaken in their allegiance, by the Yankees. Jerry says they have been begging him to join the "Infantry" and have offered him thirty dollars in gold, but he prefers his present quarters. Yankees asked the servants here if the people in the house had any watches, whether they were well armed, whether any gold or silver was buried in the lot, etc., but they got such judicious answers that they never came to look for themselves.

Did you hear that Charlie Lamar was killed in the battle at Columbus? His family came out of S. last week. The order of exile in that city is countermanded for the present. All citizens and soldiers are ordered to wear crape for Lincoln thirty days. Uncle's name was not mentioned as at the meeting, tho' they had about 50 vice-presidents and 20 secretaries.

I wrote you word in my last letter that Mary Timmons had left Aunt Lou, almost breaking Loulie Gilmer's heart thereby.

My love to all, all—

H.

MARION ALEXANDER BOGGS I (*b*. November 19, 1842)
Reproduced from a small daguerreotype taken about 1860.

Reconstruction in Washington, Georgia.

Marion Alexander to Her Sister Clifford.

Washington, July 31, 1865.

My dearest sister Mary:—

Mr. Charles Dunwody leaves tomorrow with his family for Monticello, and I intend sending this letter by him; also sister Hattie's fan if Mrs. D. can carry it. If I had known that brother Wallace could not take it, I should have made it more leisurely, and flatter myself that I could have decidedly improved on it. But it is no use regretting now, and it must go just as it is. The packet of letters sent by Express came down last Thursday and were distributed as directed. We were so glad to hear that sister Hattie was to remain with you for the present, and I take great pleasure in thinking of you as being together, only wishing that I might make one of your number, sometimes. I have said nothing to father yet on the subject of my promised visit, as the weather has been too intensely hot for me to think of moving from home, but I hope that I may accomplish it while sister H. is still with you, that being a great additional inducement.

Ed's hand is much improved and gives him very little pain now, though he fears that he may not have free use of his fingers, at least, for some time, as they can not be straightened out at all. Mr. Johnson has been performing on him with his little pricking machine, and Ed thinks it gave him some relief.

Our whole community has been wrought up to the highest state of excitement and indignation within the past two days by the unexpected confiscation of Mrs.

Toombs' house, and her forcible ejectment therefrom. The Yankee Gen'l. Wilde, who is at the head of the Bureau, embracing Freedmen, Abandoned Lands and Refugees, came up here two weeks ago with that old hypocrite French, and they have remained here ever since, making themselves busy, Wilde especially, in everybody else's concerns. They have a body-guard of Negro soldiers through whom all their commands are issued. On Saturday some of them were sent up to Mrs. T. with a written order to the effect that she must prepare to vacate the premises in twenty-four hours, as the house and lot were considered *abandoned property,*— the rightful owner, an ex-senator of the U. S. and a Major General in the Confederate Army (so-called) having left it. She would be allowed to take wearing apparel, some china, glass, etc., six chairs, and enough furniture to make one room tolerably comfortable, together with two weeks' rations! All else must be left. A Negro guard was placed at the front and back of the house, remaining there until yesterday at 12 o'clock, when Mrs. T. and Sallie left, never to cross its threshold again. Nothing that could be done to add insult to wrong was spared. Wilde took possession several hours before they left, examined everything which was sent off, and retaining the crockery, etc., walked all over the house, turned over the beds, ate peaches, and made himself at home, showing himself not only a devil, but the lowest of vulgarians. Tomorrow, he says, the land is to be divided among the Negroes. It is believed that he is acting entirely without authority, merely because he wanted a comfortable house to live in, already furnished and stored; and Mr. G. Toombs left here yesterday, resolved not to stop short of Washington, if redress can not be had elsewhere.

Cousin Sallie is very unwell, and runs great risk in being moved as she was, and when this was represented to the Brute, he only said that he had nothing to do with her being sick. I never felt in such a tumult in my life, as I did on going to bid them goodbye, and I don't know now how Mrs. Toombs forbore to call upon God to curse such a wretch. I hope I may live to see the day when the vengeance of Heaven may overtake him, and when the mercy he has shown to those defenseless women may be meted out to him, good measure pressed down and running over. You can not understand the bitterness which we feel, unless you could hear all the little details of his brutality which are too numerous to write. Poor Mrs. Toombs looked crushed, though she says she anticipated something of this kind, sooner or later. They have gone out for the present to Mr. DuBose, where they are awaiting Dudley who has been released and is on his way home. I forgot to mention that Wilde took horses, carriage, cows, everything, but the few exceptions mentioned above. He seems preparing to institute another "Reign of Terror" here.

In Dr. Robertson's absence, the other day, he tried to seize that money belonging to the Richmond Banks, which was left here temporarily by the cashiers, claiming it also as "abandoned property," but it was saved from him, though he is carrying on now a trial of that robbery case, hoping eventually to have it.

Has had several women from Danbury, or its vicinity, who are not believed to be at all implicated, confined in the Court House for days, and one of them, a Mrs. Chenault, who has an infant a month old, he has had *tied up by her thumbs in the Court House.*

Capt. Corly, the present Marshall, has nothing to do with these things. So far as he was concerned we had no complaint to make, as he always seemed anxious to promote peace, but since French and Wilde came, the whole population, white and black, has been in commotion, and I don't know when the waters will flow quietly again. Under the show of promoting harmony between masters and servants, French does all he can secretly to undermine the good feeling formerly existing between them, and already we can see the effects of his efforts. Most of the Negroes look upon him as scarcely less than Divine, and he is taking up all sorts of collections among them, re-marrying old couples and taking fees to buy licenses for them!!

Hilly and Ed are busy with their fruit kiln and are drying quite successfully with it. They do not peel the fruit except what they intend for family use, as they have, not the labor for it.

Mr. Lawton left on Friday for Augusta, and probably will go to Columbia on business before he returns. Sister Sallie is not thoroughly settled yet in the matter of servants and is still on the lookout. I think she does not intend to keep John.

We have heard nothing from Savannah since I wrote last. The Willisses expect to spend their time in Pennsylvania chiefly. Mary only weighs 80 lbs!

I hope your eyes are progressing favorably. Do write, you and sister Hattie, whenever you can. I don't seem to write any fewer letters than I did formerly, and yet I never seem to receive any.

With warmest love to each and all ever, dear sister,
Most affectionately yours,
MARION.

E. P. Alexander to His Sister Clifford.

Columbia, S. C., May 10, 1866.

My dearest Mae:—

Bessie and I have been abusing each other like pick-pockets for a month for not writing to you, and my conscience now compels me to cast out my beam, before proceeding further against her mote. She would have written long ago without being vituperated into it, but for a good deal of summer-clothes and neuralgia, which still keep her down in spite of a sempstress, peach brandy ad lib, sal ammoniac in camphor water, and a sewing machine, all of which are employed in her favor, but twins and damp weather are too much for them still.

If our family annals were very eventful I would be at a loss where to commence to narrate them to you, for I can form no more definite idea when we last heard from each other than that it was sometime since the Indians gave up the land. There has been, however, little of any interest transpiring beyond the daily growth and castigation of the numerous juveniles, so you have certainly lost nothing by our silence.

Jennie and Hampton Gibbes are still living with us with their children, who are no better than ours, and when all five of them get together I frequently imagine myself in a mad house. I have recently, however, invented a plan which gives the house a great relief and consists in having a candy tree in the yard, under which they occasionally find gum drops, etc., and from which they occasionally shake down an assortment of mixed candies, and consequently spend most of their waking hours **under it.**

We have made a number of very agreeable acquaintances in the city and Bessie is very much pleased with everything, except our house itself, which is certainly the poorest apology of a "house" that I ever saw. It has nine rooms in it, each 18½x21 feet, three on each floor, and one little end of a passage room on third floor besides, but not a closet in the house, nor one single convenience of any sort. The parlor has to be on the second floor and the doors of bed-room and nursery both come between it and the stair-case. The windows are enormously high and heavy and made after a patent which was never tried but on this house, where the contractor put it as an advertisement for a large fee. I am almost the only person in the house who can raise them. We have, however, a large garden and tho' we commenced late, we have promise of a very good one after a while.

The University progresses fairly and we hope in a few years to be a very prosperous institution and a very opulent set of professors. We are getting quite intimate with the LeContes and like them all very much.

Can't you and yours come and pay us a visit this summer? You don't know how *delighted* we would be Both Bessies join in the request and the Jr. says tell Cousin Hattie and Lucy that the "mo-est candy and gum drops grows on the trees here that they ever saw and if they'll come and see her, she will shake down more than they can eat."

I got a letter a few days ago from Gen. Longstreet, urging me to write a history of his corps, saying that his wound prevents him from doing it, and Gen. Lee has requested him to do it, and offering to furnish me with all the documents, etc. etc. and endorse the book. I am thinking of it and may try it in my three months vacation this summer.

Kiss your little ones for both of us and give them

and George a great deal of love, as well as to Hattie and hers if still with you.

Ever your affectionate brother,

E. P. A.

Marion Alexander to Her Sister Clifford.

Columbus, Ga.

Monday Dec. 24th 1866.

I would feel ashamed of myself my darling sister Mary for not having written you in so long a time, if I were not conscious of having felt a constant and earnest desire for some weeks past so to do, but without the ability to gratify my inclinations. It seems to me that I was never so little able to call my time my own as since I have been here. I say every morning that I will certainly accomplish this or that piece of work, but when the day is past I have nothing to show, although I really have so much to do.

Tonight there is quite an extensive exhibition of Fireworks down town, to which all our household except myself have gone, Sallie (Grattan) with a beau, Lucy with the Flewellens, and I am left in solitary possession, as I have too bad a cold to venture out at night. I am sorry not to see the display, but it is no small consolation to have so quiet an opportunity for a chat with you. How I do wish my dear Sister, that you could spend the Christmas with us here! We are a man-forsaken set, just now, for brother has gone to the plantation, and Mr. Flewellen and Will Shepherd are both going, but we expect nevertheless to have a very pleasant time. The preparations I see made here exceed anything I have almost ever seen, for the season, and I have had more high living here than in any private families I ever knew. We are invited to dine tomorrow with Mrs. Grimes (Mr. Ben Bowdre's sister you know) who is our next door neighbor, and as kind as any one could possibly be, and in the afternoon, we are going to our Church, where a beautiful Christmas Tree has been fixed for the S. S. children. That over, we are going out to cousin Sallie F's. to stay with her for several days probably. I have seen comparatively little of her, for though she does not live so far out, it is too lonely a walk for me to take alone, and Lucy and Sallie have both been too busy to go lately—but what I do know of her makes me want to know more and I am quite pleased with the idea of staying with her for several days, besides which, entre nous, I may thereby escape other invitations, which I confess are anything but welcome to me.

I think Columbus would soon be the death of me if it were not for Sallie Grattan, who is a substantial leader, and under whose protection I face many dangers which would otherwise put me to flight. But sometimes, even with that assistance, my natural propensities get the better of me, and I fly ignominiously from the face of mankind, as I did, for instance a few days since, when Theresa Shorter brought Dr. Foard to call on us, who is considered one of the nicest beaux here. As soon as I heard they had come, I put on my hat and darted out, scolding myself all the time, and yet unable to do otherwise. When I behave in that way, and remember that no less than 24 September gales have blown over my head, I am utterly discouraged, and despair of ever being any better. I don't know when I have so completely lost my temper, as I did about ten days ago, at having to go out to a dinner at cousin Ann Shepherd's, given in honor of her brother, Mr. James Smythe. Cousin Sallie came round early in the morning to invite Lucy, but said she would not make Sallie and me go, as it was to be an elderly party—but she came back about two o'clock and said we must go, as most of the others had disappointed her, and Cousin Ann w'd be mad if there was no one to eat her nice dinner. Dinners are my special aversion anyhow and when I found that I was obliged to go, all my corruption was stirred, and nothing but the haste I was compelled to make kept me from crying just for vexation. For once in my life, temper got the better even of my vanity, and I would not even wear what I thought becoming—but the evil spirit went off soon after I left home, and I did not find the dinner so bad as I expected.

Cousin Ann has been decidedly gracious to us, and Sallie and I have spent two nights at her house very pleasantly, once to help her entertain the new Minister, Mr. Hall, and the second time for the special purpose of playing Euchre. She provides delightfully, and the suppers she sets for us would be sufficient for twenty people. Beside the usual varieties of bread, she has one or two different salads, pickles, etc, and always jelly, ambrosia, or some such delicacy. She is a wonderfully preserved woman for her age, and keeps up with all the changes of fashion in her dress. Cousin Will is a little less bashful on further acquaintance than at first, and except that has very nice manners. They all try to tease me about him, of course, but I can see no reason for so doing, and indeed have been quite amused at the studied impartiality of his attentions to us. If he rides on horsebcak with Sallie one day, I am sure to receive an invitation for a drive in the buggy in a day or two, and when riding with him once he presented me with a paper of Gum Drops for my cough, he had even had some Chocolate Drops put in for Sallie, having heard her express a fondness for the same.

Lucy is looking much better now than when you saw her last, and is quite active. Sallie is as bright as a new penny and keeps us all waked up. Brother expects to get possession of his new plantation on the first of Jany. and has gone down now to settle up at the old place, which he wants either to sell or rent. Lucy begs you to send her by Express some white silk star-braid with a *pearl edge*. If it does not cost over 50 cts. a bunch, send her eight bunches, but she does not want to give more than that. Also send her 1 doz. bunches of plain white silk braid, narrow. Sallie and herself send very much love. I hope brother G. is with you now. He promised to let us hear from him but did not do so. I heard from home to-day—all well. Father and Mama* expect to leave for Columbia on the 2nd. This is a letter of small things, but of such our life here is made up. Do write me soon, and if not within two weeks direct to Savannah. A merry Christmas and much love to you all dear Sister, from your devoted

M.

*Marion, second wife of A. L. Alexander.

Drama of the Widower.*

Dedicated to the First of the Four United Brethren Whom It Shall Suit.

Scene I.

The dying Wife speaks to herself—

"Every dog will have his day
So will every man—
Let me tell him now the truth—
Tell him while I can."

She addresses her husband—

"Yes, I'm dying, husband, dying;
I have had a happy life—
Don't pretend that you are crying—
You'll not be long without a wife.

"I shall rest in peace, for yonder
In that country far and fair
Shirts are never made with buttons,
Stockings never need repair.

---

*This poem was read by Sarah Lawton at the Quadrilateral Dinner given by her to the four married sisters and their husbands, Gilmer, Cumming, Lawton and Hull, on Wallace Cumming's forty-second birthday, March 16th, 1869.

To which was added the following toast:

"May the first sinner to whom this poem is applicable have a hard road to travel—and may ·the remaining seven of us be unto him as seven devils to torment him."

"You will find that your affliction
    Was a blessing in disguise—
Resignation is a duty—
    You will wipe your weeping eyes—

"I shall find my youth renewing
    In that world so new and strange—
But on you will surely happen
    Just as wonderful a change.

"Ah! my eyes foresees already
    Those becoming mourning suits—
New and fashionable beaver—
    Polished manners—polished boots.

"Arts of pleasing nicely studied—
    Former things all passed away—
Daily visits to the barber—
    Hair that is no longer grey."

Here she is interrupted by Death. The Widower, greatly
overcome, is borne off, saying:

"Oh, My dear, darling, precious Wife!
She was sweetest thing in life.
I never shall another find
Exactly suited to my mind."

Scene II.

(A night has passed.)

"He asked for a scissors
    To cut off her curls—
And while they turned round
    He winked at the girls.

"They went to the undertakers
　　To get her a coffin—
And when they got back
　　The dog was a laughing.

"They went to the graveyard
　　To bury their dead—
And when they got back
　　He stood on his head."

Scene III.

Who comes here?
　　　　A Widower!
What do you want?
　　　　Another Dear!
Where's the 'tother?
　　　　She's forgot—
She rests in peace—but I do not.

He sings:

"Oh, John Anderson, my jo John,
　　Is a right good song, 'tis true;
But Darby and Joan were two old fools,
　　And for me that would never do.
For I like to be off with the old love,
　　And I'd like to be on with the new"

So the night winds sighed and the stars above
　　Looked down on the same old story—
Of first wives gone to the kingdom of love,
　　And second ones out in their glory.

Reproach him not, ye Sisters!
  Nor think the dead wife wronged.
He thought upon no other while
  To him she still belonged.

And while she lived, she lived in clover,
But when she died, she died all over.

                              S. A. L.

Harriet Cumming to Her Sister Clifford.

Home, April 1st, 1870.

My dearest and Faithfulest:

Being in the same state of mind with the fellow that wanted to be seeing "Bob Toombs all the time," I find myself constrained to begin writing to you again. I cant be quite satisfied unless I am keeping all the time in some sort of communication with you. The days when I hear something from you seem so different from the others— I am minded to keep this letter on hand for two or three days and write a little at a time—and Dear, I must beg you to keep it in some measure to yourself—and while you read parts aloud, keep parts also to yourself— I cannot put everything into a note—and you must pick and cull at your pleasure.

First, I must tell you of the scene we have been thro this afternoon. Gen. Lee and his daughter were to arrive on the train at half past Five—to pay a visit to the Lawtons. As Lulu has had measles more recently than my young folks, it was decided that I should meet him at the depot, and if she was afraid of the measles, should bring her home to my house. So Wallace drove me to the depot in the buggy—and there we waited till a quarter past six, when the train steamed in. A crowd had collected to welcome him, and as he appeared at the car-door every hat was raised and the air was rent with loud hurrahs— The crowd increased every moment, and it was almost impossible to move a step. When it became apparent that they were going to our buggy, the crowd surged round it, hurrahing and shouting—till the horse and buggy were in the midst of a sea of men. Some of them held the horses' heads; for the creatures quivered with excitement at the noise and the crowd—but they stood it nobly. After the greatest difficulty, we got Agnes into our buggy, and her Father in Gen. Lawton's, and then the question was, how to move a step. Some of the men took hold of the horses and led them at first, and the crowd was forced to open before the moving vehicle—and so at last we got under way, and were escorted by the crowd to Sallie L's very door. Agnes Lee seemed almost terrified, and kept a most anxious watch on her Father, as tho' she feared some harm would come to him— But we all reached the house safely at last, and there we left them—Agnes not being afraid of the measles.

H.

E. P. Alexander to Clifford and George Hull.

Columbia, S. C. March 16, 1871

My dear little old Cliffie:—

I had just as soon you would have this letter and know all about it as anybody else, and this is how it all happened.

First, you see Longstreet he wrote to me and he says says he you see that he had up and told a man named Mr. Ray that if he wanted a man as could dam the Mississippi worth a cent that he better get me. And then Mr. Ray, he said, "who said so besides you" and then Longstreet, he said, "you go ask Gen. Humphries, because Gen. Humphries he is head engineer of the Yankee Army and Mr. Ray is head president of the Louisiana Levee Company." So you see I went to Washington City and I asked Gen. Humphries if he would tell Mr. Ray if he thought I could dam it and Gen. H. he says "dam it yes," and so when Mr. Ray goes to Washington City next week and asks Gen. H. if he said so, too, and Gen. H. tells him that, then if Mr. Ray wants me to go and dam it, dam it I'll go and try to. But then you see Mr. Khedive of Egypt he up and says if I rather come and build a fort on the Nile that I can come and do it, and he will always call me General and will give me a harem according to rank, and then Bessie she says she don't like that, and she thinks I better dam it (Mississippi). And then you see I went to the mill and it was hot and I took off my coat and vest and hung them up and a nigger he came and took my watch out of my vest-pocket and *stole it*. And that is how it all is tonight, except they are all well, and how it will all turn out and what to do about

314

it I am sure I don't know, but if you hear of anybody damming the Mississippi, or having a harem on the Nile and building a fort, why one of them is your affectionate Brother, You Bet.

Columbia, S. C., May 7, 1871.

Dear George:—

Many thanks for your kind letter and especially for your offer of the benefit of your advice in the ways that are dark and tricks that are vain, in which my future pathway lies. I go up to Charlotte to-morrow on a freight train and back here on Tuesday, and on to Augusta perhaps that night; or possibly to Charlotte tomorrow and back by night passenger to Augusta, reaching there Tuesday A. M. But either Tuesday or Wednesday I hope to be with you.

I regret the bag-trousers and the harem, but 'twas ever thus from childhood's hour, as you may have been told beforehand and perhaps, after all, the little annoyances of Egypt, such as sand-flies and crocodiles, which I am told are very troublesome, might render life there, after all, no more blissful than it may be made here with fewer wives, tight pants, and a beaver hat.

Kiss dearest Mae and the children for me and try and reconcile them to give up all the aunties they might have enjoyed, if I had gone.

Sincerely yours,

E. P. A.

Alice Alexander Haskell to Her Sister Clifford Hull.

Columbia Nov. 22nd 1872.

My dearest Sister Mary.

Ever since I got home I have been wanting to write you to tell what I am afraid you dont *begin* to know, namely, *how very* much Aleck and I did enjoy seeing you the day he came down, and how often we speak of its pleasures since. I have however been so busy that I have had time for but little outside of my immediate household cares. Tonight Aleck has gone to ask after a friend who is expected to die from day to day, and I am seizing these moments when I feel entirely too tired to set to work, as I ought to do, and shall bore you a little instead; but as one of the brilliant Washington beaux observed to a young lady last summer "I dont mind boring such an agreeable person."

I found everything ready when I got home, for my reception, that could be done without the presence of a Mistress, but my servants being both new, and company in the house ever since, my hands have been very full. First Mr. and Mrs. Haskell came and paid us a delightful visit. I love so to have them, their life is so lonely and hard at home, and the rest is such a relief to them, and they do seem to enjoy everything so much. Last week, however, we had less congenial company. The Synod met here, and being very hard pushed for room the Presbyterians asked us to entertain some ministers, so we took two—one a young, sore-eyed-bashful newly-married, but very nice minister, after you penetrated the thick coating of starch in which he is encased, and after you have become sufficiently familiar with his appearance

ALICE VAN YEVEREN HASKELL (*b.* July 21, 1848)
From a photograph by Dana taken probably in 1887.

to cease trying to calculate the angle at which his ears stand off from his head. The other guest was a case—an *Exhorter* as they called him—ugly, prosy, stupid, or rather simple minded, to a painful degree, telling every thing he knew, but seeming so perfectly *delighted* with his visit that you could but think it a privilege to entertain any one who so highly enjoyed it. The first night he came he had a dreadful sick headache, and he was scared to a painful extent about himself. I never saw such a nervous creature about himself; you could hear his groans all over the house, and Aleck won his heart's entire devotion by his delicate attentions to him during his potations of mustard and warm water. The first taste of this beverage had a most charming effect, but he insisted there was too much mustard therein and it must be weakened. That was done and a whole tumbler full was emptied without any effect. Aleck was deeply agitated thereby and came out to consult me as to what must be done. I advised patience, and when that was played out, suggested a finger down his throat. Aleck soon returned saying *three* fingers had been unavailingly tried. I said "try, try, try again," one finger far enough and often enough *must* prevail, and finally it did. I was sorry for the poor man, but his conduct would have been reprehensible at eight years of age. However, I forgave him when I heard him praise Aleck's nursing capacities, which certainly are great.

I am so enchanted with my range, and find it burns *very* little fuel indeed. It takes coal and we are most fortunate not to be dependent on wood now, for since the horse disease is raging so here, wood is so scarce as to be selling at the rate of *$25.00 per cord* on the street. When can you come over and pay us that visit, I want to know. Has Booth come yet? I think you said Nov. was the month she was to return in. I want you to come and see how I am fixed all so comfortable and cosy. Please my dear Sister dont disappoint us, and Brother

George *must* come and expose Hendrix for imposing on the community in the matter of "Pride of Augusta."

Please when you write give me the receipt for that yeast that wont sour. I feel quite exhausted; we had a deaf Charleston gentleman to dinner, and the effort to shriek out my entertaining observations has quite overcome me. Aleck joins me in love to Bro. George, yourself and the girls.

Yours very affly.

ALICE.

Harriet Cumming to Miss E. Barnett.

Beulah,* July 5, 1874.
Sunday A. M.

Do you imagine, Darling, from my date that I have left the land of darkness and shadow behind me and come out to green pastures and still waters and an innumerable company of angels? The thought comes to me of how unutterably sweet it would be if the first one of us two that reaches those Sweet Fields could really write and tell the other of the things that are there and the Home there, as I am now about to tell you of this earthly home where for a time I am tabernacling. Remembering that in these days you know nothing of me but what I tell you myself, I must explain to you that we have vacated our house in the city for a season and are living in a sort of marooning style at a place on "The Salts" about twelve miles from Savannah, known by the poetic appellation of "Beulah"—and it deserves the name. We are not more than ten or twelve miles from the open sea and there is a broad inlet which makes up just before our door. There are beautiful oaks and green grass; and the strong, fresh sea-breeze pours in all day and all night, making me forget that it is warm weather anywhere. The scene on which I look out all day long is most beautiful to my eyes. I have a passionate love of the water, and to watch it is an ever new delight to me. The incoming and outgoing of the tides, the rolling of the waves when it is rough, and the mirroring of the sky when it is still, the little boats sailing with wind and tide, or struggling against them,—all interest me and give me a sense of enjoyment; and the green fields

*Beaulieu.

319

beyond the swelling flood speak to me of joys that lie before me. The house we occupy is a long, low rambling old affair with about 100 ft. of piazza across it on which we chiefly live and move and have our being. The upper story is not habitable, but we have plenty of room below, not only for our own family, but for friends many, and we have never taken a meal alone since we have been here, which is now nearly three weeks. Now the boys call "Mother, please come and see us swim," so I must go—

The children are very happy here. The boys learn to swim, to row, to fish, etc., and the girls enjoy it almost as much. They have their young companions with them a great deal and they enjoy the bathing immensely. For my own part I keep busy with domestic affairs a good part of every day, and I allow myself reading time and musing time, and time to enjoy such company as comes especially for my benefit.

We live chiefly from what the waters furnish and vegetables of which we can get a full supply. Housekeeping does'nt give me much trouble, even when the house is full of company, for as we only profess to be marooning, not much is expected of us.

Wallace goes in to his work on the cars every morning, and gets back about half past four in the afternoon. I think he likes the change and is willing to take the trouble it involves. He seems interested in everything that concerns our life here, and I feel as if it all does him good and keeps him healthful and cheerful. There is only one thing that I much regret and that is that it keeps us from church on Sunday, and Mr. Axson was preaching as I never heard him preach before and I felt that it was doing us all good. The two girls go in to church, but I could not carry in all the family and could not go myself and leave the children. I try to make it a pleasant and profitable day to them, and I can enjoy it myself after my own fashion. But we too often have company on that day, and I greatly miss my sanctuary food for myself and am sorry to lose its good influence on the others.

Tuesday 6th—Yesterday I was busy all day and did'nt find time to go on with my letter. Today I must lay aside the sewing and give you the time, for tomorrow I shall have company again. Leila spent the first week with me after I moved here and is to spend every Wednesday with me while I stay. She enjoys it immensely. We have a large family most of the time, varying from eight to fourteen at table, but I don't let it trouble me. I only have plain things, but plenty of them and nicely cooked.

Every morning about eight o'clock (for we have to breakfast at seven in order that the gentlemen may catch the train to town) I take my Bible, Bogatsky and Hanna's "Life of Christ" and go out on the bluff by myself. I put on a wide hat that shades and conceals me, set my chair under one of the oaks, and there give myself about an hour of time that is strength to my soul and marrow to my bones.

H.

Yellow Fever in Savannah.

Harriet Cumming to Miss Emma Barnett.

Savannah, Sept. 15, 1876.

My dear Love:—

At the close of a busy day before I lay aside my work and seek my pillow, I must begin the letter to you which I am constantly longing to write you. I am so often thinking of you and inwardly speaking of you that you seem really near me. I want to be always telling you "Be happy about me, my Darling, for I am happy." I would not be any where but here for anything that could be offered me. I should be miserable if I were away from here; should feel like Jonah fleeing from the work which God gave him to do. I have been long saying to Him "Here am I, send me," and now He is giving me abundant work which I love to do, and Darling I *thank* Him for the privilege,—

Sunday night—I was too tired to go on writing, Dearie, and had to go to bed, and since then have not found time to go any further. Cliff sent you a postal a day or two ago, saying that we were all well. Another week has gone over our heads leaving us all in health and strength, and in peace and comfort.

Dr. Axson preached us a pleasant sermon this morning —"The name of the Lord is a strong tower; the righteous runneth into it and is safe." The text was sermon enough of itself. Things around us go on from bad to worse, and, indeed, there is nothing else for us to expect for some weeks to come. Nothing can check the spread of the disease now but a heavy frost, or the fact that it has eaten up all the victims that it can find. I have been into some houses where every member of the family is

322

down,—father, mother, and children. Have seen four in the same bed with the fever. The Association hires nurses for all who need them, but the nurses are almost all negroes, and you know what kind of work can be done with so many on the hands of one person, when that person is an ignorant hireling. Yellow fever requires the most careful treatment. Nourishment and medicines must be given with great regularity, symptoms watched, vomiting prevented by vigorous remedies, warmth kept up, and in short one person of activity and intelligence would be kept well employed day and night with two patients to look after. So you may know how many of these poor creatures die for the want of care. Money and supplies have been sent us liberally and are being liberally used. But it is not possible to reach all the needs of individual cases, and among those who shrink from making known their wants there is much suffering. That is where I try to work in my small measure, and I can add many a little comfort to such, by means of the money which is put into my hands. I have sent several poor families out of the city in cases where they had friends who would receive them, if only they could get to them, and it has seemed to me the best charity I could do.

Monday night—My rounds were sorrowful this P. M. At one house where I went only because the woman had a fancy for me and was sick, and where I was not prepared for trouble, I found the husband dead and just being carried out. One child already buried and one lying very low. The mother is ill herself and the only person walking the house beside the hired nurse is a little five year old girl. The anguish of soul that the poor woman was in, must, of course, work against her recovery. I sat by her and held her hand and tried to help her to think of the Friend who will never leave or forsake us; but her cry was still "he's gone! he's gone! I'll never see him any more! There's nothing left to care for now!" Oh Darling! it makes one's heart sick to see so much sorrow. How could we bear it if we did not *know* that God is good and has his purposes of mercy in it all. To look on and lose sight of *Him*, it looks so hard and strange to see so many valuable lives taken and so many that are worse than useless left. Cliff has gone to sit up tonight with Mrs. Wilder who has been lying desperately ill for some days. I hate to have her go, but still we must not hinder those we love from doing their duty. Cliff is so calm and composed and strong in her conviction that she is where she ought to be, that I have no power to beg her to go. I want to urge it, but somehow the impression on my mind that God has put her here for some work that does not yet appear, is so strong that I make a poor effort when I try to urge her to go. I know that I should feel terribly bereft if she were gone. She is strength and comfort to me, tho' always I accuse myself of selfishness in keeping her.

I must close my letter and send it tonight, tho' it says but little of what I wanted to write you. Goodbye dear Darling. Don't be afraid of evil tidings. None can come for there shall no evil befall us. All will be well, whatever happens. While God has work for me to do I am immortal and you yourself could not be sorry if He bid me come Home. You would be glad for me as I shall be for you, if I outlive you.

I think I told you that Leila is out of town. She is about twelve miles out of the City on one of the Islands. I hear from her once in a while, but I do miss her so in our work.

Lovingly forever yours,

H.

Harriet Cumming to Her Sister Clifford.*

I.

Washington—Feb. 26—'82.
Sunday Night.

It is after one o'clock, My Dearest, but I have just gotten the poor little girl quiet and asleep, after hours of restlessness. It is not quite time to call Charley for the second watch of the night—and while I sit here, I may at least begin the letter that I would like so much to write you. Yours came yesterday— I must tell you here that I did receive the very nice long one you wrote me to Augusta—and it was only because I wrote mine to you under such hurry and worry, that I failed to reply to it. If I get time enough before I send this, perhaps I can still take up some of its points. The truth is that ever since I have been away from home, I have been in a hurry. I have always been where I wanted to give all the time that I could to those with whom I was staying—and at the same time, I have had a call upon me for much writing. I almost think now that if my hand were cut off at the wrist, it would go on writing of its own accord. Since I have been here, I relieve Charley of the writing, and the daily bulletins and letters are no small job. I never feel at leisure. Even when I sit up at night, I am divided between the nursing and the writing—trying to get ready for the morning's mail. Tonight I have had little time for the letters, because Hattie has been nauseated and restless. While I was sitting by her, stroking her hair and trying to soothe her to sleep, she opened her eyes and said

*This and the two following letters were written during the last illness of Hattie Alexander, eldest daughter of Charles A. Alexander, aged sixteen.

"Grandmother, you ought to have been named Peace—for you carry peace wherever you go—and that ought to have been your name"— It is a strange thing to see how she clings to me and seems to feel about having me near her. I can scarcely tell you how she is, as compared with when I last wrote. She does not change much from day to day. We read to her most of the day and she says it helps her to bear her pain.

H.

II.

Washington.
March 8th 1882.

My dear Old Love. I had not thought ever to date a letter to you from the old Home again at this season of the year. But here I am—and at dusk this evening, I was walking up and down the entry where our youthful feet trod thirty-nine years ago—alone this time, but bearing the thought of you in my heart as I paced back and forth. The day has been cold and dark and rainy. I tho't that the rain might turn to sleet, at one time, and then it would have been even more like "the day we celebrate."* I have had many thoughts which I would like to express to you, as I have surveyed today the path by which we have come, since that Long, long ago time—but I could never put them into a letter. Your long nice, welcome missive reached me yesterday and you may be sure that it was a pleasure to me. I would'nt disobey you and write at once in reply, if it were not the 8th of March—but tonight I have not as much writing to do as usual, and can send you at least a little letter. It is about half past eleven o'clock. Hattie had the needle at ten and has but a little while ago quieted down for the night. After she has it, she always wants me to read her Bible to her and let her ask questions and talk a little. She asked me tonight if I thought that this was to be her last sickness. I shrunk

---

*March 8th was the date on which she and her sister Clifford, when little girls, made a pact of friendship—a pact never broken.

326

from giving her an honest answer—but she pressed me, and I could only ask in reply if she would regret it, if it should be. She said that if she had her father's hand and mine, she tho't she would not be afraid to die—and then we had a long sweet talk. I did not tell her that I thought she would never get well, but I talked of the sweetness of Death and tried to set it before her as the gate of Life. She has been worse for two days past. The Doctor told me that he did not think that it could possibly last much longer —but to me it seems as if she might live weeks and even months just as she is now.

H.

III.

Friday night—March 17th.

Dearest, the end draws nigh— This morning she had the Doctor sent for early—she had been worse for two days —and she asked him to tell her truly if she was going to die. He hesitated, but when she pressed him, he told her Yes—that this was the end. She thanked him for his candor and told him that she was not afraid to die. After he left, she talked with great calmness of it. Sent for the baby, played with her, laughed merrily with her, kissed her over and over—and said she was so glad that her father and Mother wd. have the baby when she was gone. Then she began to dispose of all her little possessions—gave to each one of those she loved best, some little thing belonging to her. Said that Hattie Hull must have something to remember her by—for Hattie had always been so sweet to her. Then she was racking her brain to think of something that she could give Dr. Ficklen—something that she can buy with her own money. So she wants her Uncle George to buy her a stylographic pen of a nice kind, or a pen and pencil—or a pocket pencil, or something of that kind. The stylographic pen seems to be her preference —and she wants it sent at once. Pay for it Dear, if you can, and let us return the money here to Hattie or when

327

you come. She said tonight that she was going to beg you to come here and see her father when you came South —that he would need all the pleasures he could have.

I dont mind my night watching, tho' I suppose it does tell on old bones, in the long run— Hattie called, and I went to her. I gave her a swallow of water to moisten her parched throat and tongue. Then it was, "Kiss me— Do you love me? Ah! yes, I know you do, or you would'nt be here. Just you and God and me—that's so sweet."

Saturday 25th.

At twelve o'clock yesterday noon, she peacefully passed into the haven for which she has so longed. For more than a week—indeed for ten days, we had thought that every hour would be the last. The last eighteen hours her mind wandered, but she muttered to herself all the time, and bending your ear you would hear "many mansions," "fear not" "deep waters" "other refuge"— showing that she was trying to say the verses she so loved. She will be buried at eleven this morning. She is beautiful in death. Dressed in a full robe of Persian mull with soft crape ruffling and white ribbons—lying on her side—on the old sofa, wh. is draped in white—with long delicate vines trailing all over it—and a lily in her hand—wh. she asked to have placed there.

I go home on Monday.

H.

Letter from Richard Malcolm Johnston to Sarah Lawton.

Pen Lucy, Waverley, Md.
Dec. 3, 82.

Dear Mrs. Lawton:

I received a day or two ago some pages very becomingly and tastefully printed, in honor of your father. Along with these was a paper from Sam Barnett, which of its kind was as excellent as could be.

I did not know your father personally. I have often said to Sam how I regretted not to have known, face to face, this man whom I have long considered as the most gifted and useful private citizen that the state ever produced.

More than forty years ago when my older brother, along with Tucker Irvin, was a student of law under Judge Andrews in Washington, I used to hear him talk of the great school of girls that Mr. Alexander had established there with Miss Brackett at the head and Misses Belcher and Smith at her sides. I had an idea that Mr. Alexander, to be the founder of such an institution, must be far advanced in life. Then I heard afterwards of what he had done for our dear friend Alex. Stephens. Yet later I was surprised to find that he was not an older man.

I repeat, it was always one of my regrets that I did not know him personally, especially after I had heard Sam Barnett speak of him in terms of so high praise.

Well, my dear friend, it is well to have had such a father, to remember what sort of man he was, competent for the greatest offices, yet wholly without ambition to occupy them, a man who, above all of his time, exhibited that one may do as much in private for his country as the most renowned in public, and do so only by the force of an example of spotless integrity and a possession of highest, noblest public spirit. For your father, ever since my childhood, I have had an admiration which somehow I never had for any other man in the state. I could not but pay to him the honor which all men feel to be due to a man of transcendent abilities; more than doubly due, when such a man persists in remaining a private citizen, leaving to others to struggle for public honors and distinction. At last this is man's loftiest ambition—to do one's best for his family, his neighbors, and his country, and not only not to seek, but positively decline all rewards for such service. The great legend tells us that there were "heroes before Agamemnon." Their names were lost in the siftings of long tradition. But to my mind the best heroes are those who do what they do that is heroic silently, looking for recognition, not to men, words, spoken or written, but to their own sense of responsibility in the love and fear of God.

I condole with you at the death of such a father. But the more do I congratulate you in what you have to remember concerning him. He had lived well and he lived long. To the last he preserved the faculties that had made his career so benignant. That is a beautiful saying of Cicero (in his Cato Major de Senectute) "but the most becoming end of life is, when, with an entirely sound understanding, and unshaken sensibilities, the same nature that produced its work, dissolves it." Thus it was with your honored father. Be thankful therefore, and be happy to have had such a father, and to remember what he was and what he did.

Very truly and respy. your friend,

R. M. J.

Marion Boggs to Her Sister Clifford Hull.

I have been a long time in coming to my long-promised letter, dearest of sisters, finding but small time for writing at this busy season, and having many debts written against me. To-night the prospect of having things a good deal mixed seems to be before me, for Adam is parsing Latin sentences, and if you find Agamemnon and Clytemnestra interspersed in my remarks together with Datives and Ablatives, etc., you will understand how it comes. When William and Adam get at Latin, I feel exactly the opposite to what a little boy feels when he sees two roosters getting ready for a fight; that is, I want to get out of sight and out of hearing, too, if I can, for though it does not exactly amount to a fight, it is too much like it to be agreeable to one, who, like myself, does not know which side she is on. Adam is having to do some right hard studying this winter for the first time, and his head is so full of guns, slings, bullets, etc. that 'tis very hard to get him up to the mark in his books. I think he must be very much such a chap as E. P. A. was when he caught the "Davies Arithmetic" in his trap. The twins are going to a girls' school near by. They were very tearful when the plan was first proposed, and thought it a reflection on their manhood, or rather boyhood, that they should go to a girls' school, but since they have tried it they seem to like it much. Tom says that all the girls want Gilbert for a sweetheart, and they all want *him*, too, as long as he will *swing* them. Tom is more amiable than Gilbert, but he is so fond of teasing that he is not so popular I think. Mab says her lessons to me every day and is learning to read quite well.

Whenever Lucien hears her, he comes and says "Let me thay my lethon too mudder," and you would be surprised to see how readily he learns verses. His favorite hymn is "Let dogs delight," and he is so fond now of all that is didactic, that I am sure he is to be the preacher.

M.

Sarah Lawton to Her Daughter Nora.*

Grand Hotel, Vienna, Aug. 24, 1887.

Yesterday my General came in about 3 o'clock, found me at my little domestic avocations, sewing, studying, writing, etc., and asked me if I would like to go out for our dinner. I had been in the house all the forenoon, so I said yes, and we went to the Imperial Hotel. There we talked for some time with the Director, as to possible future arrangements there, looked at some rooms, and then dined in the restaurant. On coming out a light rain was falling, so we walked straight back to our hotel home. The porter met us at the door with a large square yellow envelope, saying "this is left for you from the Ministerium." We knew at once what it was, but when we reached our rooms and opened the seal, lo! it was written in German. Now German writing resembles Chinese as much as it does English. Dictionaries can't help you, but I did contrive to eliminate "Thursday, the 25th, at 2½ O'clock" from the scratching. So then we knew that was the day and hour fixed for your father's presentation to the Emperor. The Consul General came in soon and translated the paper for us, and his wife sat all the afternoon with me. Mr. J—— has been very much wrought up about the deferring of this presentation and has been disposed to think something lay beneath it (which we don't think). He may have written home some things on the subject, for he is very intimate with some high officials at Washington, so if the papers say anything it may have come in that way.

I am writing now while waiting for your father to be ready for dinner. I have to submit to quite irregular

*Written while General Lawton was Minister Plenipotentiary to the Court of Vienna.

hours. You all know how he is in a City, but I manage very well, by keeping on hand a little lunch. Dinner is a time consuming affair in the way we are living, and when he once goes out in the morning, he has to do all his day's work before he can return for the meal.

Thursday evening— Well, the important event is consummated! At one o'clock today your father came home and arrayed himself in his white cravat and dress suit (freshly pressed for the occasion). A carriage was sent for Mr. Lee who arrived at 2 o'clock, also in dress suit and light gloves. The President's carefully cherished letter to the Emperor was brought out. Your father conned over the little address he had prepared; he and Mr. Lee discussed and arranged just what sort of bows they would make and then they went forth. They were gone a very little while. Your father says the Emperor was ready and they were at once ushered into his presence. He was alone and your father would have gone alone if he wished, but he preferred to have Mr. Lee go in, as he might not have understood all the Emperor said in French. The Emperor was very pleasant in his manner and very polite, (he was dressed in military uniform, he has several different uniforms for different occasions) making many bows and saying kind things, and the whole' interview was easy and agreeable. He said he was very sorry he could not speak English, and that he was much pleased at the selection the United States had made of a Minister, etc., etc.

Now there will be no more ceremonies for a good long while. Only a printed list was furnished your father at the Palace today, containing the names and addresses of a great many people whom he must call on: the different families of the royal blood, dignitaries of the court, and members of the diplomatic corps—nearly one hundred in all! Most of them are absent at present. In all this I have nothing to do. About November or December I shall have to make calls also. Here the stranger leaves cards first. Up to this time we have been free to act as private individuals, but now we must enter into the restrictions and requirements of a Minister's position, in some measure. This is a country where *forms* are everything. Hitherto I have insisted on taking your father's left arm, because he hears well on that side and not on the other. Now, I must always walk and sit on his right, whether he can hear me or not, etc. etc.

We are going in the country, however, in a day or two more. We hear that Mr. and Mrs. Francis (the former Minister here he is, and the one who wrote us two long letters soon after your father was appointed) are to be here shortly, and we are anxious to see them and talk with them.

It is evening now and our French Professor will soon be here. I never pass a day without giving some time to both French and German, and I enjoy studying them so much that often it is hard for me to lay them aside. Your father is getting along nicely with French and by winter will be able to use it comfortably. He does not tackle German, but I have done so quite successfully and can make myself understood, only I can't, as yet, understand them; but I will learn.

S.

Sarah Lawton to H. C. Cunningham.

Vienna, Jan. 15, 1888.

My dear Henry:—

I have written a little account of the Court dinner which we attended and enclose it to you for you and Al and Nora and Daisy. I know you four will feel interested to hear just how such formalities are conducted. These are busy days with us—so many visits and so many cards to leave.

This week on Wednesday will be the first Court ball and the following Wednesday, the second. Next Saturday we (the General and myself) are to dine with the German Ambassador, Prince Reuss. I would prefer doing other things, dear Henry, but these are now my duties. In a month more they will pretty much be over, and we will be at liberty to spend our time as we please. I bless the institution of Lent.

We are looking forward with dread to Lulu's departure. Her staterooms are secured to her satisfaction on board the German ship Adler, to sail from Bremen Feb. 1, and she will leave us on Jan. 28, to rest two days in Dresden with her friend, Mrs. Tarleton and the "Sistine Madonna," and to reach Bremen on Jan. 31. The Consul will see her on board, and we send a faithful English Courier with her from here.

Give our best love to all, dear Henry, and be sure to remember me also to your Mother.

Yours most affectionately,

S. A. L.

(The Enclosure.)

On Sunday afternoon, the 8th of January, a messenger from the Palace left an open card, inviting the American

SARAH ALEXANDER LAWTON (*b.* January 26, 1826)
From an oil portrait painted about 1889 by Miss Lila Pollock
of Philadelphia.

Minister and his wife to dine at the Emperor's table on Tuesday 10th at 6½ o'clock. To the invitation was appended instruction as to the toilet proper for the occasion, and a request that if unable to come the Master of Ceremonies should be promptly informed. Otherwise, we knew the invitation was not to be answered. Its acceptance was a matter of course.

I sent at once to request an interview with Madame M——, an American lady of the diplomatic corps, wife of the Minister from Holland. She is a good friend of mine; has been here several years, and I knew had dined at the Palace the week previous. She sent for me to come the next day at one o'clock and when I went I was able to consult her as to many details of my toilet, and as to exactly what I must do when presented to the Empress. She said I would find everything made easy and pleasant, and I did.

Great was the commotion in this family circle on Tuesday evening over my preparations for the dinner. The General's were only the same he would have made at home. Lulu sternly presided over mine and admitted nothing that she did not approve. I was finally turned out of the work room, arrayed in my blue-gray train silk which is open in the neck and has white silk and gold braid and tulle in front, a head-dress of gold lace and feathers on one side of my head with two diamond stars to fasten it, and gold colored gloves. We drove to the Palace a little before the hour; were ushered up long staircases and past officers of the guard till we reached a small carpeted ante-room, where a servant assisted us to uncloak and a man in uniform handed us each a card. On mine was written in French, "Mde Lawton will please seat herself at table by the side of Count Nigra, Ambassador of Italy." The General's invited him in the same way to a seat beside Countess Toda, the wife of the Japanese Minister. Carrying these cards we then were ushered thro' one or two more ante-rooms into a vast reception room, where we found nearly all the guests already assembled—all standing. No seats in the room. The Countess Goess, whom we knew, came forward to receive us and appointed me where to stand, while some man showed the General to his place on the other side of the room, all the men being one side, and the ladies, the other. I found myself among acquaintances and next to the Greek Minister's wife who is a very sweet lady, and she is to be always next to me as our husbands were presented to the Emperor on the same day, so we are twins in diplomatic rank.

We were all chatting quietly together when suddenly the Countess Goess made a sign. A hush fell on all and everybody took position against the side of the room. By the door near which I was standing entered the Emperor and Empress, saluting the company as they entered. Everybody bowed and curtsied. The Countess Goess spoke to the Empress and bringing her in front of me, introduced me. Of course, I curtsied again, and then the Empress said a few commonplaces and passed on to the next new Minister's wife. There were three and each was presented in the same way. Then came the Emperor and to him we were each introduced. He made very polite bows for our curtsies. To me he said that he hoped I had found Vienna pleasant and one or two other such remarks, and to the other ladies I suppose he said the same.

When the presentation was over the Emperor and Empress walked into the dining-room and we all followed, independently, twenty-six persons. At the door an official looked at our cards which we held in our hands, and pointed to our seats. The table was set with a line of large golden bowls full of flowers, down the center. There were also glass dishes of bonbons, etc. The service was of gold—six glasses to each plate, of the plain heavy style like our old sherry glasses. Raw oysters were served first, then soup, and about ten other courses; Roman punch in the middle. After the punch china was used instead of gold plate; some exquisite kinds. When coffee came empty cups were first put before us of plain white and gilt in lovely forms. Then a golden coffee-pot was carried round and about a spoonful only was poured in each cup, and sugar and cream was offered.

I was very nicely seated. The Emperor and Empress sat in the center of the long table, opposite each other, and I was the third from the Emperor—the Ambassadress of England being next him and the Ambassador of Italy next her. Then I came and then Count Knuth, the Danish Minister, who is very pleasant. My General was not so well fixed. He was next the Japanese Minister's wife, who can speak nothing but Japanese. The Emperor's Special Aid and Adjutant General, Count Paar, was on his other side, who speaks no English, but he had agreeable people opposite. The Empress sat between two Ambassadors: the English and Turkish. Ambassadors always take precedence of Ministers, and their wives ditto. After coffee the Emperor and Empress rose. Every one stood back till they passed (not failing to bow and curtsey as Imperial Majesty swept by) and then all followed back to the salon of reception, where were no seats, and stood in order near the walls as before, the ladies on one side, men on the other. The Emperor and Empress then made, each separately, the circuit of the company, each speaking a few sentences to every person. While this went on, the guests conversed low with those near by them, and when it was done, the Emperor and Empress saluted the assembly and left the room. A few minutes more we all chatted together being then free to move around. Some persons I had not known were introduced to me, and then we all left together. As one of the Ministers said to me, "Our task is finished." To us, it was very entertaining, but to those who had been thro' it regularly once a winter for some years, I suppose it was a task. When we reached home, we had been gone just two hours.

The Reunion in Savannah.

Harriet Cumming to Her Daughter Sarah

Savannah, March 22, 1890.

Dearest Daughter:—

O for the pen of an angel to tell you all the pleasant things that we have been enjoying since last I wrote to you! But time and strength would fail me, even if I had the eloquent of which I spoke, for our joys take nearly all of my time and nearly all of my strength besides. I sent off my last letter to you on Friday morning, just before we started on our expedition to Greenwich. Sarah's carriage took herself, Alice and Cliffie; Mrs. Gilmer took Minnie and Bridget;* and I took Charley. Isaiah and the flesh-pots went out in a wagon. We had one of the pleasantest days that I ever spent. Sat on the piazzas over the water for an hour or more, and then we saw a rain coming, so we went to the house and sat on the piazza there till dinner time. The steward there had prepared delicious fried and stewed oysters and rice. Your Aunt Lou had the nicest of boneless chicken, turkey, and ham, tongue, bread, biscuit, pickles, mayonnaise, olives, etc. etc., and then ice-cream and cake, fruit, nuts, and coffee. It was a delightful dinner and we all enjoyed it thoroughly. After dinner we walked about and sat by the water and entertained ourselves well, till time to come home, and we all agreed that the day had been one of those good and perfect gifts which had come down to us from the Father in Heaven.

On Saturday afternoon Felix and Hilly came, and I had invited them all to my house at eight o'clock. It

*Mrs. Gilmer's maid.

340

poured rain but they all came, and for the first time in more than twenty years we ten sat together. Ed and Bettie got home at eight o'clock, but came over by nine, so we were a completed circle. We had all taken tea at home, but I had ice-cream and cake and wine for them, and we made merry till after eleven o'clock. As I looked around the circle at each face that was so dear, a thought that went beyond the gayety of the hour came over me, and I asked them all to fill their glasses and let me give them a sentiment, if not a toast, and then I gave—"Our Homes: the one Home of our childhood—the scattered Homes of today—and the one Home where we hoped to meet again and be once more re-united. No wanderer lost,—a family in Heaven." Our eyes were wet a little as we drank it, but my heart stirred with a mighty prayer within me, that God, who has been so good to us all in this life, would add to us each and all Life Eternal.

Today, even tho' it was Sunday, we have dined at Gen. Lawton's. It was not a formal dinner. We sat down twelve to table. Poor dear little Minnie had a headache and had to be left behind. They gave her seat to Al who came with them last night and said he was too mad because he wasn't invited to dine with us today. It was a very pleasant gathering, and after dinner Lucy and Hattie and George B. and Wallace came in. Tomorrow morning we are all to go to Launey's and have the ten photographed. I disapprove of that, but won't make a fuss, tho' I despise group pictures.

Sister has invited us to her house tomorrow night, but I think the boys will probably go on the night train. Felix, Hilly and Charley have been here this evening. Minnie came down and is getting over her headache, we hope.

I am sitting up late to write this to you, for there will be no time in the busy tomorrow.

Faithfully,

MOTHER.

Harriet Cumming to Her Sister Marion Boggs.

Home—April 25. 1890.

Precious Little Woman—The lilacs are by me, in a blue vase like unto Mother's—and I raise my eyes to them often, as their fragrance steals softly into the air. God bless you, My Darling for your sweet thought of me. The two boxes came before noon yesterday, and the flowers were as fresh as if just gathered, and the cake was sound and uninjured, and panned out famously when we cut it for tea last night. The table had quite a gala look, with all its wealth of flowers and its tall cake—and one would scarce have imagined that it was a sixty-second birthday that was being celebrated! You are right in supposing that it has been about fifty-two years since I had a birthday-cake! It had the full flavor of novelty, besides the delightful orange flavor of the filling! I seemed to see your dear face and your thin little hands as you worked over both the cake and the flowers. Ah! how I love that dear face and those thin little hands! I dont know that earth holds much of which I think with the same unspeakable tenderness.

I have kept the lilacs for my own special share of the flowers. Do you remember sending me a little box of lilies of the valley from your Columbia garden, the spring that I was recovering from pneumonia? Well, those lilies of the valley still bloom on the walls in memory's storehouse—and henceforth I think that this vase of lilacs will stand beside them. I have planted the periwinkles and hope they will thrive.

The Doctor* leaves on Monday for Dansville. Sallie will

*Doctor Houstoun.

342

not go with him. If he needs her, she can go on later—but we hope he will get along all right without her. I do want to leave it so that either Sallie, Lucy, or Hattie Hull can be with you at Commencement. If Lucy goes to see you, her visit may cover that time—but I dont know her plans—I only want to tell you that if you have no other help, and if you really want her, I'll fix it so that Sallie can be with you at that time. You are perfectly free to say you *dont* need her, and you'll hurt no feelings in any quarter—but you shall have help of some kind, if it can be compassed.

H.

The Last Reunion.

Harriet Cumming to Bessie Ficklen.

96 Harris st. Savannah.
May 12, 1891.

My dear Bess—Your sweet Mother has asked me as a favor to her, to write you an account of our Family Reunion which took place at Washington a few days ago. The half can ne'er be told, My Child—but as I know that your father will never have time to write you about it, I will try to give you some little idea of what we have enjoyed. So I'll begin at the beginning and tell you that I went up two weeks ahead of all the rest, to give Rose what help I could in preparing for her guests. You know that they were each and all those whom she and Charley delighted to honor; and so everything was put in holiday attire. Charley had everything outside made white and clean—outbuildings, fences and paling everywhere were whitewashed, the walks were freshly gravelled and Dame Nature lent her hand to the adornment by shaking out the fresh young leaves on the trees, and loading the vines with honeysuckles and roses.

Within, everything was made ready and fair and sweet, and nothing was spared that could make the old Home speak out its welcome to the long-absent children that were coming back to it. You will want to know how they were all to be stowed away in one house. So I will tell you about that.

In the first place, Rose sent everybody else out of the house, and left it empty for the brothers and sisters. She and Charley moved out of their own room and went across the hall to what we call "the *old* sitting room"—and their room was set aside for Gen. Lawton and wife. Alice and I had the two rooms upstairs in the wing. Minnie was at the head of the entry. Your Aunt Lou over the parlor, and your Aunt Cliff over the dining room. The three brothers occupied the two rooms in the cottage. On Friday noon, May 1st, Hilly arrived, having misunderstood the movement of the Sav. party, and so preceded them. At eight that evening, Minnie and Alice arrived from Athens. And so there were five of us together that first evening. But the *grand* arrival was the next day, when at 11 A. M. May 2nd, your father's car rolled into the depot, bringing Gen. and Mrs. L., Mrs. Gilmer, Mrs. Hull, E. P. A. and W. F. A. There were four carriages and buggies in waiting; for friends all over town offered their vehicles and any and everything that could be of use. The Lawtons brought Cora with them as a servant, and she seemed to belong rightly to the family gathering.

Presently the watchers on the piazza saw the dust of the approaching chariot-wheels, and forth we ran to greet them. There, by the little white gate, and under the shadow of the old oak, the ten brothers and sisters met once more, and passed on to the home where "in infancy we played." There were tears mingled with the smiles on almost every face, and few words were spoken at first. It seemed a feeling too sacred for speech.

But presently they had all passed into the house, and then began the clatter of tongues. Everybody wanted to see every room and every spot—and before they had been an hour in the house, the whole procession had marched up into the garret, headed by your Aunt Sarah and your father, and the rear brought up by your Uncle Charley with his eyes shining and his mouth stretched from ear to ear. Your father unearthed his old Xenophon from one of the shelves, and on it he pounced, and enjoyed the luxury of stamping it under his feet as he had often longed to do in the days that are past. It was the noon of a very hot day, and the temp. of the garret must have been

345

about 140— So they were soon satisfied there. Next I heard of them in the cellar. And when the rest appeared, and your Father was inquired for, he had gone down the dry well!

By that time the dinner-bell rang— And if you had seen the noble turkey that stood at the foot of the table, you might have believed that he had stuffed himself and overlaid himself with fat, and delighted to live and to die especially to grace the occasion.

Time would fail me, My Bess, to tell you all the merry talk and to describe the happy hours—but one or two scenes that will forever live in my own memory, I may speak of to you. That afternoon some of the dear friends of Auld Lang Syne came over to bid us welcome and give us greeting. When they were gone, with one accord our steps seemed to turn to the little graveyard in the grove, and the sunset found us gathered together by the peaceful graves where the dear father and mother lie sleeping. Even from their Heavenly Home I think they must have looked down on us with pleasure. And in our hearts lay deep and still the blessedness of those who can say Lord! Thou hast been our dwelling-place in all generations! Then the next sweet picture that dwells with me, is the gathering at family prayers the next morning. Your Uncle Felix led us. He read the 103rd Psalm—"Bless the Lord oh! my soul, and all that is within me, bless His Holy name." And then he led us in prayer and thanksgiving—thanking God that we were all together there, our number still unbroken —thanking Him for the parents He had given us, to whom we owed so much—that He had been our covenant-making and covenant-keeping God thro all these long years— praying that *our* children after us may remember us with as much of love and reverence as we cherish for the parents who reared us within those walls—and that when life is ended, we may all meet again in the Father's house above. Sometimes his voice failed, because of all that was in his heart—and we knelt in silence till he could speak again.

On Sunday we all went together to the little church. In honor of our gathering, the kind ladies had dressed the church beautifully with flowers—and had set aside for us the pews where we used to sit when we were children. Indeed, all the way thro, it was very sweet to see how much affectionate sympathy in our Reunion was shown by all the town. In the afternoon we all went over to the old woods, some riding and some walking. We saw again the "big gully" that your Grandfather gave you so long ago, and I can assure you that it has grown to magnificent proportions. We visited the "big poplar," the "hickory-nut woods," the Rocks, the "Spring of Delight" and many other places of historic fame—and finished by marching up "the red hill," tho the empty carriages were along with us.

The next day we visited the Mary Willis Library, and inscribed our names in the Visitors' Book—and then they all rode around to see various houses, groves &c, that were specially remembered with interest, and to view the improvements in the dear old town. At last, the hour drew on when we must part—when the car must go back and all "the Boys" return to their work. Gen. and Mrs. L. left the next morning. Mrs. G. and I the day after. And one by one, all departed. The Old Home will know us as a completed circle no more. But when this life is ended, God grant us all a happy entrance to Our Father's House on high, where we shall go no more out forever, but dwell "No wanderer lost, a family in Heaven."

Your Aunt Sarah gave to each of us a very pretty aud useful little silver spoon as a souvenir of our meeting, the name and date marked on each—and it will go down to posterity as a most pleasant reminder of this sweet time.

As for how good and generous and kind Charley and

347

Rose were, words would fail me if I should try to tell. It was a great undertaking for them to entertain us all—but they did it right royally. Their desire would have been to have *all* of our dear In-Laws with us—but our numbers were too great. And we could only carry the first and oldest representative of that honorable body*—he who had been one of us before the family was completed, and without whom it would now seem incomplete.

Your father was at his very best, and seemed to enjoy every hour—and talked so entrancingly that we couldn't bear to go to bed at night and lose so many hours when we might be listening to him. The years did indeed seem to roll back and make us young again.

And now, sweet Bess, I have told you all that my old hand can tell—and you can fill in the outline with all the sweetest pictures that your fancy can paint—and they still will not reach the reality.

You see, Dear, I have "squinched up" all my writing (as little Mary would say) to try to get it into a smaller space, that I might pretend that I haven't written you an unconscionably long letter—but I fear the truth stands out, in spite of me.

Always affectionately

AUNT HATTY.

*Gen. Lawton.

Occasional Letters.

Harriet Cumming to Her Sister Marion Boggs.

November 18, 1894.

Tomorrow will be your birthday, my precious little sister, and this is but a line to say Blessed, yea, thrice Blessed be the day that gave you to this world and to those who love you. Thanks be to God that it was to this house and this family that He sent you! And thanks be to Him that He sent me to the same, to be here to meet you when you came. Ah! Beloved! This dreary old world has been less dreary to me by far because you are in it. May He keep you here to bless all around you, till the day comes when you cry "Now let Thou Thy servant depart," and then may He let you go in peace and joy unspeakable to be forever with Him and those of us who have gone before.

I don't want you to stay till every drop of joy is drained out of life. I don't want your heart broken before you see the end of the journey. I want you spared. But He who gave you to us knows best, and He loves you better even than we do, and we need not be afraid to leave your future in His hands.

Good night, sweet child! And may new mercies and blessings come to you with the New Year—blessings rich be waiting for the coming of your feet, and the Peace of God keep your heart, prays,

Your loving sister,

H.

James Hillhouse Alexander to His Sister Clifford.*

Augusta, Ga., Dec. 8, 1894.

Dear Sister:—

I thank you for your sweet letter. It is very grateful to know that my public record is appreciated in the family, and out of it. Scores of good people are saying kind and gracious things, and they are pleasant to hear and atone for a great deal I've gone through with in public service that is even harder and more trying than people know. But all this will be forgotten in a very few days by the public. Its breath is very fleeting. It will be different in the family circle. Among us it will be a feature, that every record made is clean and wholesome, and we will take pride in saying and knowing it is so *all along the line*—and a longer line than most lines are too.

I mean to take a day or two soon and see you all, both in Savannah and Washington. I have actually to renew acquaintance with some I've seen so little of for four years past. But I've got a great deal to do in looking after my own interests that have been long neglected. I have first to get my landed property in shape to pay something in rents the coming year, for the debts I owe are hard to carry at best. I shall miss the Mayor's salary muchly, but I'd rather miss it than earn it as I have earned it.

All well at Felix's, or well as usual. Betty is here and Ed. is to be here tomorrow, I hear. Love to all at the old home.

Ever affectionately yours and theirs,

J. H. A.

*Written at the close of his term as Mayor of Augusta.

A Golden Wedding.

Sarah Lawton to Her Children.

Asbury Park, Sept. 14, 1895.

My dear children:—

I wish to write something to you all in view of the approach of the 50th Anniversary of our marriage.

The usual way of meeting such occasions is, to my mind, far below the true demand of the situation. Half a century of wedded life, with its joys and griefs, its errors and mistakes, its consequences stretching forward into eternity, is a solemn thought. The day which completes it is a standpoint from which we look back on oh! such unutterable things, and forward into such an awe-bringing unknown—its certain anguish,—its vague possibilities—its depressing fears—its inspiring hopes. I can not approach such a stand-point with a festive spirit. Indeed I can not look forward to it without terror. It is for me a time to review the past with humble gratitude to the Giver of so much good, and to commence the future with obedient trust to Him who has led us all the way with such abundance of loving kindness. But I must feel at that retrospect that now on "Jordan's stormy banks" we stand and that our feet are slipping o'er the brink.

A golden wedding, says the world—"Let us eat and drink, for tomorrow we die." I can not feel so. In such an event life seems to touch its supreme moment, and the supreme is always solemn. But solemnity does not mean gloom; it may include happiness, deep and serious, in its expression, and a full realization of all the strong and tender ties of affection. Such are my feelings regarding

351

this anniversary, which approaches from the veiled future, and of which I must think, but I can not bear to speak of it lightly. Nor could I endure the accustomed forms of "celebration" so-called. Our wrecked and weather beaten barque must not be decked with gay and gallant flags, but on its deck might gather our dear ones who would wish us joy that our voyage is so nearly over, and we are so soon to reach home.

That is all. If we live to reach the day, we will spend it quietly, and meantime, do not let us talk about it.

One other thing I wish to say. Your father and I both feel that it would give us pain to have presents offered us on that occasion, and we hope that none of our children will think of doing anything of the sort. Their love is all we ask.

We wish to give our children each some token of affection in memory of the day. Your father says "presents should go downward, not upward"—But we wish them to have something lasting, something which will go to their children and be ever associated with the day; so I shall seek to select wisely some small token for each one—and that will be our celebration.

MOTHER.

I heartily approve and join in the wish that the views expressed may be carried out.

FATHER.

The First Break in the Circle.

Marion Boggs to Her Sister Clifford.

Athens, Ga., Dec. 2, 1895.

I have a constant desire to be writing some of you these days, Sister dearest, because I suppose all hearts are drawn together by our common sorrow.*

The thought of what we, what so many have lost, in losing Sister comes more and more over me, and yet I am sure it is with no real appreciation of the fact that she has actually gone out of our lives. Time only will bring us that. I don't believe that with all the pleasure we have had in each other as sisters, we have ever realized until now how much we have been parts of each others' lives.

Loulie has sent me one of those pictures.** It is very lovely to me; a far better likeness than any other that is known to me. There seems no look of death in the face; only rest and peace and victory.

I wonder if the shadow of another parting is already sweeping toward us? Lucy writes that Brother Lawton is failing rapidly.

I have missed the children (George and Dorothea Baldwin) very much. Dorothea was on her best behavior and I think tried conscientiously to do what she thought she ought. She is a child of such unusual sensibility of feeling, that we were all struck by it when the time came for her to go. She made us laugh very often too with her funny sayings. Once she said, "I've been caressing Bibbie because he looks so like a grown man with that collar on." Another time, "Aunt Marion, I felt a little sad when I came in to supper, but my cup of tea has quite enlivened me!"

M.

*The death of Louisa Gilmer.
**Taken after death.

E. P. Alexander to His Sister Clifford.*

Greytown, Nicaragua, June 10, '97.
My dear sweet Sister:—

A visitor (an Englishman named Climie, one of the Nicaraguan Commissioners) left with me to read the poetical history of an Evangelist named "Silver Jack," and it recalled something you have shown me sufficiently to make an excuse for me to copy it and work off a bit of a letter with it to you—bless your heart—wherever you are. Uncle Sam's postoffice can find you, I reckon. I hardly think you can have seen any of my letters home, for Miss Teen has had to send them around to our Kids, who, I expect, have about worn them out, so I will give you a brief resume of my movements.

I sailed from New Orleans on May 1, about a week before I had expected to. Had a splendid smooth voyage and was not sick at all, and reached Limon, Costa Rica, May 6 at 9 P. M.

I had a cordial greeting from the Costa Rica officials (with champagne) and next day was sent in a special train to the Capital, San Jose, 103 miles up in the mountains. This railroad ride was really the most interesting thing of my trip, for I had never read anything of the road before. But it first ran about 40 miles through forest, plain, and jungle, along the coast; and then it started up into the mountains and climbed a mile high in less than 40 miles, among the most tremendous cliffs and precipices, on the flanks of two volcanoes, Irazu and Turri Alba, each of them over two miles high, and lifting far above us, all

*Written on his first trip to Nicaragua, where he was sent by President Cleveland to arbitrate a boundary dispute between that country and Costa Rica.

354

covered too with the dense and curious tropical forest. There is no finer scenery or bolder railroad construction on the Canadian Pacific. A little way over on the Pacific slope we came to San Jose, a city of about 15,000, mostly low, square, mud-brick houses, with tile roofs, but with some good modern structures and a fairly good hotel. Here I spent a day and had many courtesies from the Pres. Iglesias and his officials, and meeting some really nice people (one of the Cabinet, Dr. Ulloa, and a Dr. Nunez specially). Next day our Commission started to come here. First, by rail to a station, Junta, where we spent the night; next day on horseback through the forest, some 8 miles, where I first saw wild monkeys, macaws, toucans, etc. Then in canoes for two days down a mountain river, and through long narrow deep lagoons, like green cañons thro' the tall forests, where every single tree, fruit, flower, vine, bird, beast, reptile, insect, and even the fish were new and strange to me. None of my comrades in the trip spoke more than a few words of English, so I could get little information in reply to my questions, and I almost gave up asking any, and simply tried to take in and remember all I could. Then we had one day out in the Caribbean in a little scrap of a 22 ft. sloop, crawling along the coast, broadside to the heavy ocean swell rolling in and making the wretched little cockle shell, and all its passengers, heave and pitch, and toss and roll, till it was a wonder that any human soul would stay in such a tormented body. And all that brought us to "Colorado Mouth," and there a good little steamboat came next day and brought us the last 20 miles here—with a bit more tossing, but not lasting unendurably.

Here the whole populace met us with a band, artillery, and champagne. This place was once on a great boom, while the Nicaragua Canal Company was spending six millions. Then the Company failed and this town has since nearly dried up. But they think that even a Boundary excitement is better than none; or that in some way settling the boundary question may help the canal, so nothing has been spared to make me comfortable. I have a nicely fixed-up room and servants to myself, and a man who speaks English to live with me and run it and keep it stocked with all the fluids and solids the town affords, so that I may entertain when I choose. It is isolated and has verandahs, and is as cool as any house here can be. And, judging by the thermometer, the temperature here is not excessive, 88° to 90° is the very highest I have seen in the shade. But the humidity is great and that makes one feel just on the verge of being uncomfortably warm all day; and in the evenings when it gets to be dead calm then you are over the verge till ten or eleven o'clock at night. Any exercise makes one uncomfortably warm at any time and even writing makes one's pad perspire. I have been agreeably surprised in one thing, however, and that was to find very few mosquitoes here—not near as many as I left in New Orleans.

This is the "rainy season" here from May to November, but it is an unusually dry one just now. Rains only about once a week. I have fished and hunted a very little on account of the heat and also because woods and under-growth are so dense one can hardly go anywhere. I've caught no fish to speak of, but have killed a very large wild duck, evidently the progenitor of our domestic Muscovy, and some very pretty wild pigeons with pink bills. Have seen very few snakes, but an hour ago some children brought by the house a sort of non-venomous constrictor 9½ feet long which they killed on the edge of the town. Of the insect pests one hears of I have had experience with only one—the jigoe. He is about one-fourth the size of a pin head, and always goes for the toe-nails under which he burrows and nests. Several of our Commission have had to have them removed, and one has been laid up for a week. I had one little fellow get on me but I caught on to his presence so quickly that he could do no harm.

Our Boundary Commission got to work on May 15, but could not agree upon the starting point of the line on the sea-shore. In fact, that is the principal cause of dispute in the whole business, and that I will have to settle. On June 14th I am to hear the argument and contention of each side, and then on June 30th rebuttal arguments are to be handed in, and then on July 1st the case will be in my hands. I may have to have some surveys and maps made and it will probably be in August when I render my decision. It is too soon for me yet to form any idea when I can get home.

Please write to me sometime and give me the family news, etc. Direct your letters "via New Orleans and Bluefields," and you will designate what is usually the quickest route, though the postoffice people generally know it. Letters take from 12 days *quickest* to 16 average and 20 slowest record.

Give my warmest love to all of yours.

Most affectionately,

E. P. A.

Harriet Cumming to Her Sister Clifford.

Baltimore, Nov. 2, 1897.

Your note has come, darling. It is a comfort to put out a hand and *feel* those that are left. Only you and I now, of the older sisters. I stand now at the front—the oldest of my generation—of all our family connection. I thought she* would want to stay and try to stay a little longer, but perhaps when the Home prepared came in sight she couldn't consent to wait. Even the dear earthly ties and wishes grew weak and faint, when she saw that it was but a step or two to the end. The heavenly radiance had long been on her. We could see the angel soul thro' the thin veil of flesh, and I trembled when on Wednesday night Lulu came in with us after prayer-meeting and said "I am sorry to tell you that mother has a touch of the Grippe." She said she had a postal from Daisy and that her mother had fever, but did not seem especially sick and the Doctor said there were no complications. On Thursday I had a note from Daisy saying that she was that day sending me a cape that Sarah had bought for me before she was taken sick.

Lulu says Sarah kept her bed first on Monday A. M. of last week, but that from the first she seemed not to want to take anything to help her except opium. She said "her work was done and they must let her die."

I am stunned, darling. My heart aches and sinks, but I don't even try to realize what has happened. I so rejoiced to think of her coming this Fall and that she would see our new home and know what sort of life I was to lead.

*Sarah Lawton.

I do not know how to live without her. I leaned on
her so much. But it won't be far now to the end. Love
to my sake.

Faithfully,

H.

E. P. Alexander to His Children.

Rivas, July 13, 1900.

Oh you Dear Ones, all of you, and just getting dearer and dearer all the while the further and the longer that I am away from you! Here I am at my journey's end, safe and sound in wind and limb. When I move from here again every inch I go will be homeward.

I finished up book No. 4 yesterday afternoon at Surtown and I left it there to be mailed on Sunday by a steamer to Panama. (But it was not left after all). Soon after finishing it, Commandante Sanchez, who lived in the house in which my room was, brought in his wife to introduce to me, and a prettier little Senora I've never seen in all this country. And tho' she spoke no English and I no Spanish, we managed to exchange a question or two and then she went and brought in as pretty a little four months old boy as could be found anywhere, and if ever there was a proud little mother she was the one. She told me his name (for his grandpa, but I forget it), and then she made me tell my children's names. Then I had what is so far the greatest disappointment which has happened to me on this trip. In Panama I had bought a little box of gum drops to suck at sometimes when half sea-sick. Two other little kids were hanging in the door, and it occurred to me to give them some gum drops, and the box to the little mother for the four months old. So I jumped up and searched my baggage thro' and thro' in vain, and then remembered leaving the gum drops in the upper berth in my stateroom on the "Sidney." And the worst of it was I couldn't explain to them what I was fussing round about. If I get a chance I would like to send something to that kid yet.

Well, I had a good cot and slept nicely. The berths on the "Sidney" were narrow, short, and hot, and I hated them. I do despise to have the footboard touch my feet.

This morning I was awake at 5 o'clock and up and out at 6, and I went down to the wharf to look around. I saw some soldiers fishing there and I borrowed a line and fished with them to their great amusement. In about ten minutes I caught a splendid big fish, bigger than all they had caught put together. It was about black bass in shape, silvery in color, with fine gold zigzag lines and rather big eyes. They called him curbena. My fellow was over a foot long, and would weigh over a pound, and he bit and pulled very prettily.

By the way did I tell in the last book of my visit to the Cable offices? Four ocean cables come to Surtown and the outfit of the office is very extensive and elaborate, and with no end of beautiful and delicate machinery. An Englishman, Mr. Crow, was in charge and was very polite, and I promised to send him a magazine article on deep sea cables, of which I told him.

Well, at 7:30 A. M. this morning we had a good coffee breakfast, and then we started at 8:30 on the 18 mile ride to this place. This ride has been a good deal on my mind ever since I decided on this route, for this is the rainy season, and the whole country is one vast quagmire, in which the roads soon become broad canals of mud full of bottomless holes. The descriptions they gave me of their trip over to meet me, and the accounts of the natives did nothing to reassure me. Old Mr. Holman, the American Consul, told me "just to prepare for the worst." Fernandez, the matter-of-fact Costa Rican, talked of mud holes "up to the mules' necks," and finally when they brought me my mule and tied her tail up to the saddle behind my back to keep it from dragging too much in the mud, it really began to look serious. But I have never been afraid to stand my chances, and they had gotten me a fine, stout little mule, but old and grey and experienced, and they lent me leather leggins well up on my thighs, so I bade farewell to every fear and just determined to plunge at everything that came, even if I broke a leg or a neck. As I went up to mount the old lady she dropped her left ear over towards me like an ear trumpet, as if she invited a confidence, and so I told her the whole responsibility would be on her, 170 lbs. of it, and she must just do the best she knew how. My trunk I had to leave to come by an ox cart, which is to start today, and to take two or three days on the road, but after seeing the road I fear it will be a week. I put some under-clothing and two shirts and a pair of pants in my satchel, and one of the servants took that on his horse and another took my umbrella.

These people are certainly the most hospitable in this world. Three or four officials and residents insisted upon accompanying us about four and a half miles across the principal range of hills (some 600 ft. high), that part of the road being considered "good." And, indeed, comparatively speaking it was, for these hills were steep and the water could run off generally. But the gullies it washed, and the tremendous ruts made by the oxcarts, with wheels sawed out of big forest trees, were enough sometimes to make me wonder what the next minute would bring forth. And before these gentlemen bid us good bye and turned back (where we entered into the morass country and the road was admitted to be *bad*), I had become convinced that Lorena, my mule, was not to be entirely relied upon. She displayed some fondness for the rear part of our procession (of about ten or twelve), and sometimes she seemed to want to hesitate, where hesitation meant sinking deeper every second, so I borrowed a rather keen pair of spurs, and I told Lorena that I meant business, and did not propose to be trifled with, for what did she get fed for? Well, after that the road just got to be ridiculous, to be called anything at all, and I can't pretend to describe it. But more than once when poor Lorena would seem to be about to give up and stop, I would just *lift her up* on those spurs as if with a steam derrick, and the mud would fly as if a shell had hit in it. Part of the way we got a native guide to take us three miles thro' a plantation, avoiding (they said) the very worst portion. But that three miles was as near impassable as anything could be, and yet be passed, thro' woods where roots and stumps and vines and bushes and thorns and trees, etc. only made the mud holes even worse; and across boggy meadows, where grass prevented any choice of ground. But we pushed the horses for all they were worth and made speed over every good place, and made the whole 18 miles in five hours. And I really enjoyed every foot of the ride: the beautiful meadows, hills, woods, trees, birds, flowers, and all such things all around me all the way, I can't begin to tell you of. I am dreadfully spattered, but "it will all brush off after it gets dry." I only dismounted once in the whole ride, for one five minutes' rest for mules, and yet came is as fresh, and steaming just as well, as when I started.

About three miles out from Rivas we were met by the Governor and the Chief of Police and Dr. Castrillo of the Nicaraguan Commission, who came to welcome me. And now here I am at quarters engaged for me in advance at the house of Senora Reynolds, a widow. The Senora is about 60, tall and full in figure, and stately, with grey hair. In color is about a quadroon, or a trifle darker. As an assistant, apparently, is Senora Santos, (her daughter,) only a shade less tall and full, about an octaroon in color and she speaks English, the only one in the house, except a Senorita Mathilde Santos who is full white, but somehow falls a little off in personal pulchritude, considering how far I have come to see her. I am assured that she reads and understands and can speak English, but she refuses to admit it to me.

The house is a typical old Nicaraguan house, built

around an open court of flowers and shrubbery, with big brick-tile floor, level with street, and high steep roof, extending over 10 foot pavement in front, and verandah in rear around the court. My room is 25 ft. square and fully that high, or higher in the middle, open up to the ridge pole of the roof, of old time tiles; double doors open on street in front and verandah in rear, in which all meals are served. There are no windows but a grated one in each door, so the room is rather dark, but it is always airy and cool. Only furniture is a table, a washstand, a canvas cot, a rocker, and four chairs, and a few pegs in one corner on the wall. The tile floor has been worn by the feet of generations. In a cage in the court is an Oriole, the same I used to call "Charlotte bird" in Greytown, because one of their favorite calls is "Who kissed Charlotte." This fellow does not sing much. Another interesting pet in the yard is "Al Caravan," a domesticated wild bird of the country, like a small heron, long legs, big eyes, and keeps a house clear of roaches and all insects.

The table is just splendid and profuse. It is now Saturday noon and I have just finished breakfast: six dishes of meat, including Vienna sausage, roast chicken, meat pie, roast beef, etc., eggs, rice, plantains, and potatoes. And the Nicaraguans keep my room stocked with all sorts of liquors, and they provided, also, an officer of the army to follow me about as an orderly and a valet to sit in my room all the while. I begged off from the officer, but Jose, my pretty little valet, sits in a chair behind me now. I had him at work for over two hours this morning getting the mud off my coat, and he did it pretty well too. I then sent him out to bring me some mangoes (I have often eaten mangoes but have never had enough). He could not find mangoes but got me oranges and sapote instead. Tomorrow I will try and beg off from him also.

Mrs. Reynold's husband was a Texan, and was a sort of professional Chief of Police at Panama when it was a

hard town to manage, and afterward here. Mrs. Santos'
husband is now a political refugee in Costa Rica, so she
is a grass-widow. Mathilde is her daughter, age 17, and
there is another, Marie, fifteen, who is better endowed with
looks. I pick up fresh points, you see, about the household
as the day wears on, it being now afternoon. I have given
Jose holiday and sent him off until tomorrow morning, and
I am sure we will both enjoy it.

Children, do you know it begins to look to me not
only certain that I can reach New York by August 14,
but even *possible* I may do it by August 7. I have been
looking over the work the Commission have done, and
what is to do. Everything in the field is finished except
a few monuments which we need not wait upon, for
ordinary workmen can finish them after we have signed
the books and gone. So there is nothing to do but to
sign up the books as soon as all the work is entered
on them. They say they can finish that in four or five
days.

Oh, my Lord! have mercy on me! Mrs. Reynolds has
just shown me in the Rivas paper that a "Demonstration
of the Sympatica of the Government" is to be shown me
at Managua. How like a fool I will feel! I would far
rather ride back over those 18 miles to Surtown! You
all can't even pray for me, for it will be over before you
know of it. I am sorry to end my letter so sadly, but
there is not a piece of balm in all Gilead good for a case
like this. Only, bless your dear hearts, you and yours
all, little and big, if anything on earth could make me love
you more, and find more rest and delight and comfort in
the very idea of owning you all, it would be the contemplation of these "scenes of confusion and creature complaints," through which it seems that I will have to go.
I only pray that I may not seem to others more than half
as big a fool as I will to myself.

But ever and always most affectionately,

FATHER.

E. P. Alexander to His Children.

Managua, July 24, 1900.

Well, my dear ones all, the great day has come, when we are to close our labors amid the simultaneous rejoicings of the two countries. At four o'clock at a solemn meeting in the presence of Congress and the President, I will attach the last signature to our records, and then the telegraph will give the word everywhere it reaches and every town will begin to shoot guns and to play bands and rejoice generally. Then tonight is a banquet with 100 guests, and your poor old dad has got to make a speech on each occasion. The first one and the biggest I have written out in full and it is translated into Spanish by Munoz and is all ready to be fired off. Munoz seems to think it will do very well.

Wednesday, July 25.—Well, beloved ones, at last the letters and telegrams of congratulations are answered up to date, and now I can begin to tell you briefly how everything passed off. At 4 P. M. yesterday an Aid of Pres. Zelaya came for Fernandez (the Costa Rican) and myself in the President's carriage—a very stylish one and with the biggest and fattest horses I almost ever did see. Compared with what one generally sees in this country they would take your breath away. It was only two blocks to drive, however, and then we drew up where about 500 soldiers were drawn up to receive us, with a band playing American and Costa Rican Hail Columbias. The ranks of soldiers presented arms, and we walked between them about a block to the entrance of the Congress Hall. The President and Cabinet and all the dignitaries were already assembled and seated, and we

EDWARD PORTER ALEXANDER (*b.* May 26, 1835)
From a photograph by Fr. Bery Johnston of Washington, D.C.,
taken about 1907 for reproduction as the frontispiece for General
Alexander's *Military Memoirs of a Confederate*.

marched in and sat behind a table or long desk reserved for us, draped above with the three flags. The whole hall too was draped and decorated with wreaths, and everything was made as fine and pretty as could be. I sat in the middle and the Commissioners on each side of me. I was surprised to see the big turnout of Prince Albert coats and silk hats and gloves. I had neither, but I had what was infinitely more appropriate—a nice palm-leaf fan, and I hope I have set a fashion in Nicaragua that may bless future generations. I had on moreover a nice new cutaway suit in black, and I will leave it to posterity to say if I was not right. For oh that hall, filled and packed as it was, was hot! I had to start my fan in less than two minutes, and in about five minutes the President had another, and after a while a Secretary had another, and every other poor man in the room was a-mopping and a-fanning with his handkerchief.

As soon as we were all settled we began with a formal meeting of the Commission,—reading aloud our final proceedings and then signing them. Then the cannon and the bands began, and the telegraph started off the whole of both countries. Then the benevolent looking bishop (he reminded me of my father's old carpenter, Jack Ryans, of slavery days) had a little showing, which I suppose was a blessing for us all. Then the orator of the day, Senor Maldonado, ascended a little platform and made a splendid speech. Everybody said so, and it so looked in gesture and sounded in inflection, but of course, I couldn't understand it. But, my darling children, I did wish you were all there just to see the gestures and to listen to the inflections for about ten minutes after he began about me. I know you would have all thought that your old daddy must be "some pumpkins" after all. There were more guns and band, and then came my turn. I couldn't do so much on gesture because I had to read out of my little book (which I will send along with this and you can see both my little speeches) but I did my best on inflection. And then there were more guns and band, and Munoz got up and said my speech over in beautiful and flowery Spanish, and got a good round of applause and still more guns and band. Similarly Fernandez followed, and then champagne was handed around, and President Zelaya made a short address in Spanish, and then we drank and then cigars were handed and we smoked, and there were some stray addresses and then we broke up, and Fernandez and I drove home again with the Aid and the fat horses.

I just had time then to take a nice cold bath in my private bathroom and put on my dress suit for the big banquet. It was given at Angel Caligari's Hotel Italia. The tables were set on three sides of the great square verandah around the open central court, and there must have been about two hundred seats. I will send a menu with this book. The service was excellent, the cooking the same, the decorations and flowers elaborate, and all accessories were up to date and in style.

The President sat in the middle of the middle side. I was placed opposite with Fernandez and Castillo on the right and left. Above the President were the three flags, draping an oil painting of the President and a life-size and very excellent crayon likeness of myself done in two days by an artist here from a Gettysburg photograph I happened to have.

We all met first in a large room where cocktails—so-called—were handed, but they were capacious glasses of nearly pure whiskey and mine just took my breath away. Then we went in and got our seats, each with a beautiful big card, and then the eating and drinking began. The first wine was a nice sherry and after that came my favorite Chateau Yquem, which is among the wines as your dear mother was among women,—the one I loved. But I had scarcely had more than a glass of it when I began to feel a sort of feeling in my ankle-joints which is my thermometer to tell me when to begin to go slow.

It was that wretched cock-tail. I might have drunk a whole bottle of Chateau Yquem and never known that it wasn't mineral water. However, the great art of enjoying a dinner is not to take a single drop or mouthful too much, and so I took the warning and kept myself well inside the line, and on the whole was never at a dinner which I enjoyed more.

Soon after the dinner got well under way some military officials began to circulate as busy as bees carrying the cards of guests who wished to drink the health of other guests. For instance, one would come up to me bringing the dinner cards with the names of several gentlemen way off some where, but who wished to drink with me. I would then look across to where they were, and we would all bow and drink. Then after awhile I would join Fernandez and Castrillo perhaps, and we would send our cards on pilgrimages, and we would drink in every direction. I think I drank with all the 200 guests, and with some of them several times, but I regulated the size of my drinks by the sensations of my ankle-joints and didn't take a drop too much or a drop too little, and so I felt fine.

When we got to the dessert and coffee and champagne, the speaking began. I had managed to hurriedly write a short speech in the back of my same little book which you will find there. Up to my delivering that everything had been on the solemn and patriotic order, and I doubt if there had been even a ghost of a smile in the whole crowd. But I had written my little remarks with a little faint streak of very subdued humor in them, and now when I came to speak, with a little Chateau Yquem in my veins, I made the very utmost of it and added to it a little, and gave it loud and clear and slow, and with all the inflection I could, and it caught everybody in the whole crowd who understood any English at all, and then Munoz translated what I had said and got all the rest of them. Especially were they all pleased with the big "boom" which I told them Nicaragua would soon have, coming from peace and the Nicaragua Canal. I don't think the word had ever been heard before, and I made it sound big and *loud*, and explained what it meant. And after they got it good, somebody made the big bass drum of the Band go "boom" beautifully, and that brought down the house. All the rest of the evening every once in a while the old drum would say "boom."

Since I have been writing this I went out to see a procession with rockets and flags, etc., religious, political, or both, and also to buy a little book to continue this letter in, and some small boy recognized me and shouted "General Alessander, Boom."

Well, about 11:30 we broke up and all in a good humor, and I really believe now that the Nicaraguans like me as much as I like them.

E. P. A.

Supplementary Details.

The foregoing Genealogical Table has been compiled and condensed by Lucy Harvie Baldwin for the purpose of showing only such ancestry of Sarah Hillhouse Gilbert as were of special note. It is believed to be correct.

The various genealogies, histories and records referred to in the following Supplementary Details should be consulted by those wishing fuller information concerning all other ancestry.

(1) HENRY WOLCOTT.

(of Galdon Manor, Tolland, Somersetshire, Eng.).

Born 1578. Married January 10th, 1606. Elizabeth Saunders. Died May 30, 1655. Was County Squire and Justice in England. Came to New England with Rev. John Warham, 1630. Became a Founder and Original Proprietor of Windsor, Conn., 1635. Was Magistrate, and in 1637 Member of the First General Assembly of Connecticut. Was "Assistant," or Member of the Governor's Council, or Member of "Upper House" (Senate), for twenty-four years.

See Wolcott Memorial; Hist. of Dorchester; Hist. of Windsor (Styles) ; Porter Gen.; and all Colonial Histories of Connecticut.

(2) JOHN MASON.

Born in England, 1600. Married Ann Peck, 1637. Died January 30th, 1671-2. Served in English Army in Netherlands with rank of Lieutenant. Came to New England with John Winthrop in 1630. Settled in Dorchester, Mass. Planned fortifications in Boston Harbor. Removed to Windsor, 1637. Commander-in-Chief of American Forces during Pequot War, 1637. On his return was made Major General of Connecticut Forces, which position he held thirty years. Removed to Saybrook at the request of the inhabitants, and was invested with command of the fort. Was Commissioner for the United Colonies, 1647-'54-'55-'56-'57-'61. Removed to Norwich, 1660, and was, by election and appointment, Deputy Governor from 1660 until his resignation in 1670. He wrote "A Brief History of the Pequot War," edited by Rev. Thomas Prince, and published in Boston. Reprinted in New York by J. Sabin & Sons, 1869.

See all Colonial Histories of Massachusetts and Connecticut; Calkins' Hist. of Norwich; Hollister's Hist. of Dorchester; Genealogies of Jocelyn, Fitch, Stranahan and Dow Families; and Appleton's Ency. of Am. Biog.

(4) AARON COOKE.

Born in England in 1610. Married Johanna Ford, 1637. Died September 5th, 1692. Came from England to Dorchester, Mass., 1630. Was one of the party who journeyed through the wilderness and founded Windsor, Conn., 1635. Removed to Massachusetts, and was an Original Proprietor of Westfield, Mass. Was Captain and Major of Connecticut Forces; Representative to General Court, 1660 to 1668.

See all Colonial Histories of Connecticut and Massachusetts; Styles' Hist. of Windsor, and condensed genealogy of Cooke Family in Porter Genealogy, Vol. 1.

(6) MATTHEW GRISWOLD.

Born 1620. Married Anne Wolcott, 1646. Died September 27th, 1698. With Major John Mason, "drew the boundary between Pequot and Massachusetts," 1654. Lieutenant of Train Band of Lyme, 1677. Deputy to General Court, 1678-85. Commissioner for Lyme, 1689-94.

See Gen. of Griswold Family in Mag. of Am. Hist., February and March, 1884; Hyde Gen.; Colonial Records of Connecticut; and all Histories of Connecticut; Calkin's Hist. of Norwich; Salisbury's Hist. of Griswold Family.

(7) JAMES FITCH.

Born 1622. Married Priscilla Mason, October 2nd, 1664. Died November 18th, 1702. He led the Colony that founded Norwich, 1660, and was one of the legatees of Joshua Uncas. Became an Original Proprietor of Windham, Conn.; and was Chaplain to the Army during King Philip's War, 1670-71. Preacher of Election Sermon (1674)—the first one ever printed—a copy of which is preserved in the Library of "Yale College." Cotton Mather, in his "Magnalia Christi Americana," calls him "Second Classis of the Church in the Americas."

See Hist. of Norwich; Hist. of Hartford; Life of Rev. Thomas Hooker; Condensed Gen. of Hillhouse Family in Hyde Genealogy; Appleton's Ency. of American Biography; Old Homes of Norwich (Perkins); Cotton Mather (as above).

(10) WILLIAM PITKIN I.

Born 1635. Married Hannah Goodwin, 1651. Died December 15th, 1694. Settled in Hartford, 1659. Prosecutor for the Colony, 1662. Appointed by King Charles II Attorney for the Colony, 1664. Treasurer for the Colony, 1676-7. Commissioner to negotiate Treaty of Peace with the Narragansetts, 1676. Continuously Member of General Court, 1665-1690. Occasionally during this period Commissioner to the United Colonies. Member of Colonial Council, 1690-1694. One of the Commissioners to draw the boundary between Massachusetts and Connecticut, 1693. Envoy to Sir Benjamin Fletcher in New York, 1693.

See condensed Gen. of Pitkin Family in Porter Gen., Vol. 1 (p. 70), Appleton's Ency. Am. Biography, Vol. 5 (p. 32).

(13) SAMUEL PORTER II.

Born 1660. Married Johanna Cooke, Feb. 22, 1683. Died July 29th, 1722. Representative to General Court, 1699-1704. Sheriff and Judge of the County of Hampshire, . Mass.

See Porter Gen., Vol. 1 (p. 16).

(14) WILLIAM PITKIN II.

Born 1664. Married Elisabeth Stanley, 1686. Died April 5th, 1723. Member of War Committee ("Queen

Anne's War"), 1704. Chief Justice of Superior Court, 1713. Member Colonial Council, 1697-1723. Commissioner of War, 1706-07.

See Appleton's Ency. Am. Biog., Vol. 5 (p. 32).

(18) WILLIAM HILLHOUSE.

Born 1728. Married Sarah Griswold, 1750. Died November 10th, 1816. Chief Judge of County Court forty years, 1767-1807. First appeared in Legislature, October 14th, 1756, where he continued as either Member of Lower House, or of Governor's Council ("Assistant") thirty years. Lieutenant of Troop of Horse, Third Regiment, Connecticut, 1757. Member of Council of Safety, 1776; Major of Second Regiment, Horse, 1776.

See Biographic Annals of the United States Civil Government (p. 204); Hollister's Hist. of Connecticut, Vol. 2 (p. 641); Calkin's Hist. of New London (p. 506); Records of the State of Connecticut (p. 24).

(19) ELISHA PORTER.

Born February 9th, 1742. Married Sarah Jewett, 1762. Died May 29th, 1796. Was Representative, 1770-1774, and afterwards Chief Judge. Held rank of General in Revolutionary War, commanding Regiment which marched, April 21st, 1775, to Boston (from Grenwich, Mass.), and fought at Battle of Bunker Hill. "Distinguished for bravery" at battle of Saratoga, and his Regiment "served with distinction" (1776) in Canada, under command of Brig. Gen. John Sullivan.

See Am. Archives, Series 4, Vol. 4 (p. 411); Porter Gen. (p. 196); Dr. Jeremy Taylor's "Note Book," printed in the "Proceedings of Massachusetts Historical Society" meeting of June, 1875, Vol. 14 (p. 93).

The Alexander Family.

I Generation.

DR. ADAM ALEXANDER.

Born at Inverness, Scotland, March 3rd, 1758; was reared there by two maiden aunts, named Jamieson. He attended the University of Edinburgh; studied medicine; came to America in 1776; entered the American Army as Surgeon; taken prisoner by the British at the Siege of Savannah; afterwards released in order that he might use his surgical skill in behalf of a wounded Officer.

He married, March 10th, 1802, Louisa Frederika Schmidt (born in Stuttgardt, March 23rd, 1777), daughter of Egydius Heinrich Schmidt (born May 5th, 1738; died August 23rd, 1795), and Dorothea Christina Kinselbach, his wife (born in Stuttgardt, June 7th, 1740; died in Sunbury, Ga., January 9th, 1812). An impression of his letter seal, owned by Mrs. C. A. Alexander, is used on the title page of this book. He came to America (Charleston, S. C.) about 1785, and was a cotton merchant.

Dr. Adam Alexander died in Sunbury, Ga., March 3rd, 1812. Louisa Frederika Alexander died in Savannah, Ga., October 1st, 1846.

Their children (being of the II Generation) were:

(1) Adam Leopold. Born Sunbury, Ga., January 29th, 1803. Died Augusta, Ga., April 9th, 1882.

(2) Louisa. Born Sunbury, Ga., July 10th, 1807. Married Anthony Porter, of Savannah, December 16th, 1824. Died August 5th, 1888. (No issue.)

Descendants of A. L. Alexander.

II Generation.

(1) Adam Leopold Alexander, son of Dr. Adam and Louisa F. Alexander, married April 29, 1823, Sarah Hillhouse Gilbert (b. October 23, 1805; d. February 28, 1855), daughter of Sarah Hillhouse and Felix Gilbert II (b. ——, 1778; d. November 27, 1813), came (with his brother William) to Washington, Ga., from Virginia. He was the son of Felix Gilbert and his wife, Maria Grant, daughter of Peter Grant, all of Rockingham County, Va.

Adam L. Alexander graduated at Yale in 1821. At the time of his marriage he moved to Washington, Ga. Was planter there until 1872. Moved to Augusta, Ga., and lived there until his death, April 9th, 1882.

He married, second, December 5th, 1865, Jane Marion Glenn (nee Dunwody), born 1821; died 1885. No issue.

The children of Adam L. Alexander and Sarah H. Gilbert (being of the III Generation) were:

(3) Louisa Frederika, b. June 9, 1824; d. Nov. 19, 1895.

(4) Sarah Gilbert, b. Jan. 26, 1826; d. Nov. 1, 1897.

(5) Harriet Virginia, b. April 24, 1828.

(6) Mary Clifford, b. June 14, 1830.

(7) William Felix, b. May 7, 1832; d. Aug. 16, 1907.

(8) Edward Porter, b. May 26, 1835.

(9) Charles Atwood, b. Nov. 4, 1838; d. Jan. 30, 1907.

(10) James Hillhouse, b. June 6, 1840; d. Dec. 4, 1902.

(11) Marion Brackett, b. Nov. 19, 1842; d. Nov. 21, 1901.

(12) Alice Van Yeveren, b. July 21, 1848; d. Oct. 29, 1902.

III Generation.

(3) Louisa Frederika Alexander, daughter of (1) Adam L. and Sarah H. Alexander, married, December 18, 1850,

Jeremy Francis Gilmer (b. North Carolina, February 23, 1818; d. Savannah, Ga., December 1, 1883).

J. F. Gilmer graduated from West Point, 1839 (Engineers). Fought in Mexican War. Resigned in 1861. Made Lieutenant Colonel C. S. A. 1861. Major General, 1863. Chief Engineer of Confederate States from 1862 to end of war.

Their children were (being of the IV Generation):

(13) Louisa Porter, b. Sept. 3, 1852.

(14) Henry Halleck, b. Nov. 7, 1854.

III Generation.

(4) Sarah Gilbert Alexander, daughter of (1) A. L. and S. H. Alexander, married November 5, 1845, Alexander Robert Lawton (b. November 4, 1818; d. July 2, 1896), son of Alexander James Lawton (of St. Peter's Parish, Beaufort District, S. C.) and Martha Morse, his wife. Alexander R. Lawton was educated at West Point; commissioned Second Lieutenant of Artillery, U. S. A., 1839; resigned January 1, 1841. Joined the Savannah Bar 1843. Brigadier General, C. S. A., April 1, 1861; Quartermaster General, C. S. A., 1863-65. United States Minister to Austria, 1887-89.

Their children were (being of the IV Generation):

(15) Corinne Elliot, b. Sept. 23, 1846; d. Jan. 24, 1877.

(16) Louisa Frederika, b. June 9, 1849.

(17) Nora, b. March 1, 1855.

(18) Alexander Rudolph, b. Aug. 9, 1858.

III Generation.

(5) Harriet Virginia Alexander, daughter of (1) A. L. and S. H. Alexander, married January 12, 1853, Wallace Cumming (b. March 16, 1827; d. February 6, 1877), son of Joseph Cumming (b. Augusta, Ga.) and Matilda Poe (Baltimore), his wife.

Their children were (being of the IV Generation):

(18) Charles Maxwell (died in infancy).

(19) Sarah Gilbert, b. Nov. 7, 1855.

(20) Mary Nesbit, b. Sept. 20, 1859; d. Sept. 23, 1876.

(21) Wallace II, b. July 13, 1863.

(22) Joseph, b. Oct. 23, 1865; d. March 18, 1892.

III Generation.

(6) Mary Clifford Alexander, daughter of (1) A. L. and S. H. Alexander, married December 7, 1854, George Gilmer Hull (b. January 25, 1829; d. April 24, 1885), son of Asbury Hull (b. 1796; d. 1866, Athens, Ga.) and Lucy Harvie (b. June 20th, 1798; d. 1859), daughter of William Harvie (Virginia). Asbury Hull served in the Legislature both as Speaker of the House and President of the Senate. Was for forty years Treasurer of the State University, and first President of the Southern Mutual Insurance Company.

Their children were (being of the IV Generation):

(23) Lucy Harvie, b. March 25, 1857.

(24) Harriet Alexander, b. Oct. 5, 1859; d. Feb. 21, 1909.

III Generation.

(7) William Felix Alexander, son of (1) A. L. and S. H. Alexander, married, first, April 28th, 1853, Louisa Toombs (b. 1833; d. 1855), daughter of Gen. Robert Toombs, (no issue); and, second, January 6, 1863, Lucy Grattan (b. August 10, 1838; d. October 14, 1899), daughter of Peachy Grattan, of Richmond, Va., and Elvira Fergusson, his wife.

W. F. Alexander graduated, Yale, 1851; planter, 1855-61; entered service C. S. A. 1861, and served (Major) until the close of War.

The children of W. F. Alexander and Lucy Grattan were (being of the IV Generation):

(25) Elvira, b. Jan. 4, 1869.

III Generation.

(8) Edward Porter Alexander, son of (1) A. L. and S. H. Alexander, married April 3, 1860, Betty Jacqueline Mason (b. May 7, 1835; d. Nov. 20, 1899), daughter of Alexander Hamilton Mason (Va.) and Jane Allen Smith, his wife.

378

E. P. Alexander graduated West Point, 1857; appointed Second Lieutenant Engineer Corps, 1860. Resigned 1861. Entered C. S. A. as Captain of Engineers 1861. Served in Army of Northern Virginia until surrender at Appomatox, 1865. Was Chief of Ordnance and later Brigadier General of Artillery and Chief of Artillery, Longstreet's Corps, until end of war. Was Professor of Mathematics and Engineering at University of South Carolina, 1866-70; General Manager and President of various railroads (including Louisville and Nashville and Central of Georgia), 1871-92; Government Director Union Pacific Railroad, 1885-7; Engineer Arbitrator of Boundary Survey between Nicaragua and Costa Rica, 1902-05.

Their children were (being of the IV Generation):

(26) Bessie Mason, b. Nov. 10, 1861.

(27) Edward Porter II, b. Sept. 21, 1863.

(28) Lucy Roy, b. Sept. 21, 1863; d. April 28, 1900.

(29) Adam Leopold, b. July 24, 1867.

(30) William Mason, b. Nov. 23, 1868.

E. P. Alexander married (second), October 1, 1901, Mary Landon Mason (b. Aug. 28, 1861), daughter of Augustine S. Mason, Hagerstown, Md.

III Generation.

(9) Charles Atwood Alexander, son of (1) A. L. and S. H. Alexander, married (first) April 8, 1862, Ida Calhoun (b. August 15, 1841; d. December 23, 1867); (second) November 4, 1880, Rosa Calhoun (b. February 10, 1848); both daughters of Edward Calhoun (South Carolina) and Frances Middleton, his wife.

Charles A. Alexander entered the "Liberty Troop," C. S. A., in 1860. Commissioned Captain 1861, and served to the end of the war.

Their children were (being of the IV Generation):

(31) Harriet Virginia (daughter of first wife), b. July 28, 1866; d. March 24, 1882.

(32) Ida Calhoun (daughter of second wife), b. Aug. 21, 1881.

(33) Carlotta Rosa (daughter of second wife), b. Jan. 20, 1886.

III Generation.

(10) James Hillhouse Alexander, son of A. L. and S. H. Alexander, married June 25, 1863, Sarah Irvin (b. April 18, 1841; d. April 4, 1903), daughter of Isaiah T. Irvin (Washington, Ga.) and Lizzie Joyner, his wife.

J. H. Alexander entered the Confederate Army at age of 21. Commissioned Captain (Signal Corps) 1862. Major (Bureau of Engineers) 1863 to end of war.

Their children were (being of the IV Generation):

(34) Irvin, b. March 10, 1866.

(35) Hugh Hull, b. Dec. 27, 1867.

(36) Elizabeth, b. July 25, 1869; d. May 12, 1901.

III Generation.

(11) Marion Brackett Alexander, daughter of (1) A. L. and S. H. Alexander, married November 2, 1870, William Ellison Boggs, D. D. (b. May 12, 1838), son of George W. Boggs (South Carolina) and Isabella Ellison, his wife.

Their children were (being of the IV Generation):

(37) Adam Alexander, b. Sept. 29, 1871.

(39) Gilbert Hillhouse, } b. Oct. 2, 1875.
(38) Thomas Richmond, }

(40) Marion Alexander, b. Aug. 24, 1877.

(41) Lucien Hull, b. Jan. 4, 1882.

III Generation.

(12) Alice Van Yeveren Alexander, daughter of (1) A. L. and S. H. Alexander, married November 23, 1870, Alexander Cheves Haskell (b. Sept. 22, 1839), son of Charles T. Haskell (Charleston, S. C.) and Sophia Lovel Cheves, his wife.

Alexander C. Haskell enlisted a private in the Confederate Army, 1861; was made Lieutenant and afterwards Adjutant and Captain of same Regiment, 1861; then Assistant Adjutant General and Chief of Staff to Brig. Gen. Gregg, serving until the end of the war. ,

Their children were (being of the IV Generation):

(42) Alexander Cheves, b. Aug. 15, 1871.
(43) Louisa Porter, b. July 25, 1872.
(44) Mary Elizabeth, b. Dec. 11, 1873.
(45) Anthony Porter, b. Jan. 27, 1875.
(46) Marion Alexander, b. June 5, 1876.
(47) Charles Thompson, b. April 25, 1878.
(48) Frederika Christina, b. Dec. 10, 1880.
(49) Adam Leopold, b. Sept. 1, 1882.
(50) Alice Van Yeveren, b. June 21, 1884.
(51) Suzanne Courtonne, b. Feb. 16, 1886.

IV Generation.

(13) Louisa Porter Gilmer, daughter of (3) L. F. and J. F. Gilmer, married June 19, 1890, Jacob Florance Minis (b. November 12, 1852), son of Abram Minis, of Savannah, Ga., and Lavinia Florance (Philadelphia), his wife.

IV Generation.

(16) Louisa Frederika Lawton, daughter of (4) S. A. and A. R. Lawton, married April 11, 1876, Leonard Covington Mackall (b. Baltimore, June 17, 1843; d. May 6, 1890), son of Dr. Leonard Mackall (Baltimore) and Frances Bennett, his wife.

Their children were (being of the V Generation):

(52) Leonard Leopold, b. Jan. 29, 1879.
(53) Corinne Lawton, b. Feb. 27, 1880; m. April 14, 1903, Gari Melchers.
(54) Alexander Lawton, b. May 23, 1888.

IV Generation.

(17) Nora Lawton, daughter of (4) S. A. and A. R. Lawton, married April 7, 1886, Henry Cumming Cunningham (b. April 5, 1842), son of Dr. Alexander Cunningham (Washington, Ga.) and Anna Frances Mayhew (New York), his wife.

Their children were (being of the V Generation):

(56) Sarah Alexander, b. April 26, 1887.

IV Generation.

(18) Alexander Rudolph Lawton, son of (4) S. A. and A. R. Lawton, married April 27, 1882, Ella Stanley Beckwith (b. August 9, 1860), daughter of Rt. Rev. John Watrous Beckwith, Episcopal Bishop of Georgia, 1868-1890, and Ella Brockenbrough (Virginia), his wife.

Their children were (being of the V Generation):

(57) Alexander Robert III, b. Aug. 16, 1884.

(58) John Beckwith, b. Oct. 17, 1886.

IV Generation.

(19) Sarah Gilbert Cumming, daughter of (5) H. V. and W. Cumming, married June 14, 1877, James Patrick Houstoun, M. D. (b. November 3, 1847; d. January 29, 1892), son of Edward Houstoun (Savannah) and Claudia Bond (Florida), his wife.

Their children were (being of the V Generation):

(59) Harriet Alexander, b. April 17, 1878; m. Nov. 3, 1904, Chas. Kerr (Baltimore).

(60) James Patrick, b. Aug. 22, 1880.

(61) Mary Cumming, b. Oct. 30, 1884.

(62) Claude Edward, b. April 8, 1888.

IV Generation.

(23) Lucy Harvie Hull, daughter of (6) M. C. and G. G. Hull, married June 27, 1882, George Johnson Baldwin (b. August 18, 1856), son of Daniel H. Baldwin (b Phillipston, Massachusetts, 1825; d. New York, 1887) and Kate Philbrick (b. 1830; d. 1898), his wife, daughter of Samuel Philbrick (b. New Hampshire, 1797; d. Savannah, 1855) and Elvira Priscilla Bascom, his wife (b. Massachusetts, 1803; d. Savannah, 1879).

Their children were (being of the V Generation):

(63) George Hull, b. April 23, 1883.

(64) Daniel Hoard (died in infancy).

(65) Dorothea Clifford, b. Feb. 22, 1889.

IV Generation.

(24) Harriet Alexander Hull, daughter of (6) M. C.

and George G. Hull, married April 27, 1893, Mark Cooper Pope (b. August 16, 1861), son of William H. Pope (Washington, Ga.) and Susan Cooper, his wife.

Their children were (being of the V Generation):

(66) Mark Cooper II, b. Sept. 22, 1896.

(67) Lucy Harvie, b. Jan. 21, 1898.

(68) Clifford Hillhouse, b. April 11, 1899.

IV Generation.

(25) Elvira Alexander, daughter of William F. and Lucy G. Alexander, married November 12, 1897, Edgeworth Baxter (b. July 18, 1868), son of Richard Bolling Baxter (Sparta, Ga.) and Kate Rucker (Athens, Ga.), his wife.

Their children were (being of the V Generation):

(69) Lucy Alexander, b. March 18, 1900.

(70) Elvira Grattan, b. April 25, 1903.

IV Generation.

(26) Bessie Mason Alexander, daughter of (8) E. P. and B. M. Alexander, married December 28, 1886, John Rose Ficklen (b. December 14, 1858; d. August 3, 1907), son of Joseph Burwell Ficklen (b. Falmouth, Va., 1800; d. 1874) and Anne Eliza Fitzhugh (b. Virginia, 1816; d. 1907), his wife.

Their children were (being of the V Generation):

(71) Porter Alexander, b. Oct. 25, 1887.

(72) Elizabeth Fitzhugh, b. May 11, 1890.

IV Generation.

(27) Edward Porter Alexander II, son of (8) Edw. P. and B. M. Alexander, married June 18, 1889, Agnes Grady (b. June 12, 1872), daughter of Cuthbert P. Grady and Susan Armistead, his wife (Baltimore, Md.)

Their children were (being of the V Generation):

(73) Edward Porter III, b. Nov. 4, 1891.

(74) Agnes Grady, b. May 31, 1896.

(75) Susan Armistead, b. Sept. 13, 1898.

IV Generation.

(28) Lucy Roy Alexander, daughter of (8) Edw. P. and B. M. Alexander, married January 8, 1889, William Jones Craig (b. May 4, 1860), son of John Craig and Annabella McKenzie (Augusta, Ga.), his wife.

Their children were (being of the V Generation):

(76) Elizabeth, b. April 5, 1891.

(77) John (died in infancy).

(78) Roy Alexander, b. Dec. 10, 1896.

IV Generation.

(29) Adam Leopold Alexander II, son of (8) Edw. P. and B. M. Alexander, married January 15, 1902, Nellie Holman Baldwin (b. July 25, 1869), daughter of Daniel H. Baldwin and Kate Alice Philbrick, his wife. (See No. 23.)

Their children were (being of the V Generation):

(79) Adam Leopold III, b. Oct. 21, 1902.

(80) Eleanor Baldwin, b. June 9, 1906.

IV Generation.

(30) William Mason Alexander, son of (8) Edw. P. and B. M. Alexander, married November 14, 1900, Julia Adelaide Moore (b. July 14, 1872), daughter of James W. Moore (Augusta, Ga.) and Anna P. Wilson, his wife.

Their children were (being of the V Generation):

(81) Anna Wilson, b. June 22, 1903.

IV Generation.

(34) Irvin Alexander, son of (10) Jas. H. and S. I. Alexander, married July 21, 1903, Daisy Davidson (b. March 4, 1878), daughter of William J. Davidson and Martha Bohler (Augusta, Ga.), his wife.

Their children were (being of the V Generation):

(82) James Hillhouse II, b. Oct. 19, 1904.

(83) Martha, } b. June 29, 1906.
(84) Elizabeth, }

(85) Harriet Clifford, b. Sept. 26, 1907.

IV Generation.

(35) Hugh Hull Alexander, son of (10) Jas. H. and
S. I. Alexander, married June 10, 1891, Mary Burton (b.
September 23, 1868; d. February 19, 1908), daughter of
Thos. J. Burton (Burke County, Ga.) and Sarah Shewmake,
his wife.

Their children were (being of the V Generation):
(86) Louisa Porter, b. June 5, 1893.
(87) Sarah Elizabeth, b. July 25, 1902.

IV Generation.

(36) Elizabeth Alexander, daughter of (10) Jas. H.
and S. I. Alexander, married June 14, 1894, Llewellyn G.
Doughty (b. September 25, 1864), son of Dr. Wm. H.
Doughty, of Augusta, Ga., and Julia Felder, his wife.

Their children were (being of the V Generation):
(88) Jean Irvin, b. Aug. 18, 1896.

IV Generation.

(37) Adam Alexander Boggs, son of Wm. E. and
(11) Marion A. Boggs, married July 3, 1895, Emma
Converse (b. August 12, 1872), daughter of James W.
Converse II (Boston) and Hattie, his wife.

Their children were (being of the V Generation):
(89) Marjorie Converse, b. May 11, 1896.
(90) William Ellison II, b. May 14, 1899.

IV Generation.

(39) Gilbert Hillhouse Boggs, son of . Wm. E. and
(11) Marion A. Boggs, married August 24, 1904, Emily
Newbold, daughter of Wm. A. Newbold (Philadelphia) and
Martha S. Bailey, his wife.

Their children were (being of the V Generation):
(91) Gilbert Hillhouse II, b. Oct. 31, 1905.

IV Generation.

(42) Alexander Cheves Haskell II, son of A. C. and
(12) Alice V. Haskell, married May 3, 1904, Laura T. Guion

385

(b. July 23, 1871), daughter of Benjamin S. Guion (Charlotte, N. C.) and Catherine Caldwell, his wife.

Their children were (being of the V Generation):

(92) Alexander Cheves III, b. Feb. 2, 1905.

(93) Benjamin Guion, b. Jan. 9, 1907.

(94) Louis, b. Feb. 21, 1909.

IV Generation.

(43) Louisa Porter Haskell, daughter of A. C. and (12) Alice V. Haskell, married June 3, 1903, Reginald Aldworth Daly (b. Ontario, Canada, 1876).

Their children were (being of the V Generation):

(94) Reginald Aldworth II (died in infancy).

IV Generation.

(45) Anthony Porter Haskell, son of A. C. and (12) Alice V. Haskell, married (first) April 17, 1901, Sallie Ann Black (d. 1902); (second) August 5, 1903, Lorian Smith (d. June 21, 1906); (third) November 7, 1907, Grace Chappell.

Their children were (being of the V Generation):

(95) Alexander Cheves IV (son of Sallie Ann Black), b. April 25, 1902.

(96) Anthony Porter II (son of Lorian Smith), b. July 20, 1904.

IV Generation.

(46) Marion Alexander Haskell, daughter of A. C. and (12) Alice V. Haskell, married June 17, 1908, Gaston Caesar Raoul (b. March 1, 1874), son of William G. Raoul (Louisiana) and Mary M. Wadley (Georgia), his wife.

Their children were (being of the V Generation):

(97) Alice Van Yeveren, b. July 18, 1909.

IV Generation.

(48) Frederika Christina Haskell, daughter of A. C. and (12) Alice V. Haskell, married December 25, 1902, Willoughby George Walling (b. May 23, 1878), son of Willoughby Walling and Rosalind English, his wife.

Their children were (being of the V Generation):
(98) Willoughby Haskell, b. April 23, 1904.
(99) William English, b. April 19, 1907.

IV Generation.

(50) Alice Van Yeveren Haskell, daughter of A. C. and (12) Alice V. Haskell, married October 17, 1906, Christie Benet (b. December 26, 1879), son of William C. Benet (Perthshire, Scotland) and Susan McGowan, his wife, of Abbeville, S. C.

Their children were (being of the V Generation):
(100) Christie, b. Aug. 13, 1909.